THE PASSION OF PRIVATE WHITE

THE
PASSION
OF
PRIVATE
WHITE

DON WATSON

SCRIBNER

LONDON NEW YORK SYDNEY TORONTO NEW DELHI

First published in the Australia by Scribner Australia,
an imprint of Simon & Schuster Australia, 2022
First published in Great Britain by Scribner,
an imprint of Simon & Schuster UK Ltd, 2023

1 3 5 7 9 10 8 6 4 2

All photographs © Neville White

Permission to reproduce scenes and dialogue from Kim McKenzie's
The Spear in the Stone (1983) was granted by Ronin Films and
The Australian Institute of Aboriginal and Torres Strait Islander Studies.

Simon & Schuster UK Ltd
1st Floor
222 Gray's Inn Road
London WC1X 8HB

Simon & Schuster Australia, Sydney
Simon & Schuster India, New Delhi

www.simonandschuster.co.uk
www.simonandschuster.com.au
www.simonandschuster.co.in

A CIP catalogue record for this book
is available from the British Library

HB ISBN: 978-1-3985-0693-0
EBOOK ISBN: 978-1-3985-0694-7
AUDIO ISBN: 978-1-3985-2256-5

Printed and Bound in the UK using
100% Renewable Electricity at CPI Group (UK)

To the people of Donydji.

Approval for this book was granted by Donydji community
members Joanne Yindiri Guyula, David Guyamirrlili Bidingal
and Peter Wanamal Guyula.

The anthropologist is less able to ignore his own civilisation and to dissociate himself from its faults in that his very existence is incomprehensible except as an attempt at redemption: he is the symbol of atonement.

Claude Lévi-Strauss

'For what man knoweth the things of a man, save the spirit of the man which is in him?'

Corinthians 2:11

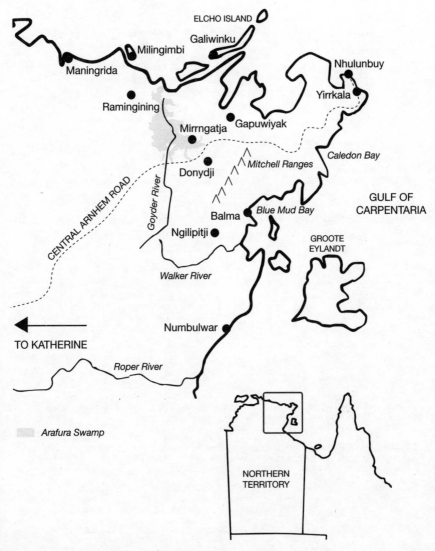

North-East Arnhem Land

ARAFURA SEA

ELCHO ISLAND

Galiwinku

Milingimbi

Maningrida

Ramingining

Mirrngatja

Gapuwiyak

Nhulunbuy

Yirrkala

Caledon Bay

Donydji

Mitchell Ranges

GULF OF
CARPENTARIA

Balma

Blue Mud Bay

Goyder River

CENTRAL ARNHEM ROAD

Ngilipitji

GROOTE
EYLANDT

TO KATHERINE

Walker River

Numbulwar

Roper River

Arafura Swamp

NORTHERN
TERRITORY

PART I

The purpose of anthropology is to make the world
safe for human differences.

Ruth Benedict

ONE

Neville emerged from the crush in the airport terminal, wearing a green work-shirt with half a dozen pockets, a notebook and pencil protruding from one of them, and his old army slouch hat, memento of the war in which he served. Bony and lean as a whippet. 'Old mate,' he said, and very soon he was calling me 'cobber' and 'cob'. Neville is old-school Australian, though he's neither taciturn nor laconic in the way of the caricature. His words flow quickly, much like his gait. 'Quick' describes him: quick to laugh, quick to anger, quick, sometimes, to judge. His once black hair was well on the way to white, and his restless greenish eyes seemed to have sunk a little deeper in their sockets. The cheekbones pushed at the thin flesh on his face. The Arnhem Land sun had done its worst on his skin.

The plane comes into Nhulunbuy every evening, flying 1000 kilometres north-west from Cairns across the Gulf of Carpentaria to the Gove Peninsula. It is a mining town and many of the disembarking passengers are people connected in various ways to the mining operations. The others are likely to include white bureaucrats or consultants involved with the Indigenous community, or Indigenous leaders and operatives returning from consultations. A more thorough survey would likely find people intending to go bush-bashing in a four-wheel drive, fishing for barramundi in the tropical waters or hoping to see a crocodile.

This was August 2005, the northern Dry. Neville had not long turned sixty. He was twenty-three when I first met him, and while there had been long periods when we never saw each other, I generally knew what he was up to in all the years since. I knew for instance that he lived among the trees on the north-eastern fringes of Melbourne and that he had built a successful academic career at La Trobe University, where we met in 1968. I knew his first marriage had ended in divorce and that he had married again. And I knew he spent half his life at a remote Aboriginal settlement in north-east Arnhem Land.

At a counter in the terminal, Max Pearson, thighs like gateposts descending from his shorts, waited for his Toyota renters. I shook his massive hand. Max came up from Melbourne forty years ago and never left. He ran a travel agency as well as the car rental business and owned a shed on the town's fringes which he wanted to turn into condos. We walked through the curtain of thick warm air and took possession of one of Max's Toyotas – the coveted HiLux. North-east Arnhem Land is mining, hunting, and fishing country, and Aboriginal country, so it is also Toyota HiLux country.

It was in Max's cavernous shed that Neville and I spent the night, on the concrete floor listening to the rats and the bats, imagining the snakes searching for them in the dark. *I* was imagining them at least: Neville had taken the anxiety pills doctors prescribed three years earlier and seemed to be asleep. But you could never tell with Neville: he might have been wide awake in some dark, perplexing corner of his past or working out tomorrow's priorities.

It was over twenty years since I had asked him to speak to my Australian history students. He presented them with a lecture of such breadth and intensity that they all sat, as I did, in barely comprehending silence. With slides he displayed data and diagrams to illustrate Aboriginal kinship structures, language, ceremonies and religious beliefs. He described their relationship with the land, the patterns of their seasonal migration, the manner of their food gathering. He also said, with data and photographs to prove the case, that living on homelands away from the towns and eating a mainly traditional hunting and gathering diet made for measurably better health and wellbeing. If they grasped little else, his audience learned that a hunting and gathering society was no simple thing. Dr White, as he had recently become, might have subverted another prejudice in his mainly proletarian audience, for it was impossible to look at or listen to him and maintain the view that scholarship was only for the pallid and polite classes.

Neville had about him a bit of the 'Anthropologist as Hero', Susan Sontag's designation for people who pursued 'one of the rare intellectual vocations which do not demand a sacrifice of one's manhood'. (It was an odd choice of words given the number of famous women in the field, but we know what she meant.) 'Courage, love of adventure, and physical hardiness – as well as brains – are used by it,' she wrote.

In the early morning glare, Nhulunbuy spreads itself across the dry grass and pink-tinged gravel. At one end there are leafy residential streets, a light industrial quarter at the other, and in between there is a bakery, a supermarket, banks, two motels, an 'aquatic centre' and café combined with a camping store called Captain Cook. There are schools, a hospital, a church of the Assembly of God and various air-conditioned arms of the public service. The mine, the alumina refinery and the loading jetties are to the west and out of sight, along with a village of several hundred mine-workers' aluminium huts. The Arnhem Club, one of two main watering holes and a poker machine parlour, is by the water on the east side of town.

Sprawling between the scrub and mangroves, the town owes its existence to a massive bauxite mine and refinery. It is built on a 300 square kilometre mining lease excised from the Arnhem Land

Aboriginal Reserve in 1963, though the reserve established thirty years earlier had been 'for the exclusive use and benefit of the Aborigines'.

Nhulunbuy, a European town with modern European services and modern European habits, including gambling machines and liquor stores, was more for the use and benefit of the Europeans: some, however, benefited from their share of $9.5 million paid annually by the mining company to the Indigenous people of the Northern Territory.

The European name for Nhulunbuy is Gove, like the peninsula, after an airman who was killed there. During World War II it was an air force base. Then it became a refuelling post for international flying boats. But back then few white Australians would contemplate living in such a place. It was too hot and too wild and unknown.

For the last forty years, all the Indigenous people of north-east Arnhem Land (Miwatj) have been known as Yolngu – which means 'person' or 'people' or 'human being'. They number about 3000 and all are members of one or other of several dozen intermarrying culturally connected clans. About forty distinct but related dialects are spoken, all mysteriously *un*related to the languages spoken by the clans in the lands immediately surrounding.

The Yolngu live in an area of 26,000 square kilometres, a little bigger than Sicily, bounded by sea to the north and east, and by rivers in the south and west. Most live close to the richly resourced coast; some are scattered in the tough interior. Their ancestors are among those who left traces of their presence in the region 50,000 years ago (some researchers claim evidence for 65,000 or more), but it is possible that the Yolngu's immediate predecessors arrived in north-east Arnhem Land from the Gulf Country to the south a mere 5000–6000 years ago, a migration that might be explained by the rising sea levels which created the Gulf of Carpentaria. These, at least, are the views of some European scholars. The stories which bind the Yolngu clans are spun of more poetic material.

Twenty kilometres south of Nhulunbuy, and outside the boundaries
of the mining lease, Yirrkala had been a Methodist Mission for forty
years. In 1976 it became a Yolngu town on Yolngu land, and home
to the Buku-Larrnggay Mulka Centre – a mecca for tourists and
dealers hunting for a bark painting (a 'gamanungu') or a decorated
pole (a 'larrakitj') of the kind once used for storing the bones of the
dead, but now painted or carved in designs of the local clans. 'Mulka'
is a sacred ceremony. 'Buku-Larrnggay' is 'the feeling on your face
as it is struck by the first rays of the sun', which is to say when you
are facing east, towards the Arafura Sea where it becomes the Gulf
of Carpentaria.

We spent half the morning loading the HiLux with food and building
materials. Neville had settled into his characteristic short, rapid strides:
the driven soul's indifference to anyone else's capacities or inclina-
tions. You follow at the same hectic rate or find yourself stranded. At
the front door of a house in an empty street in Nhulunbuy, a snowy-
haired, jockey-sized man appeared. He picked up a blanket from the
verandah and ambled across the parched grass. On this day he wore
a pair of football shorts and a brown check shirt, and over the next
few years I rarely saw him in anything else. The plastic water bottle he
carried turned out to be as much a fixture as the shirt and shorts, and
the trace of wryness that creased his face. He accepted Neville's warm
embrace and exchanged half a dozen words with him in a language
I did not understand.

Neville introduced him to me as Tom. He shook my hand, offered
a grin and climbed in beside me. Tom spoke Ritharrngu, the language
group (or 'matha' meaning 'tongue' or 'voice') to which his Bidingal
clan belongs. He had only a few words of English. At the bakery café
across the road from the Toyota agency we got a toasted sandwich and

a cappuccino. Tom took a pill from a bottleful provided by the medical centre.

Tom Gunaminy Bidingal was the senior man at Donydji, the remote community to which we were travelling. Son of Bayman, stepson of Bayman's brother Dhulutarama, hunter, warrior, keeper of clan knowledge and phenomenal pedestrian, he had known Neville for more than thirty years. The pills were to quell his anxiety about a man called Cowboy from the Madarrpa clan of the Ritharrngu, who had arrived at the Donydji homeland a couple of months earlier and declared his intention to take over the place and turn it into a cattle station.

That was why Tom had moved into Nhulunbuy: Cowboy's silent and malevolent – Tom believed dangerous – presence on the homeland had psyched him out. But Neville had persuaded him to come back. Neville would support him. That's what Neville did.

We set off towards Yirrkala but veered right onto the track you would take if you wanted to drive the 1000 kilometres to Darwin or the 1800 kilometres to Alice Springs – or the Indian Ocean for that matter. The Bulman Track, or Central Arnhem Highway, runs from the east Arnhem Land coast 700 kilometres to the Stuart Highway just south of Katherine. Because it runs across lands belonging to the Yolngu clans, a permit is required to drive on it. But hardly anyone bothers to get one. The road was built for the mining companies that have leases all over north-east Arnhem Land. Many of the road signs gave European names to the streams we crossed. Neville seethed. These were Yolngu lands and there was a Yolngu name for every creek and watercourse. To ignore them seemed wilfully offensive.

Here and there watercourses straddled by jungles of pandanus and paperbark cut across the woodlands. Signs advised drivers to watch out for buffalo. Little mountains of manure in the dust indicated that they had crossed in the night. Other signs said we should be careful crossing the streams. Neville was, though I thought only to a degree. In this July most were still flowing; in the Wet, they are often impassable. There were patches of recently burned bush and some still burning; patches that had been 'cool burned' and now looked like manicured gardens; and dense, scrambled patches that had not been burned and should have been.

The Yolngu burned the undergrowth constantly, setting it alight in the cool of the mornings and evenings and whenever the winds were light and the temperatures relatively low. Burning served many purposes: travel was easier over regularly burned ground, with less risk of injury or snake bite, and it was easier to see enemies – and, these days, buffalo – approaching. Burning regenerated edible plants and created fodder for game. It attracted birds of prey which were also eaten, and it cleared swamplands so tortoises and snails could be easily collected.

But Neville, who had been walking in Yolngu country for thirty years and learning from Tom and his family for just as long, told me it was not all 'cool' burning: the clans deliberately left lank, unruly patches by the junctions of creeks and on knolls as fuel for hot fires they lit in the Dry season ('dharra dharra'). Then the hunters took up positions from which they could readily ambush game fleeing from the infernos, along with hawks and kites which also lay in wait. The explorer David Lindsay told the Adelaide branch of the Royal Geographical Society in 1887 that he had met a Yolngu man who, after burning a patch of scrub, had 'over a dozen snakes around his neck.'

The Yolngu burned in accordance with custom and law, and with the unalterable need of a hunting and gathering society to know the land intimately and keep it productive. Now that the seasonal migrations have ceased and hunting provides only a portion of their food requirements, many of the logistical reasons for burning have been lost and with them the methods mandated by custom.

It was the gist of Claude Lévi-Strauss's 'structural anthropology' that the structure of human society is an expression of the structure of the human mind, and as all human minds are structurally much the same, we find in each society practices that have counterparts in *all* societies. In the hunter-gatherer societies of Amazonian Brazil he found customs and behaviour essentially equivalent to many in modern Western society, qualities often superior to it and skills the west lost long ago. Which made the 'sad tropics' of his title (*Tristes Tropiques*) all the sadder because, whatever comparisons might be made between hunter-gatherer and agricultural and industrial societies, the fact was that the hunter-gatherers would not survive contact between them. The hunter-gatherers Lévi-Strauss scrutinised in the 1930s were in catastrophic decline. 'I am a traveller in my own day hastening in search of a vanishing reality,' he wrote.

Tom knew what those words meant. Men of his generation – the last of the nomadic hunter-gatherers – saw the ancient regime of land management crumbling. Tom was deeply conservative. He feared for all the traditions of the clans, and lived determined to stop the vanishing. Neville was his accomplice.

This was the only road west, west-sou'-west in fact. Donydji was 280 kilometres away, three to four hours from Nhulunbuy. Long sections of the track were deeply corrugated and rattled vehicle and brain alike. We belted along, veering from one side to the other in search of the better going, maintaining speed yet avoiding the deep banks of sand piled up at the edges. Every now and then the road ducked down into a creek bed, some dry, some with a foot or two of water left to surge through before bouncing up the other side. Tom stared ahead, speaking only when Neville asked a question in his language. He had big things on his mind: he was going back to stare down a coup.

Half an hour along the way, on a gentle rise, the bush gave way to grassland grazed by Brahman cattle. Sturdy sheds, fences, yards and races, and an imposing house sprouting many aerials stood on the ridge. As we passed by the cattle station, Tom and Neville exchanged a few words. The place is operated by the Gumatj clan, saltwater people. Tom disputed their right to the land, and even if they had a right, he disapproved of their raising cattle on it. What might be perceived as the Gumatj moving with the times, he saw as abandoning tradition, selling their culture to miners, tourists and politicians. Neville passed on this information as we thundered along. He told me there were signs on the boundaries of the cattle station that said: 'No Hunting'.

The lands and the people of the Ritharrngu clans are known by the words for the nape of the neck ('dapu') or the back ('diltji'), which is their location relative to the people who live on the coast or by the tidal estuaries – the saltwater people – who face the sea. They are the 'durdi' (base of the spine) or 'luku' (foot). We were travelling from the foot to the neck. The Gumatj are Yolngu like the Ritharrngu, but Tom has always told Neville the inland clans are different, and nothing the coastal people say or that is said about them can be taken as true of the Ritharrngu. Tom wanted nothing to do with the Gumatj and nothing to do with the Northern Land Council, the representative Aboriginal body on which the Gumatj are the most powerful voice.

Neville slowed to let a slender, metre-long black snake cross the road. A few miles on, he slowed again, this time for a bustard with silver wings. Tom sighed and muttered, and Neville translated: 'No

gun! Another meal gone begging!' Half an hour later, when a lizard
bolted across the road in front of us, we stopped and Tom chased it
into scrub and hurled a rock at it, but he missed and climbed back in
with the same ironic grin.

We pulled off the road to eat a sandwich. Neville asked Tom what
this plant was, what that bird was, and wrote down his replies in his
notebook. Over three decades he had filled hundreds of little red and
black books, made hundreds of tape recordings. He had told me of
long walks with Tom through seemingly featureless scrub, and Tom
uncovering this or that invisible thing as if he had just crossed a room
to pick it up.

Tom knew the 1200 square kilometres of Bidingal land from both
experience and custom, from what he learned by walking it and from
knowledge handed on to him constantly recited in ceremony, songs
and dances. He knew in astounding detail physical features and the
cultural and religious meaning invested in them. Neville had checked
Tom's geographical knowledge of the ancestral lands against his own
GPS mapping and found it to be precise. He had in abundance the
fine-grained knowledge required to survive. He knew, Neville said,
'hundreds of species and their habitats, annual cycles, names and generic
classifications.' He knew how to process them, how to prepare them for
food, tools or ritual. He knew how, where and when to find them. He
had the remarkable ability of hunter-gatherers to see things in nature
that untrained European eyes cannot. Above all, he had the 'inside'
knowledge: he knew the things not present in external reality, but
which contained the truth about it and on which explanation depends.

The Bidingal (pronounced more like 'Bringal') of his name is a
species of aquatic plant (*Nymphoides*), reflecting the fact that his family
and their riverine lands are inseparable, and that the people depend
on the freshwater streams and the habitats surrounding them for
survival. The same identification with the land is apparent in the clan

dialect name, Ritharrngu: it comes from 'ritharr', meaning the young shoots of a grass that grows near the streams after rain (*Coelorachis rottboellioides*) and hurts one's feet when walked on. The Bidingal are one of five Ritharrngu clans, though one of them, the Barrupa, is now extinct. In Tom's father's youth, the Bidingal fought bloody battles with the Barrupa. The other Ritharrngu clans are Madarrpa or Malabarritjaray, the Gulungurr and the Bunanadjini.

Seventy years before this, the anthropologist Donald Thomson came upon Ritharrngu hunters on their traditional land: 'sometimes in little hordes, at other times in family parties consisting of a man and his wives and their children; occasionally just a hunter or two, their faces and bodies smeared with grey mud or clay so that their quarry – red kangaroo or wallaroo – would not "smell" them.' Twenty years ago, Tom hunted like that. On his chest, just visible in the V of his check shirt, were the raised horizontal cicatrices made at one of the several rites of passage he has been through, each one (anthropologists call them 'grading ceremonies') revealing more of the knowledge of the group and raising his status by degrees. Now he was the chief repository of all the religious knowledge of the clan. He knew the obligations, the ceremonies, the rituals, the rules, the law, the land. He knew what was sacred and what profane. And the history: 'All that has been, is now, and lies in store.' The little man in the football shorts eating a salad roll was the clan embodied. So long as he survived, the clan and the world as it was understood by the clan would survive. Tom was also old enough to know the recent history of the group, through first-hand experience and the tales told by his elders: when the clan were still making the seasonal treks; when they periodically fought with rival clans, were raided and made raids, engaged in violent blood feuds; when incised 'message sticks' were used to communicate with other clans; when stockmen from the pastoral stations were still killing them.

The cattlemen had come in the wake of David Lindsay, front man for colonial capital, who trekked along the Goyder River to the western edge of the Arafura Swamp, hunting out commercial prospects, in 1883. He saw signs of precious metals, as well as land he thought capable of carrying vast flocks of sheep and herds of cattle and growing sugar cane. Along the Goyder – 'swarming with wildfowl and full of fish' – and elsewhere, Lindsay saw soils that at some future date would support 'a large agricultural population'. As well as the cattlemen, prospecting parties came – one was reported to have killed forty Yolngu in retaliation for two on their side speared. The soil was too poor for sugar, and no one took up agriculture, least of all the Yolngu, who had spent thousands of years immune to its seductions.

The Yolngu harassed Lindsay, speared four of his horses and drove off others. Three hundred attacked one day, he said, though it seems an unlikely number, and how they managed not to hurt any in the party of six is difficult to comprehend.

Lindsay described the Yolngu in the usual clichés and the usual contumely: they were 'cowardly and treacherous', though he fancied they could be 'civilised to a great extent'. But that was a task for somebody else: 'Were I to go there again I would shoot the first blackfellow I saw,' he wrote.

Though hunted mercilessly, the Yolngu fought back against the stations and their resistance must have been one of the reasons the owners gave up and left. Enough of their cattle remained to breed a continuing wild population that the Yolngu call 'bullocky' and still hunt.

Then the missions came to rescue them from the rough justice of the frontier, but more particularly from themselves. Tom's people would not leave their lands. Tom dodged the missions and hated the miners who came in force as the missions were departing.

Before all the Europeans, there were the Makassans. He wasn't old enough to remember their seasonal visits to catch and process trepang and trade with the coastal clans, but the memory of those years is preserved in Yolngu language and art, and in such items of the material culture as the long pipes, with bowls fashioned from 50mm bullet casings or the claws of mud crabs, that until very recently they smoked.

Tom's father Bayman was a man whose authority and dignity were not diminished by the disfigurements inflicted by the tropical disease, yaws. When Bayman died, Tom and his brothers, all adults, were adopted as custom dictated by Dhulutarama, Bayman's brother who was, like him, 'respected and feared in equal measure.' Dhulutarama also inherited, in line with (levirate) custom, Bayman's wives, some of whom were sisters of his own wives. His favourite in old age was Gunbangal, Tom's mother and the mother of his brothers. Dhulutarama was short and slight of stature, as the Ritharrngu tend to be, but wiry and strong, 'charismatic with a fierce temper', Neville said, and his authority was beyond challenge.

Tom had several brothers: Lesley (Ganmayn), Bobby (Djiminurru), Adam (Wupatha), Roger (Yilarama), Jimmy (Ngarriwaanga) and Christopher, and an adoptive brother, Ronnie (Malapar). Early deaths had left Tom as the senior Bidingal man.

Neville was the one with the scientific mind. Tom, in Lévi-Straussian terms, was the representative of *non*-scientific thought, 'wild thought' – *la pensée sauvage*. Twentieth-century modernism – art, literature, psychiatry – owed Tom a lot. Modern ethnography owed him just about everything. The scientific mind 'measured, weighed and modelled at a remove', sought meaning in such elements as it could discover beneath the surface. Tom had no need to seek the meaning beneath the surface: he already knew it. Tom took his environment for what it was, and he ordered its elements into a 'mythopoetic formula', which Neville had spent thirty years coming to understand.

For Tom the world was essentially as it always had been and always would be, and people were to live in the world as it had been given. The venerable Australian anthropologist W. E. H. Stanner surely meant something like this when he called the Dreaming or Dreamtime of Aboriginal cosmology 'abidingness', and their philosophy 'a mood of assent'. The implication that one should simply remain, and bear patiently, is not so unlike the lesson Yahweh tries to teach his chosen tribe of early agriculturalists in the Book of Job, and it seems likely that Stanner deliberately chose a word that owed something to Ecclesiastes where we are told that for everything there is a season, and the Earth 'abideth forever'.

The Yolngu's 'mythopoetics' rest on a foundation of four women – the Wagilak Sisters and the Djanggawul Sisters. Living with the Yolngu in the 1920s, the American anthropologist Lloyd Warner found the Wagilak Sisters were ever present in their minds. They abided there. They might have been in Tom's mind as we drove. We might have crossed their Dreaming path.

The Wagilak Sisters are the original lawgivers among the Yolngu clans. They are the beings who gave meaning to the world. Their meeting with Yurlunnggur, the Yolngu version of Muutj, the Rainbow Serpent, is the central narrative of their creation story. The Sisters travelled from the south towards the Arafura Sea, striding like emus, bright lorikeet feathers trailing from their armbands. At Ngilipitji, site of a legendary quarry, they left spear heads in the stone. As they travelled, they hunted and foraged and camped and made fires, just as the Yolngu do. They hunted kangaroo, goanna and echidna and foraged for yams, tortoises and eggs – everything the first people, the Djuwany, hunted and the Yolngu clans still hunt. The Wagilak Sisters sang and, like Adam, 'whatsoever [they] called every thing, that was the name thereof'. They sang the names of places and the boundaries of the clans. They gave the clans their names and their different languages. They gave them the rules of kinship and marriage and much of the rest of the sacred law that still survives. They gave them creation ceremonies that also survive. Their passage, and those of other creation figures, are marked by sites which remain significant to the clans in their vicinity.

Deep in a lagoon lay the serpent Yurlunggur – the Great Father. The younger of the Wagilak Sisters gave birth to a baby nearby. When she went to get a sheet of paperbark for its bed, blood from the placenta spilled into the water. (In another telling it was the other sister's menstrual blood.) The serpent smelled the blood – smelled it as profane. It rose to the surface and, as it did, fine rain began to fall. The Sisters made a hut. They slept, but the rain grew heavier, the land flooded – thus was the Wet installed – and the serpent made thunder and lightning which woke the sisters. They danced, but their dances did not stop the rain. The Sisters again fell asleep in the hut. The snake swallowed the younger Sister first. Then her baby boy. Then the older sister. He rose into the sky, where he met two other serpents. The serpents spoke different languages but managed to understand each other. One asked Yurlunggur what he had eaten recently. Yurlunggur confessed to eating the Sisters and the baby, but said he intended to vomit them. And a few days later, vomit them he did. And the cycle of life was established.

The story varies. In one version Yurlunggur swallowed and vomited the Sisters and the boy three times. The boy survived and the Sisters were turned to stone. In another, the serpent involuntarily vomited them after he had been besieged by a species of stinging caterpillar which the Yolngu still try to avoid.

It was the Sisters who divided society and the world into the two moieties, Dhuwa and Yirritja. The Sisters were themselves Dhuwa, like the clans that bear their name, and the story is a Dhuwa one. Their gift was not the world itself but the identity and character of all who lived in it. A person's affiliations, religious beliefs, ceremonial duties and marriage options would be determined by his or her moiety. They laid down the taboo on incest and the avoidance practices that maintain it. As each clan was a member of one of those two patrilineal moieties, so was everything else in the cosmos: every person, plant, animal and insect, and all the heroic ancestral beings.

The ancestral heroes of the other great story, the Djanggawul Sisters and their brother, came from the east and in a canoe followed the path of the morning star, or in some versions the sun, to the region of Milingimbi. They brought with them sacred objects – 'raŋgga' – the most important of which was a symbolic uterus, a plaited conical mat ('ngainmara'), versions of which are still made: women and children sleep under them, or women use them to obscure their view of male rituals they are forbidden to see. The Sisters also brought a dilly bag (a 'bathi') with powerful secrets inside and feathers outside, another symbolic uterus. Like the Wagilak sisters, the Djanggawul story is the subject of important ceremonies, and a great song cycle attaches to it.

The Wagilak Sisters named living things; the Djanggawul Sisters created life. In some versions the Djanggawul gave birth to the ancestors of all the Yolngu. But the Djanggawuls left the dilly bag and its power-giving secrets in a tree, and the men stole it.

The woodland of straight, slender stringybarks and woolly-butts with black trunks and silvery upper branches – occasional bloodwoods and flowering silky oaks, cypress pines, cycads and sorghum grasses – gave way abruptly to expanses of treeless grasslands. They seemed to be the product of human clearing, but Neville said they were a natural feature and probably caused by aquifers.

Neville gripped the steering wheel with hands in fingerless gloves to keep the sun off. He was in remission from a melanoma. The fingers were bent at improbable angles, knuckles outsized and knobbly. The breaks and dislocations were a legacy of the days when he played suburban Australian Rules football for a year or two after returning from the war in Vietnam. He broke his fingers on the heads and bodies of his opponents. Hardened veterans in the team were disturbed by what they saw him do. For Neville, it was as if military combat had been the model for football. Years later he told me that if he had not done violence on the football field, he would have done it elsewhere.

As a student, he once stayed in my flat for a week. It was like living in a war zone. He set traps. I could not walk through a door without the risk of a heavy object falling on me. How much of this physical edginess came from his upbringing, how much from a native disposition for real and feigned violence, and how much from army training and Vietnam I have never known. Whenever he approached, I tensed in readiness for a two-fingered jab to my solar plexus, neck or ribs: intellectual curiosity, unfailing solicitude and generosity, and the threat of sudden, unprovoked assault. I never had the feeling in those early days that Vietnam was behind it, and he never gave me to believe otherwise. It was just Neville.

After a few years without seeing him, one Saturday afternoon in the late 1990s we met by accident at a paper recycling depot in Melbourne. He was haggard and pale, in treatment for cancer. He talked about the work he and his second wife, Alicia Polakiewicz, a doctor, were doing at Donydji, monitoring the people's health and investigating their genetics. He told me I should join him next time he went. Years later, Alicia rang and asked me to his sixtieth birthday party. By then he had begun to take members of his old Vietnam platoon to work at Donydji. Some of them sent jocular birthday messages with photos from their army days. Neville kept smiling but he was agitated and barely sat down all evening. It was at the party that Alicia told me in detail I had not heard before that he'd been diagnosed with post traumatic stress disorder (PTSD), or 'Vietnam syndrome': that he was paranoid and cranky and, when he wouldn't take his meds, very difficult to live with.

'Dreaming is an active continuous time, an animating presence in the land, reactivated whenever Country is traversed by its keepers, or song and ceremony performed.' So was Tom travelling through the same landscape as Neville and I were? How many paths of the ancestral beings were we crossing, and did our crossing them trigger something in Tom's mind – a mind conscious of the different clans linked by the 'nexus of adjacencies, chains of connection, a network of fissures and lesions', as one anthropologist called them? If every human culture develops its own way of seeing, did Tom see a different world?

For Tom, the ancestral route of the dog is fixed forever, and there is no puzzle in the saltwater crocodile painted on the wall of the cave where no saltwater has been for several thousand years, because the ancestral crocodile stopped here on its way from the east; the ripple-stone of the old sea floor is where the crocodile sat down. 'Man never creates anything truly great except at the beginning,' Lévi-Strauss said. What then of a people for whom the beginning is inseparable from the present, who bring the beginning with them in the Dreaming – the philosophy of life that Bill Stanner called the 'everywhen'?

Now Neville and the man beside him, who began as a suitable subject for his study of an aspect of human evolution, were friends –

classificatory brother and brother-in-law, kin, and mutually dependent to a rare degree. And after nearly forty years studying and spending long periods living with Tom's people – trying to see the world as Tom saw it – and driven as he always has been by his own urgent and mysterious imperatives, it seems possible that Neville saw the land he was belting through in ways as much like Tom's as they were like mine.

Neville had arrived at Donydji in the Dry season of 1974. He had been told that, alone among the Yolngu clans, the people living here had never left their lands. Here, and only here, would he find a clan whose traditional knowledge was intact. He had clambered out of a Methodist Aviation Fellowship plane with an army mosquito net and a plywood box containing enough food to last him for two or three months. The plane flew away.

The men had just speared a buffalo. It lay some distance away and they had returned to camp for their steel-wheeled wheelbarrow, which a mining company had left behind. The men called it, with conscious irony, the 'tractor'. 'Tractor' was one of only a couple of dozen English words they had, and Neville had no Ritharrngu. But they shook his hand and led him through the bush to the fallen buffalo. Soon after, he was pushing and pulling the barrow laden with a great bleeding haunch of the beast through deep sand toward the camp.

In 1974, fifty or sixty people lived in lean-tos, shades and more substantial huts made of boughs and bark. A long bark hut housed the unmarried women – widows and wives with absent husbands. Platforms constructed from the same materials and standing three or four metres high awaited the Wet season (Gunmul) when families perched on top while smoking fires smouldering beneath them discouraged mosquitoes and sandflies.

They were Bidingal Ritharrngu and other Ritharrngu clans, and Wagilak clans who were traditionally the preferred marriage group. Neville joined the close-knit Bidingal family headed by Bayman and Dhulutarama, but for a long while he slept in the Wagilak camp. He was made Wagilak and therefore his moiety was Dhuwa. In time, a Wagilak man would offer him one of his 'fiery' Ritharrngu wives. Every night at Donydji the men sang and played the 'yidaki' (didgeridoo) and clapsticks. They hunted every other day. They never left the camp without their spears and clubs.

Neville was made welcome (though Tom remained faintly removed) and he has spent a part of every year since at Donydji with his 'other family', and, perhaps, his other self.

You know you're getting close to Donydji when you see the 'tumuli', the massive boulders in piles and strewn among the trees. This is the stone country, the western foothills of the Mitchell Ranges. Among the clans, these lands go by the name Gurumala. We dipped down into the bed of the Donydji Creek, went surging through the pool of water and there, on a long straight stretch, was a sign pointing south that you'd never notice if you weren't looking for it.

The track in from the road wound through deep white sand and scrub. Neville squeezed the truck between the trees and rocks and navigated cavernous holes. Ten minutes later, we came onto a rise at the top of an airstrip of red gravel and bone-dry grass, half a kilometre long and wide enough to land a jumbo jet. We drove down it, as it cut through the scrub and termite mounds to a scattering of half a dozen clapboard houses, mango trees, dogs in profusion and rusting skeletons of forsaken Toyotas, picked clean and parched by the sun. A tank perched on a ten-metre steel tower and an even taller aerial stood by a phone booth where three or four rangy youths were gathered. Behind a tall wire fence someone was erecting a new building. The lean-tos and bark huts had long gone, but there seemed to be about the same number of people as Neville had found thirty years earlier.

Men sat in a couple of groups under trees at one of the settlements. At the other end, 150 metres distant, women were gathered under shade cloths. At one of the women's fires where we unloaded food – tea, sugar and flour the bulk of it – an old, old woman, toothless, incredibly thin and blind, lay in the dust.

We dropped Tom off in front of his oversized house, which had been built by a government contractor the year before. He left the car without a word, walked up the steps, sat down cross-legged on the porch and surveyed the scene.

A hundred metres away, in a cowboy hat, navy singlet and wrap-around sunglasses, a big, heavy man – at least twice as big as Tom – faced away from the camp and towards the scrub that fringed it. His dogs – cattleman's dogs – were bigger than any of the camp dogs. He sat apart from the other men, not on the ground like they did, but in a director's chair by a fire with his broad back to the rest of population. Two women, his wives, attended to him. His rifle stood on its stock, resting against the chair, and on the ground beside him lay his spears. No one went near him. No one, it seemed, even wanted to look in his direction. This was Cowboy.

Sporadically, from a couple of buildings – one of them with a new green Colorbond roof – came the sounds of hammering and electric saws. Burly white men and lean young Yolngu men moved about. The building with the green roof was to be a workshop and a training centre. In the last three hours of the trip from Nhulunbuy we had not passed a single human habitation, yet here, under an immense sky on the vast savannah, was a light industrial scene. It seemed more than improbable. It might have been a cult of some kind, or an army exercise.

Neville had his quarters by a ragged windsock on the edge of the airstrip. A lock-up aluminium hut from a mining camp now stored his camping equipment and food. A couple of tents pitched beside the camp were billowing in the breezes. For shade, a plastic tarpaulin had been strung from the hut, and under this awning, chairs, a table and some benches created a kind of kitchen. Steeping the air in the fragrance of white cypress, the fire smouldered nearby, bursting into life each time someone threw on a stick from the adjacent woodpile to boil the blackened billy. Behind the kitchen, an old grey caravan rested on tyres from which the air had long departed. 'La Trobe University' was stencilled on the side of it: 'Donydji Biological Research Project North-East Arnhem Land'. It had been there for twenty years.

In the heat and general stillness, little kids ran shrieking and laughing. They dragged each other around on a rusted-up, long-abandoned motor mower, or on any scrap of wood or metal that would roll or slide across the dry grass. They hung in the mango trees. They hurled green mangoes at each other. The girls sat in circles on the ground, talking and laughing. The boys kicked balls about. Somehow they found the energy to run.

Half an hour later, I noticed Tom ambling from his porch to one of the groups of men sitting on the ground, legs crossed, under a tree. He sat down with them.

'We must advance as nature prescribes, by slow, laborious imitation; we must follow custom; we must accept the mandates of the Gerontes – the old men who embody and enforce tradition. We must be content to move slowly.' So wrote the classical scholar, Jane Ellen Harrison, about human societies.

TWO

Neville's father was Leo White, an Australian featherweight boxing champion. In the ring, Leo was the famed Kid Young. He fought sixty bouts under that name, and forty before that under various aliases he adopted so his mother wouldn't know what her son was up to.

The Whites had been one of the poor Irish-descended families living adjacent to Donaghy's rope works by the railway line in Geelong, the industrial port 100 kilometres west of Melbourne. Boxing was a way out and Leo took it. He became Australian champion in 1941. In his five years at the top, it was said that whenever he fought in Melbourne the railways had to run extra trains from Geelong. Through boxing, Leo lifted his family several social rungs, to Manifold Heights no less, a much superior address.

When Neville was born there in 1945, Geelong was a working-class town connected to the sheep barons of Victoria's Western District who educated their offspring at the exclusive Geelong Grammar School and shipped their wool through the port. Leo was Catholic, his wife Gwen Presbyterian. Gwen fed and cared for them. Leo – a featherweight force of nature – trained boxers, most of them Aboriginal. Neville and his younger brother went to the decidedly proletarian Geelong West Technical School. In keeping with tribal custom, Neville surfed at the nearby beaches, played Australian Rules football for the local team, formed a one-eyed lifelong attachment to the local AFL team, the Geelong Cats, went to Mass some Sundays, and with his father and brother hunted rabbits among the rocks and tiger snakes on the basalt plains beyond the town.

What was different in his childhood was the boxing gym attached to the house and the Aboriginal presence in it. Neville's boyhood was a world of left jabs and right crosses and feints and thumps and clinches, manoeuvres he was still repeating forty years later. And he was still hearing his father's voice calling to his charges: 'Left! Left! Jab! Jab! Underneath! Underneath!', while a cockatoo in a cage repeated the instructions. There were always a lot of people around Leo's gym, the white ones mainly of Irish stock and most of them given to practical joking and horseplay. The legendary boxing impresario Jimmy Sharman was a regular. Chief Little Wolf, the American professional wrestler, famous for the feather headdress he wore in the ring, and for his 'submission hold', the Indian Death Lock, sometimes came for a meal.

Out the back, in earshot of the gym and a frequent visitor to it lived Father Tressider. Mrs White went occasionally to the local Presbyterian church, but Neville was raised Catholic. Father Tressider taught Neville the Roman Catholic catechism on Friday afternoons after school. His parents were Labor voters, but it was not a political family. Geelong West was divided on religious lines: if you were going to take a Protestant girl to the local dance you had to know how to fight, Neville says. And Neville did. Religion aside, his parents, he said, had 'very different personalities'.

Most of the fighters Leo trained were young Aboriginal men he either gathered into his fold from Sharman's travelling boxing tent or recruited in North Queensland. In Queensland, Aboriginal people lived under the oppressive conditions of a 'Protection' Act first introduced in 1897. Living 'under the Act' meant living at the mercy of easily corrupted white 'Protectors'. The most feared of the Protectors' arbitrary powers was their right to remove Indigenous people from their homes to remote missions and government reserves, the worst of which were hellholes. To be, in the view of a Protector or a local cop, 'disruptive', was sufficient grounds for removal. 'Mixed blood' was enough. For Aboriginal women and girls, becoming pregnant to a white man was enough.

It was at the most notorious of these settlements, Palm Island, that Leo's greatest fighter, George Bracken, was born. Bracken's father was Indian, originally Brackenridge. His mother was Aboriginal, from the rainforest country of North Queensland. George fought in Sharman's travelling tents, until Leo took him on and made him an Australian lightweight champion. The early days of my knowing Neville were agreeable not only in the way of all new friendships, but in finding myself just one remove from near mythic figures that secretly stalked my sport-addicted boyhood. George Bracken stood in the front rank of my idols. I listened to his fights on the radio and followed every turn of his career in the newspapers. As Leo White was his famous trainer, he too had lived in my young imagination.

Leo had boxed in Sharman's tent when he was starting out in the game in the 1930s, and he took young Neville to watch in the 1950s. Sharman was one of three operators whose tents travelled up and down the east coast, from the tropical north in winter to Melbourne and Sydney in the southern summer. In the tents, Black and white boxers of varying ability staged fights of varying authenticity. What was undeniably genuine was the passion of the crowd: the men and women who poured in made heroes or villains of the contestants on impulsive whims or the deepest prejudice. Racism – and social Darwinism – was an unrestrained element in the drama. Black 'boys' rarely fought each other. The promoters knew a Black versus white fight had a lustier dimension. Among largely white audiences, 'racial' contests usually excited hostility towards Black fighters. Yet it was far from unknown for the skills of the Aboriginal fighters to earn applause, or for customers with natural sympathy for an underdog to cheer them on. George Bracken probably scored on both those counts and on another one – he had the looks of a screen idol. And for all the racism, injustice and hardships of the life, the tents were places where Aboriginal men could step out of mendicancy and despair and, if only for a while, earn some recognition and respect.

George Bracken had grown up near Ingham in North Queensland, and as a youth worked as a stockman on a nearby cattle station. He went back for a month in 1959 and took the fourteen-year-old Neville White and his boyhood friend Neville Scarlett with him. They spent some of the time with the Bracken family, some on horses mustering cattle on Lucky Downs station, and some collecting words from Warrgamay people around Ingham. The Warrgamay language is now considered extinct. Mrs Bracken told Neville about her being taken as a young girl on a very long walk to see, as she discovered at the end of it, the bones of her grandmother resting in a rock overhang.

Two years later, Neville White went back to Lucky Downs. Bracken was nearing the end of his career and, after a dispute with Leo, had moved to the stable of a rival trainer. Neville felt George worked him extra hard and at the most unpleasant station tasks, and he wondered if it was to make him pay for whatever his father's offence had been, or to teach him a little of what an Aboriginal man's life was like.

When he had been a young stockman, Bracken had to go to the police station to collect his wages, or what was left of them after the police had taken their cut. The system was still operating when Neville was there. The threat of repatriation to Palm Island guaranteed compliance in all things, including official theft. With his earnings from boxing Bracken drove a new Chrysler Valiant.

A couple of Queensland police officers stopped him, roughed him up and demanded to know how a 'boy' like him came to have a car like this. George told Neville the only place a Black man had a chance to be equal – or better – was in the boxing ring. Their only other resort was language: having been confined to the back stalls at the pictures, they could repay the insult in a language that white men didn't understand.

From his father's gymnasium, his days on the cattle station and time spent talking to Bracken and his mother, at seventeen Neville knew more than most white schoolboys about life for Aboriginal people and did not share the common bigotry. Not that Neville wore his heart anywhere near his sleeve. At twenty-three when I got to know him, sympathy and indignation were generally concealed in a language that would now be thought unspeakably offensive. Then, it was the general manner.

The stints in Queensland sparked Neville's intellectual interests in ethnography and shaped his moral universe. His notion of what made a good person, what would make *him* a good person, would always be connected in some way to the injustice done to Aboriginal people.

Australians born in the decade after World War II – the baby boomers – grew up in the shadows of war. Wars fought by their fathers and grandfathers. Nuclear wars. Wars of national liberation in the old colonies on their doorstep. Future wars they might have to fight.

War and the remembrance of war was all but a religion. Amid loud echoes of empire, its rituals were performed by bristly old diggers bedecked with medals. The imperative of duty and the glory of sacrifice lived on in the elders. In every city, town and school, on Anzac Day, Remembrance Day and Empire Day children mouthed Kipling's

hymn 'Recessional', hummed 'Land of Hope and Glory', bowed their
heads for the Last Post and kept them bowed for a full minute until
Reveille unbowed them and signalled the moment to murmur 'Lest
we forget'. At the centre of this, our 'mythopoetic formula', were men
who had looked death in the face. The tales they solemnly told –
Christ-like Simpson and his donkey, the evacuation of the Gallipoli
peninsula, valiant conscripts fighting their way up the Kokoda
Track – all taught the lesson of bravery, resilience, sacrifice (or
martyrdom) and sticking to your mates. Above all, to be grateful: for
Australia, for Britain, for your ancestors.

A patriarchy of old soldiers oversaw the governance of post-war
Australia. Decorated military men filled most of the ceremonial
positions and many of the most powerful. The governor-general
was the British imperial warrior, Field Marshal Sir William Slim:
'Slim of Burma', who smashed the Japanese on the Irrawaddy. Before
being sent to Burma, Sir William had been wounded in Eritrea,
and a quarter of a century before that he had been wounded at
Gallipoli. In Slim's time in Australia, two of the most populous
states also had governors who had been wounded at Gallipoli. Their
immediate successors, and the governors of all the other Australian
states, most of them British, all bore the prestige of distinguished
military careers.

Cabinets and party rooms, boards of companies and public
institutions, school boards and universities; wherever there was
power there were men with soldiering credentials. The Returned
Servicemen's League (the RSL) was the nation's most powerful
pressure group, and, especially through its countless clubs, a pervasive
influence on the culture. RSL badges – on top the British crown,
beneath it red for blood, white for selflessness and blue for aid to any
mate under the sky – marked out the veterans of battle, the men of
worth, the custodians of the tribe's lore.

With direct access to Cabinet, the RSL was both the nation's most influential advocate for the welfare of returned soldiers and war widows, and its most belligerent conservative voice. Royalist, racist and anti-communist, the League demanded more spending on defence and the introduction of compulsory military service, including an obligation on conscripts to serve overseas.

The anxiety expressed in the White Australia Policy, and to some extent contained by it, had been there at the nation's founding. Australia's white settler society was always mentally besieged by visions of teeming millions to the north eyeing off Australia's wealth and empty spaces. 'Asian nations are imbued with an ambition to populate Australia,' the Queensland RSL branch president said. They would 'inundate' the country. If Australia did not keep them out 'we could eliminate our own race,' he said.

In the era of the cold war, the RSL's views were not fringe, but mainstream and, in several influential quarters, beyond challenge. The anti-colonial movements that followed the end of World War II in South-East Asia ignited old fears and generated new ones. As if the sheer mass of population were not enough to propel them southwards, now a malevolent revolutionary ideology galvanised their ambitions. From the north, Australians heard of little but turmoil and insurgency. The communists had won in China. Half of Korea had gone the same way. Indonesia had thrown out the Dutch. Vietnam had thrown out the French. The British, having been thrown out of India, were making a last stand in Malaya before departing altogether.

The Australian government sent 17,000 troops to fight communists in Korea, and 340 were killed. Seven thousand were sent to Malaya, where another 39 died. When the federation of Malaysia was formed, the charismatic hero of Indonesian independence, Sukarno, declared it a neo-colonialist plot. Australians might have wished it were so. Australian military personnel and a squadron of RAAF Sabre jets were stationed permanently at the old British military base at Butterworth on the Malay Peninsula. The defence experts called the policy 'Forward Defence'. The general populace translated it as 'Better to fight them up there than in our own backyard.'

Behind the policy lay the belief expressed by the United States' President Eisenhower in 1954 that in the decolonising world if one country fell to communism others too would fall – like dominoes. The theory held that Vietnam was the domino on whose resistance the fate of all South-East Asia depended. Underwritten as they were by the Soviet Union and communist China, the forces of North Vietnam and the Viet Cong were, in the words of the Prime Minister Robert Menzies, a 'direct military threat' to Australia. The wise course – indeed the only one – was to join with the one country determined to stymie international communism, and manifestly capable of doing it. That country, of course, was the United States.

In Australia, the Domino Theory fused readily with the xenophobia in which the nation had been conceived. Yet the old racial fears were now part of the problem. In the new strategic environment, the White Australia Policy had become an embarrassment and would soon be officially abolished. But the prejudice it embodied, the ignorance it nurtured and the fear it subdued were not so readily expelled.

Even as Britain withdrew from the region and threw in her economic and strategic lot with Europe, Australia's prime minister assured the mother country that she still had first call on Australia's loyalty. The people were not of a mind to rebuke him. Far from being an impediment to Australian identity, divided allegiance gave it hybrid vigour. After more than half a century of nationhood most Australians remained content in their British heritage and institutions and grateful for the status and comforts granted by their colonial past.

No such 'crimson thread of kinship' joined them to the Yanks. True, they had saved Australia in the war. They had near as dammit saved the world. But grateful as they were, the friendship owed less to affection than self-interest. So long as the Americans were seen to offer the only hope for deliverance from the hordes of Asia, no one had to like them to believe they were indispensable.

In mid-1965, having been persuaded by the military's top brass that ground forces were the answer to the 'South Vietnam problem', the Australian government sent a battalion of regular soldiers to fight with US troops in South Vietnam.*

Not everyone thought it sensible or right. In the national parliament, Arthur Calwell, the Leader of the Opposition, committed the Labor Party to opposing Australian participation in the war. As if knowing it was political suicide, he told his colleagues what to expect: 'Your motives will be misrepresented ... your patriotism will be impugned ... your courage will be called into question.' This came to pass, as did his prediction that the war would become a quagmire from which the US could not escape. And it also came to pass that, in November 1966, the Australian people rejected Calwell's argument and handed the government a thumping victory.

The year before the battalion went to Vietnam, the Australian government, 'bearing in mind all the various commitments, at home and abroad', introduced a scheme to conscript twenty-year-old men for national military service. The government no doubt also judged that, as young American men were being conscripted to fight a war in Australia's vital interests, it was only fair – and politic – to conscript some of its own as well.

---

* The US had asked for less: President Johnson suggested 200 advisers and some naval craft, and the Australian government itself was not contemplating much more than that until an Air Force chief offered the Americans a battalion and left them with little choice.

Because the army did not need, and in any case did not have the ability to train, all of Australia's twenty-year-old men, the government decided to train only some of them. It came up with a plan to put 184 marbles in a barrel, each marble inscribed with two dates, and every six months invite a distinguished citizen – preferably sporting a RSL badge – to draw out as many marbles as the army thought appropriate to requirements. All men whose twentieth birthdays fell on the drawn dates were required to report for National Service.*

At the third of these national service rituals, on 10 September 1965, one of the marbles had Neville Graeme White's birthday on it.

I can think of no better way to grasp the conscript's lot than to ask myself what I knew when I was twenty years old. They may as well have thrown a goat into war as throw me. Being at once suggestible and dogmatic, driven much more by elemental urges than reason or wisdom, much that I took for truth was only half true or plain false. Little that I know or believe now I knew or believed then. Most of the opinions that crowded my mind I would now think vain, foolish or nonsensical. Fifty years later it is clear to me that half of who I am had not been born when I was twenty, and much of the born half lived on borrowed lore. But it is precisely because they are goatish that twenty-year-olds are sent to war. Physically fit but intellectually unfit and vulnerable, desperate to emulate or outshine their fathers (when they are not inclined to kill them), they are primed for death or glory.

Fifty years ago, many of us took to the streets to oppose the draft. Now military conscription strikes me as a greater wrong than

---

*   Exemptions and deferments were common, and in later years so was non-compliance. In all, between 1964 and the abolition of conscription in 1972, of the 804,286 twenty-year-old men who registered for National Service, only 63,735 served their two years in the army.

I thought it then. Whether by legislation, executive order or other coercive means, or by luring them into battle with the promise of material benefits and esteem society has hitherto denied them, or seducing them with patriotism, mateship and lies, to draft young men for war is a crime against humanity. At least it would be if humanity, in virtually all its social forms, were not constitutionally inclined to think it tolerable, if not a condition of manhood. And if so many young men did not feel compelled to imitate the example of their fathers.

At university we knew Neville thought the war in Vietnam was wrong: not just futile, but wrong. It was not his experience in Vietnam that led him to this view. He held it before he was conscripted and all through his training. He held it while he was in Vietnam. He'd been against it when he was studying for his diploma in textile chemistry at Gordon Institute, the technical college in Geelong. Neville Scarlett, whose passions were botany and politics, was more radical and, when he went to the University of Melbourne, became an activist. He also became an influence on his old schoolfriend, debating with him, often arguing, and putting him in the way of political tracts. Neville Scarlett was not called up: had he been, he would have become one of a small band of draft resisters.

Neville White objected to the selective form of conscription Australia had adopted, but he had no argument with the idea of compulsory national service. He decided that his participation did not represent support for the war in Vietnam. It was experience, a road to take, a test – and he believed in tests.

Neville was called up in the second draft but deferred while he finished his diploma. He briefly took a job at a textile mill in country Victoria, before entering the army with conscripts from the third intake. When he boarded the train with other conscripts at Geelong, all on their way to the army training base at Puckapunyal, Neville

Scarlett was on the rail platform with a placard, protesting against conscription and the war. Scarlett remembered it as a dark, depressing day. The atmosphere was 'gloomy'. 'There was no cheering. It felt bad.'

Neville White spent 1966 and the first half of 1967 being turned into a soldier at Enoggera in Brisbane, where the battalion was based, and at Canungra, the jungle warfare camp south-west of Brisbane in the ranges of the Gold Coast hinterland. He spent the second half of 1967 as an infantryman in Vietnam. Some veterans say that the psychological damage began well before they reached the battlefield. The purpose of a military regimen is, after all, profoundly radical: to take young men – we might as easily call them boys – from their homes and workplaces and everything else that is familiar to them, and in unfamiliar places strip them of their personalities and instincts so they may be reconstituted as members of a fighting force, a band of brothers reflexively obeying the imperatives of the group. Everyone is 'reduced to the same level' as one National Serviceman told me; to 'shit', as another one said. The military call it discipline. 'Discipline,' Field Marshal Montgomery reckoned, 'can help a man lose his identity and become part of a larger unit. It is in this way that discipline will conquer fear.' Forget any notion of a cause: it is 'devotion to the comrades who are with them and the comrades who are in front of them' that 'steels' good soldiers. And we should not think 'fire in the belly' spurs them on. According to Montgomery, a good soldier goes into battle with 'a cold feeling inside him'.*

By the time the army has finished with him a recruit has been stripped of his individuality and recast in a common all-purpose mould. Incorporated. His identity and all previous attachments

---

*   'They need to be trained not to care', Siegfried Sassoon tells the psychologist
     W. H. Rivers in Pat Barker's *Regeneration Trilogy*. If you do care, it's 'too cruel'.

have been surrendered. So long as the army has him, the battalion or the platoon will be his family, in some ways also his religion. It will lay down the tenets of his belief and obligations, of which the most important is loyalty. These are his mates: their lives depend on him and his life on them. He must never leave, betray or any way let them down.

Between learning of his call-up and his induction into the army, Neville marked off the days on a calendar. He wrote above those months, 'The Agony', and under it 'The Conflict Within'. He blacked out each day of his training. He headed a page of quotations 'National Service Liberation Movement' and among the words under it was the dictum Atticus derived from Thoreau in *To Kill a Mockingbird*: 'The one thing that doesn't abide by majority rule is a person's conscience.'

He resented the 'unbelievable political propaganda' to which they were subjected from the moment they arrived at Puckapunyal. And he did not accept the view almost universal in the media that a US victory was inevitable and imminent. He had read the documents relating to Vietnam's war of independence, against the Japanese and the French. He knew that Ho Chi Minh had asked the Americans to support him against the French and been rebuffed. He knew that had a vote been held in 1956, Vietnam would have been unified under Ho's leadership. He believed that fear and sycophancy, not reason and justice, had got Australia into the war. He did not believe in the Domino Theory, on which the argument for the war rested. The argument was at least as old as Saint Augustine: To prevent the destruction of your country it was just and right to kill the destroyers. It was just to fight so the 'good might live more peacefully among the wicked'. But Neville did not believe that the country was on the verge of destruction and didn't think it was so easy to say where the goodness and evil lay. So Neville thought he had no justification for killing.

Neville's resistance to Australian main force ideology did not make him an outcast in the army. His fellow conscripts and his platoon commander, Barry Corse, saw his anti-war books and the anti-war material that lined the inside of his locker. Corse told him he had better keep his political sentiments out of sight. But Neville was good soldier material. He could match it with most of them physically, spoke the ordinary man's lingo, could tell a story and was unfailingly interested in the lives of others. No less than any of his friends, he soon felt almost unnaturally fit and intensely bonded in a cohesive, proud and selfless band. He believed in the mateship creed and yielded to no one in the exercise of two of its vital organs, chiacking and practical jokes. His fellow trainees, working-class and rural Anglo-Celtic Australians in the main, ribbed him less for his politics than for regularly having his nose in a book.

A few of the conscript mates quietly shared some of Neville's political sentiments. But the army did not, and by the end of their training the mates were army, specifically 2nd Battalion, Royal Australian Regiment. Second Battalion had a proud record fighting communist forces in Korea and 'searching for communists' in Malaya. Its motto was 'Duty First'. At the end of their training the conscripts were brought together in a room and asked if among them there were any not prepared to fight communists in Vietnam. Neville raised his hand.

As his mates flew off to Vietnam in the last week of May 1967, Neville was transferred to the Army Medical Corps, which the authorities thought a good fit with his tech school knowledge of chemistry and biology. Given a Cornelian choice between betraying his principles or the men he trained with, he chose not to betray himself. He worked in the laboratory of One Camp Army Hospital near Brisbane, testing soldiers' urine samples for signs of venereal disease, and wondering if he had made the right decision.

Was he casting friends aside as if the bonds between men had no place in his moral code? Might they be thinking he had judged them? Was it moral to serve out his time in perfect safety while they risked their lives in battle? In the hospital there were men who had been wounded in Vietnam. Could he live with himself if any of his mates were killed or crippled? Would he be haunted by their ghosts and their reproving stares?

He would hardly be the first to fight a war in which he did not believe. His father had fought a hundred men for whom he felt no enmity. Some of history's mythic soldiers had done just that. He had chosen morality over mateship. But mateship *was* morality, wasn't it? What was mateship but exalted friendship? 'Once for all, then ... Love and do what thou wilt', Saint Augustine said. His comrades were on a battlefield prepared to lay down their lives for each other while he was poking around in a laboratory, as if he had no heart in him, no pulse. To be a mate was to submit to a moral code: that he decided was the moral imperative.

He told the army he wanted to join the men he had trained with, in the infantry, not the medical corps. He got to Vietnam three weeks after the rest of the platoon. The platoon commander Corse, was not sure. Could someone who thought the war was wrong be trusted to do what soldiers must? Would he hesitate when hesitation was fatal? Would he put his mates at risk? The mates didn't think so. They knew what he thought about the war, but for all his books and lofty ideas, they liked him. He was a good soldier. He was one of them. So, in mid-June 1967, Lieutenant Corse, who was a mate to all his men, found Neville in Nui Dat and told him to grab his bag. He was taking him to 9 Platoon.

*

Neville spent three weeks in Nui Dat before 9 Platoon took him in. In that time, he got to know a man by the name of Tim Cutcliffe from Orange, 250 kilometres west of Sydney. Private Cutcliffe and Neville had arrived on the same plane as 2nd Battalion reinforcements. In their few days together in Vietnam they became friends. Neville thought Cutcliffe was 'a strong, good man', and in an army photo he looks like one – before his youth bears down on you. They had several long conversations. Cutcliffe was eager to be assigned to a platoon and go on patrol. He told Neville the only thing he regretted was having an argument with his fiancée just before he left.

A few weeks after he and Neville arrived, Tim Cutcliffe stepped on a mine. Neville heard the explosion. He saw the body bag go past on its way back to Orange. Cutcliffe was twenty-one. Conscripts were 37 per cent of the Australian soldiers in Vietnam and 42 per cent of the casualties. Neville says he has always felt 'deeply guilty' that he didn't write to the young man's fiancée.

Some Australians stood on mines Australian troops had laid to protect the perimeter of Nui Dat. It was one of those military stuff-ups. The Viet Cong dug them up and re-laid them. The VC were not only expert at laying mines, they deployed an array of ingeniously simple booby traps to kill or cruelly injure, but above all, to stop advancing enemy platoons and leave them open to attack: shallow pits with sharpened bamboo spikes smeared with shit or anything else likely to cause infection when a spike pierced a human foot, or deeper pits and longer spikes of steel with jagged tips for impaling human torsos; vipers hidden in abandoned backpacks or tethered at head height in leafy screens; hidden grenades connected to trip wires that might not kill a man but would take his legs and genitals. That was the other function of booby traps – to sow fear and demoralise the enemy, derange him, knock him off his game. The Americans had B52s and napalm: the Viet Cong had spikes and pits and snakes.

The constant danger of mines and booby traps, the fear of ambush and the ambushes they set themselves were as hard on men's nerves as the firefights. Patrolling was a platoon's constant occupation, day after day, and standing to an hour before dawn and dusk. Fighting communism was a very different thing to watching anti-communists talk about it on Sunday morning television.

Late in October 1967, Neville was on patrol with 9 Platoon near Nui Dat. It was hill country, farmland refashioned into scrub by bombs and napalm. The twenty or so men of the platoon moved with the practised stealth of a hunting party. A few steps, then stop and listen, then a few steps more. The technique famously worked against communist insurrectionaries in Malaya and the conscripts had rehearsed it together for a year. A platoon is an organic thing. In the way of a flock or swarm, the twenty were as if one mind and one body, each part conscious of unusual movement or sudden apprehension in another, the whole preternaturally alert to the immediate environment.

On this day, Private White and two other riflemen were scouting ahead when they heard what sounded like someone chopping wood with a machete. They signalled the American lieutenant commanding the platoon, who indicated they should move forward and investigate. A machine gunner and the section commander followed. The men advanced until, in a clearing beyond a screen of vegetation, they made out a Viet Cong soldier sitting on a hammock and eating his lunch. They assumed he was a sentry, and that the sound they had heard must have come from a VC company nearby.

The section commander signalled back to the American lieutenant who had a bit of Hollywood about him, a few hints of Colonel Kilgore in *Apocalypse Now*. He wore glasses with thin steel rims. On his hip he carried a revolver with a pearl handle, and he had a cut-down semiautomatic Armalite strapped to his left forearm with the trigger

adjacent to his index finger. He signalled to the section commander
to shoot the sentry. The section commander signalled to Neville and
the other two riflemen, and through the leafy screen the three of them
fired from about 20 metres in quick succession. The sentry fell to the
ground. A few moments later, two Viet Cong soldiers ran into the
clearing. Both were shot by the Australian machine gunner, who then
called for ammunition, and Neville took it to him.

With enemy fire coming from the other side of the clearing, the
remainder of the platoon closed in on the fray. Amid the shooting,
the wounded sentry called out in agony. The American lieutenant
ordered Neville to take the medical kit and attend to him. He chose
him because he was officially attached to the Medical Corps. But
Neville was serving as rifleman. He had asked for the role, to do what
his mates were doing and take the same risks. The American lieutenant
did not know this, or that Neville had arrived in Vietnam three weeks
after the rest of his battalion and missed the basic training in field
medicine the rest of the platoon received. Barry Corse would have
known that Neville was the wrong man for the job. In fact, Corse might
have thought putting one of his men in mortal danger to save the life
of an enemy soldier was not a job worth doing. But Corse had been
temporarily assigned to a US platoon, and the American to 9 Platoon.

Neville didn't know how to inject morphine with the World
War II syrette in the kit, or how to apply a field dressing. Nor did he
know why he had been ordered to save the life of a man he had just
been ordered to shoot.

But he did know that his was not to reason why. He rushed with
the medical kit to the wounded sentry. He saw one bullet had torn a
chunk of flesh from his biceps, one had hit his leg and one his chest.
The man was in great pain. Neville had to remove the cap on the
morphine syrette, pull away the wire loop at the end to break the seal
on the hollow needle, insert the needle under the skin at a shallow

angle and squeeze the morphine tartrate from the tube. When at last he managed that, he was at a loss with the World War II dressings. First, 'expose the wounds', the handbook said. The leg and arm were relatively easy – once he had the dressing out of the packet. But wounds to the chest (known as 'sucking wounds' because of the sound made by punctured lungs) had to be sealed (with the packet) to prevent the lungs collapsing. They needed to be sealed at both the entrance and exit points, the man's chest and his back, and the bandages then wrapped round the torso and tied at the front 'on the intake of breath'. As he turned the soldier towards him, a photograph fell from the breast pocket of his tunic. It was a photograph of a man with a woman and two children. The man in the photo was missing half of one ear, like the wounded man.

More than the sudden wild excitement of battle and the agony of the man on the brink of death, his own ineptitude jangled Neville's nerves. His mates were doing what they had been trained to do. Battle was imposing order on them, forcing them to surrender every impulse to the lessons of their training and the will to survive. But Neville had only chaos. Doubts he thought he had resolved came lurching at him. Eighteen months of training had come down to his own little sideshow of the absurd.

Aware that they had stumbled on a large enemy encampment and with sporadic fire coming from the other side, the American lieutenant radioed for artillery. The barrage arrived promptly but the lieutenant's coordinates were wrong, and the shells began falling perilously close to the Australians. The lieutenant gave the order to get out quickly. Neville had the dressings on after a fashion when the American lieutenant approached, looked at the sentry and, with scarcely a movement, fired three rounds from the Armalite in a line down the man's torso so that his belly was opened and the rice he had just eaten spilled onto the ground. Charlie Howe, the radio operator, who was

standing beside the lieutenant, says the sentry must have sensed what
was going to happen, because Charlie noticed – and remembered ever
after – that a second before he died, the man's eyes, which had rolled
back with the morphine, rolled forwards and looked up at the men
standing over him.

Then 9 Platoon retreated, full tilt and full of the adrenaline and
nervous emotion that follow the breathless deeds of battle.

Fifty years later, Neville did not know why he was ordered to save
the Viet Cong soldier and why, after he had done his best to save
him, the American turned his gun on him. Charlie Howe knew
why. As the radio operator he heard everything. Shot because he
was the enemy, the VC soldier was then to be kept alive because the
Americans wanted to interrogate him. He was shot dead because
the lieutenant judged he would not survive interrogation and there
was no other reason for trying to save him. The seeming madness from
which Neville was trying to emerge was reasonable in the logic of
battle. The lieutenant had followed this logic, and the platoon had
followed the lieutenant. But it would never settle in Neville White's
mind. It would never alter the images cemented there, or the
mortification he felt when the American officer killed the sentry.

Six weeks later, Neville's war ended with brutal swiftness. The army
was legally obliged to get the conscripts out at the end of their two
years, and unless they had formally requested a further twelve months,
there could be no extensions. His military service completed, in the
middle of an operation early in December 1967, Neville was plucked
from the platoon, helicoptered to Saigon and put on a plane home. He
left behind Charlie Howe, Alan Osborne and others he had chosen
over everything who had six months more to serve. He would not see
them or anyone else from the platoon for twenty years.

Both he and David Glyde, the beefy machine gunner who left a month before Neville, felt guilty for years, even 'ashamed', Neville said, for abandoning them. They felt worse when news came that on 26 January two members of the platoon had been killed in action. One of the dead Neville knew well, a section commander from the regular army. The other was a medic, a young Scottish migrant who had been with the outfit for just a few days when, under fire, he went to the aid of a wounded Australian soldier. The *Sydney Morning Herald* announced the deaths on the same page as the sports results. The Melbourne *Age* put the news in two column inches on page 12. Both newspapers supported the war. A column inch for each life given to save the country from destruction. So the good could live peaceably among the wicked. It piled anger on the guilt.

When the subject came up in a conversation I had with him in December 2021, Neville grew agitated. He rang Charlie Howe at his home 1500 miles away in northern New South Wales and asked him how he felt about his leaving the platoon so abruptly. Charlie told him not to worry. No one thought they were deserting them. They knew the rule. Neville handed the phone to me. He wanted me to hear it too, as if I needed convincing. Late that afternoon he sent a message asking me to phone him. I did. His skin was itching, as it always does when his mind is agitated. He said he knew his recurring dream would come back that night: he would be under fire, trying to get the field dressings onto a wounded soldier who was moaning with pain like the Viet Cong sentry had. But it would not be the VC – it would be Charlie or Dave, exemplary soldiers, the loyalest of friends. And his mind would be in chaos, and he'd be failing.

He had phoned Charlie a year or two earlier, when he read about an Australian SAS soldier, diagnosed with PTSD, who said his fellow soldiers had taken away and killed a wounded Afghan civilian he had been caring for. Was that not much the same as killing the

Viet Cong sentry in the clearing, Neville wanted to know. Charlie told him what he told him after our conversation: the bloke was in terrible pain and he was going to die anyway. Shooting him was the right thing to do.

Neville had told me about the booby traps and the mines. But being blown to pieces, or impaled on spikes, or bitten by vipers, or losing his genitals was not the stuff of his nightmares. His terror was failure, specifically failing a mate, failing the group, failing himself. A psychologist might say that it was failure to truly belong; that Neville's nightmare was an expression of our deepest fear – the fear of being left out of the group with which we identify. Someone else might say he had been thrown into an impossible dilemma, and the moral injury, the rage and the nightmare would be undying.

From Melbourne airport Neville was taken to the military base in the suburb of Watsonia, and from Watsonia he made his way back to Geelong. He just walked out: the army didn't want to know. Before leaving, he stole as much of his file as he could find in the office and destroyed it. 'I didn't want the bloody army getting in touch with me again.'

'They brought us back under cover of darkness,' he said, and then, 'we were dispersed.'

It was not the lack of welcoming street parades – not many World War I and II soldiers received those – but the way their service was terminated: abruptly removed from their units, flown home and, barely forty-eight hours after their last patrol, dropped back into the community as if they had been away on a business trip. After training them to believe that the bonds between them were unbreakable and that they were embarked on a noble, nation-saving quest, the army cut them adrift.

A few weeks later, Neville was handing out anti-war pamphlets on the footpath in front of Woolworths in Geelong West. He wore his 2nd Battalion colours on his shirt pocket. He also wore abuse from passers-by who called him a communist.

Late in January, just a few weeks after General Westmoreland told the National Press Club in Washington that the end was beginning to 'come into view', the Viet Cong and North Vietnamese struck at a hundred cities and towns in South Vietnam, including Saigon – and made Westmoreland, the US president, his administration, and the Australian government look like knaves and fools.

Like everybody else, Neville read about the Tet Offensive in the newspapers and watched on television as the Viet Cong brought the fighting to the streets of Saigon. *Un*like nearly everybody else, Neville had friends in the fight. Among others, Alan Osborne, Tom Donovan and Charlie Howe were still there.

Charlie Howe became a section commander. In 'Operation Coburg', which lasted from 24 January to 1 March, 9 Platoon was positioned 20 miles south-west of Saigon to hold off the North Vietnamese Army as it surged towards the capital. They were involved in daily fighting with the NVA. Any concerted enemy strike would have routed them, but the North Vietnamese overestimated the Australians' strength and never mounted the assault the platoon expected. Luck, they all knew, was the big player. Charlie reckons he owes his life not only to that enemy miscalculation, but to a left-handed Viet Cong scout who scanned the terrain ahead of him from left to right. Had he been right-handed and scanned right to left, he would have seen Charlie before Charlie saw him and Charlie would have died. And the scout would have lived.

*

The year Neville took up his life again, 1968, was the year Australians began to turn against the war. After months of fighting, the NVA and Viet Cong lost all the ground they had gained in the Tet Offensive. Their losses were atrocious: as many as 50,000 soldiers died, half or more of the forces they threw into battle. But the military defeat was a political victory. Tet was the moment at which the world – and millions of American citizens – came to doubt that the US could win, then to realise that they had been lied to by leaders who had known for years that the war was unwinnable.

After February 1968, though the press and more than half the population continued to support the war, the opposition grew wider and louder and the case became familiar: the war was not against advancing communism, but a civil war. Ho Chi Minh was not a puppet of communist China or the Soviet Union or an agent of international communism, but a patriot seeking to reunify his country. The Viet Cong and the NVA – who the Americans and Australians called slopes, gooks and nogs – were tenacious fighters for a just cause taking on and beating the most powerful military machine the world had ever seen. The aggressors were not the communists, but the United States. The United States government had fabricated justifications for their escalation of the war, and the Australian government had lied about US calls for Australian involvement. American and Australian soldiers were neither heroes nor victims, but pawns – complicit in atrocities. Their cause being just, Viet Cong and North Vietnamese atrocities were excusable, and it was more convenient to make Ho Chi Minh an imperishable revolutionary hero than to notice that the men in Hanoi were prepared to sacrifice Vietnamese lives at an even more ghastly rate than the Americans could manage.

*

He had enjoyed his work as a textile chemist in rural Wangaratta, and the company was keen to have him again, but, like others returning from the war, Neville did not want to go back to where he had been before the army. Perhaps it was that starting somewhere else made more sense of their experience; that returning to their pre-war routine made Vietnam akin to a holiday or leave; that it would feel a little unhinged, and possibly unbearable, to go on as if nothing had changed. They *had* changed, even if they did not know how much. Starting in a new job affirmed the significance of what they had been through.

In January 1968, Neville caught the Victorian Railways bus from the city to La Trobe University, way out on Melbourne's northern edge. Halfway there he was overwhelmed by doubts. He had only a diploma from a technical school. Why would a university, even a new one like La Trobe, take him? He asked the bus driver to let him off at the next pub. The pub was an uncongenial rough house called the Olympic. He had a beer, walked the last couple of miles and asked the Biology Department if they would accept him without a Matriculation certificate. La Trobe was just a year old and still adventurous. They welcomed him in.

For all the remembrance of war and the talk of war, and their faith in God, monarchy and the white race, my parents' generation bequeathed us peacetime privileges they didn't have – no generation had had them. They gave us schools and universities wherein some of us found reasons to shun most things they stood for and find enlightenment. Most of the young men and women who went to La Trobe in its first few years were the first in their families to go to university. The great majority declined the invitation to heresy and insurrection, and most of those who accepted it staged their rebellion without irreversible breaches of custom or law. They made quite a din just the same and defied many minor conventions, and when they joined in protest with small but strident cohorts of wild-eyed insurgents, the campus took on a distinctly radical appearance.

Neville had just outgrown his army haircut when he arrived in the first week of March 1968 and saw hairy young men, none of them more than a couple of years younger than he, in paisley shirts and flared trousers and swaying to American songs about love-ins, peace and wearing flowers in their hair. I don't know which was stranger: that he so readily made light of his experience, or that we did. But none of us had lived long enough to understand how recent all our experience is, and that mortifying events are never wholly in the past.

Neville disliked what the Americans were doing in Vietnam as much as any campus revolutionary: but when he thought of the Americans, he thought of the lieutenant with the steel-rimmed glasses, the pearl-handled revolver and the Armalite strapped to his arm. He hated napalm – he'd smelled it; and Agent Orange – he'd been soaked in it. He thought historical justice favoured Ho Chi Minh's side of the argument. He thought these things, but he could not think them in a way that betrayed his experience or his duty to the platoon. His reasons were burdensomely complex and could not be simplified or fed into slogans.

He joined the Moratorium demonstrations in the streets of the city, but the sight of students flying Viet Cong flags and wearing National Liberation Front badges, and hearing some in the crowd call his fellow soldiers 'criminals', left him, he said, 'troubled' and 'angry'. He did not – probably could not – think that because the war was wrong he and his comrades were wrong. For patriotism, bravery, loss, suffering, sacrifice, fear, violence, duty – for Neville's experience of the battlefield the anti–Vietnam War movement had no affirmative words, or sympathy, or respect.

At La Trobe, he was unusual in having friends on both sides of the Science/Humanities divide. In addition to his science subjects, he took philosophy. Knowing what he wanted from a university education also separated him from those, like me, whose main purpose had been 'experience': for which read mainly pleasure. Fifty years later Neville said he had 'wanted to understand more about why people differed.'

He used to think about it in army training, shooting at bogeymen in conical hats and black pyjamas. Vietnam did not reduce all men to a base level of emotion and behaviour, but it reduced some to that state. Not all Vietnamese men came offering their sisters to Australian soldiers, but some did. Not all soldiers on leave treated Vietnamese women the way some men did. Not all soldiers treated the Vietnamese with contempt, but among the Americans, if not the Australians, contempt was 'nearly universal'. Vietnam showed Neville how 'some people are reduced by the sort of environment . . . that war creates'. And some are not.

THREE

About eighty people were living at Donydji that Dry season. They gathered in groups by hearths and half a dozen houses set roughly in a crescent. Tom's new house stood at the eastern end of the settlement, where the senior men spent their days. The old women and the young unmarried ones spent theirs 200 metres away at the western end. Married couples and their children lived in another domain; and in a run-down green house from which snatches of plaintive country music wafted, the unmarried men were accommodated. Not that I was then aware of these or any other patterns or logic underlying life at Donydji. Nor did I know then that the chords backing the sorrowful songs were being played on a little electronic keyboard ingeniously connected to a solar panel on the roof.

Donydji's children seemed to be as happy and healthy as any children ever were. They greeted Neville whenever he passed and gave every appearance of loving him like some funny, indispensable uncle. He laughed with them, and obviously loved them in return. Their smiles and laughter were almost enough to explain Neville's dedication to the project.

Neville took me to meet the senior men. I sat on the ground enveloped in a silence punctured only occasionally by talk – of what, of course, I had no notion. The Ritharrngu are 'the most strongly nomadic' of the Yolngu, the anthropologist Donald Thomson said when he encountered them in the 1930s, and their language was understood more widely than any other in north-east Arnhem Land. Yet nomads were not always travelling, and the hunting part of hunting and foraging allowed much time for reflection – so much time that another anthropologist, Marshall Sahlins, called them the 'first affluent societies'. '[H]alf the time,' he said, 'the people do not know what to do with themselves.' It seemed that the countless hours these now part-time hunters of Donydji spent in still, silent communion with the cosmos was a recreation with roots in the ancient way of life.

Women, the foragers, worked much longer hours and brought in much more food – fish, turtles, reptiles, yams, seeds – than the men. At Donydji at least, they brought the firewood as well. And they prepared the meals. In the old days when travelling, they carried more, including children and the bones of the deceased. When we left the men and visited one of the women's hearths, the wages of their greater effort seemed to show. The very old woman, who could not sit but lay on the ground, was called Dhawungurdu. Her sister, now dead, was Rayguyun, the first of Dhulutarama's six wives. Betty was the last. Until his death a decade earlier, Dhulutarama, whose wily, theatrical character reveals itself in Neville's photographs, was the undisputed elder of the clan.

It was Rayguyun who told Neville that the first white man she saw when she was a girl shot at her, but missed, and as he kept shooting, she ran into the bush. She told him that stockmen from the Murwangi cattle station on the fringe of the massive Arafura Swamp had tried to wipe out her clan. When the white men came to their camp the children hid up in trees, but they were shot and fell to the ground 'like rotten fruit,' she said. 'The cattle boss was hunting us down. We fled from the cattle boss. We were running away scared of him. The stockmen were killing us. They were murderers.'

She told the story without apparent anger, Neville says. It was just something that happened, as things do. Her father disappeared for a while. He returned wounded but he survived. He took the women and children up into the Mitchell and Parson ranges, where they lived in rock shelters while the men fought the war with the stations in the woodlands and the swamp. Only when the station was abandoned, and the white men had gone, did the survivors go back to their lands.

At Donydji there are rocks and trees of significance to all Ritharrngu clans in Arnhem Land. It is a totemic landscape, the 'Waanga Ngaraka' – 'the place of my bones'. In 1967, when miners and geologists were swarming over Arnhem Land, the mining company BHP put in the airstrip that to this day serves the Donydji homeland. Some members of the Ritharrngu and Wagilak clans, traditional owners and managers of the lands, reckoned the airstrip might serve their interests and lent the company a hand. But when a geological survey team working nearby drilled into sacred rocks known as Djawk, the mood changed.

Ritharrngu clan leaders from other parts, including Cowboy's father, Munuma of the Madarrpa Ritharrngu, whose traditional lands were south-east of Donydji in the central Mitchell Ranges, blamed Bayman and Dhulutarama's Bidingal Ritharrngu clan for failing to protect the rocks. Fiery meetings were held. The Bidingal very likely had to pay some form of compensation. Bayman and Dhulutarama decided that to protect the site in future, they would give up their seasonal journeying and set up a homeland there.

What had been a seasonal camp and significant religious site by Donydji creek in 1971 became a permanent home for the Bidingal Ritharrngu and the Wagilak clans with whom they traditionally intermarried and were culturally entwined. Now countless centuries of nomadism ceased. The timeless and sacred converged with the material advantages of an airstrip and a road offering access to worldly goods and services. They went on hunting and foraging, but the seasonal movements stopped. The habit of hiving off into separate bands to share resources more efficiently, or when tensions developed, also stopped. They would have to manage the tensions, live with disagreements and jealousies within the homeland – or clear out to the towns. For all a homeland might offer, the people living on it would never quite stop being refugees.

In those early days the present rough road into Donydji continued down the northern side of the airstrip. Miners and tourists in their four-wheel drives often stopped to take photographs of the people in the camp. Neville organised a permit system. The Donydji men took a book across the airstrip and asked the travellers to sign it. Neville abandoned the scheme after a year or so and burned the book, which was full of mockery and abuse the Yolngu could not read.

As Madarrpa Ritharrngu, like all other Ritharrngu groups, Cowboy had undisputed ceremonial links to Donydji. He had been raised on the Roper River cattle stations 200 kilometres to the south, where his father had been taken as a boy during a period of intertribal violence in the 1930s known as 'wartime'. Like his father, Munuma, Cowboy had worked with cattle. And like his father when Neville first met him, he wore moleskin trousers and a big cowboy hat.

Many Indigenous men became stockmen on the cattle stations, a vocation in which they excelled. Many Indigenous women became domestic servants, unpaid like the men. The alternative was life on the fringes of the frontier settlements – an entry into a life of beggary and abuse. A few brief encounters aside, the Bidingal chose neither option: they stayed on their lands. Perhaps Cowboy had not been through the gates of hell, but he was descended from something like it. He emerged a moderniser, a worldlier bloke (in the European sense) than anyone at Donydji. Unlike Tom, who

had only a few words of English, Cowboy spoke and wrote it
well enough.

Arriving for a funeral a few months earlier, he had hung his
ceremonial wares up on a line as a symbol of his rightful connection to
the place and his stature as a man of knowledge. He knew the songs
and at funerals he was a recognised song man. But his ceremonial
knowledge was not matched by his knowledge of the country. No one
could deny his links to Donydji, but he had never lived on the Bidingal
land, and for Tom and his younger brother Christopher, and everyone
else at Donydji, that disqualified him.

After the funeral, Cowboy had taken possession of a community
house close to the three-metre fence that surrounded the construction
site of the new school. Whenever a plane landed on the airstrip, he
greeted the pilot and passengers as if he were the man in charge.
He dealt with the contractor building the school on the same basis.
If he could cause Tom to lose his nerve, his putsch just might succeed.
And if it did, he was going to turn Donydji into a cattle station.

For Tom the idea was poison. Yolngu did not raise cattle.
Cattle would destroy the country. They would destroy the Yolngu.
Cowboy would have said Tom was talking as if the old times, the old
country and the old Yolngu still existed. But they were gone and it
was no good pretending that they hadn't. Tom would have said they
were gone for you whose father gave up his lands, but not for us whose
fathers stayed.

What's more, Tom thought Cowboy's conduct of ceremonies was
dangerous – that he had stirred the fates – and Tom did not want
to be caught up in the consequences. For Tom, the clan's existence
depended on sacred knowledge. They must observe the rules or else
invite calamity. The deaths of three of his brothers attested to the risk.
It was on his knowledge of the rules and his adherence to them that
the homeland's future and his authority rested.

Before starting on the school building, the contractor, a taciturn gent, had put up the wire fence to keep the community out and built himself a little house so that he could be comfortable and unbothered by his surroundings. When Neville took Tom to the contractor and translated as Tom explained that he, not Cowboy, was rightfully in charge, the man listened to Tom's complaint and said he would think about it.

Cowboy had not helped his case when, soon after arriving, he declared that a rock near the women's houses was sacred and chastised the community for touching it. He put a netting fence around the half-metre rock and soon it was overgrown with dry grass. No one else in the community thought the rock had any spiritual significance. The women had found it useful for sharpening their axes. Worse for both his credibility and his peace of mind were mistakes he might have made at the funeral ceremonies. He was still sticking by all his claims to knowledge, but he was also wondering if he had made himself a target for Galka, the shape-shifting assassin of the Yolngu world. That was why he was facing the scrub with his rifle and spears within arm's reach. Neville wandered over to him and told him that near the Gapuwiyak turn-off he'd met a thin Yolngu man he hadn't seen before, but he looked like he'd come from a ceremony and had said he was looking for Cowboy.

Half an hour after this conversation, Cowboy added a Dolphin torch battery to a list of groceries he gave Neville, who was going to Gapuwiyak, the hub-town 80 kilometres away. Then, he hooked up a spotlight on a three-metre pole he cut from the bush and connected it to the contractor's generator.

Mid-afternoon, Neville declared a tea break and the workforce of late-middle-aged Vietnam veterans and young Yolngu ambled from the buildings to his fire, on which a large pot of water had been set to boil. The vets, all big men and all sweating heavily, poured the tea and slapped sandwiches together for their Yolngu assistants and trainees. Tom and his brother Christopher strolled up to be served. With a grin, Tom asked for and got a cigarette from Neville. Neville's a lifetime non-smoker, but he keeps a packet in his shed and hands them out upon request. Every day, usually on her way back from taking food to Tom, an almost spectrally thin woman in a floral dress stood twenty metres from Neville's camp and signalled for a cigarette. Neville grinned and took her two.

Betty was a Wagilak woman from down near Ngilipitji by the Walker River. When young, she had eloped with a man who was Dhuwa like her – a 'wrong' man. She had two children with him. Dhulutarama, who, with the three he inherited from his late brother Bayman, had five wives, went down to the Walker and brought Betty back to Donydji as his sixth. She was the mother of David, one of the workers. David, of the beautiful face and soulful eyes, lived with his wife and children in a miserably small hut between Neville's camp and the workshop. He and his family needed a new house and a toilet that worked.

Two veterans from Neville's old platoon, Charlie Howe and Fred Howell, had left Donydji the day before I arrived. Three remained. One had pitched his tent near Neville's by the airstrip, the other two had made their beds in the new workshop 100 metres up the fringe of the airstrip.

The workshop was a fine thing with green Colorbond walls and roof, and big enough to easily accommodate three or four Land Cruisers on the concrete floor. Neville had raised the money through Melbourne Rotary and the vets had built it. The workshop was one of two centrepieces in his plan for Donydji. The other was the school, then being built by the contractor.

Homelands didn't change the lives of the women half as much as they changed the lives of the men, especially the young men. The women went on foraging and cooking, weaving and caring. But for the men – the young men at least – leading sedentary lives and relying less on hunting and more on store-bought food made it a struggle to find purpose. This was what the workshop was intended to correct. The young men could learn skills there, fix vehicles and make things, and be paid for their labour. The vets were already training them.

This was the second year the vets had come to Donydji. This time, like the last, they would stay for two months or more. As well as the workshop, they had repaired and installed plumbing, dug drains, put in gully traps, fixed pumps. Now they were cleaning out, renovating and painting one of the houses that had been built with government funds twenty years earlier. At least a dozen young men and teenagers were gathered round, watching how the work was done, receiving instructions and doing a lot of it themselves. Some were preparing walls for painting; some were learning how to attach shelves to walls, some were listening to a vet explaining fractions. The vets seemed to be not only good tradesmen, but natural teachers. The worksite hummed with enthusiasm.

Meanwhile Neville, who is no tradesman, marched with his quick little strides, as if keeping the separate parts of the camp in touch with one another and bearing tidings to which no one else was privy. It was not just that he spoke in a language the white men could not understand, or that among them he alone knew the name of every soul in the settlement and his or her relationship to every other soul, or that he had known many of them for thirty years and many since they were born; his constant movement around the camp was a sign to everyone that a grand plan was underway, and that he knew where things were up to and what at length would be realised.

At the end of each day's work, the white men gathered their towels and soap and followed a path down to the creek. There, in a pool under giant pandanus, while dazzling bee-eaters darted through the air above and a kingfisher watched from a low branch, we stripped off and lowered our generally ample, pale, naked flesh into the water. Alan ('Ossie') Osborne, thickset with a defiant jaw, was the quiet, gently mannered one. He was deaf in both ears, slightly stooped and because of a bad back he walked slowly, as if in a shell. For years he had taken anti-inflammatory drugs. Though no government department has ever acknowledged it, he is sure the damage was done when, loaded up with weapons and ammunition, he was jumping out of helicopters in Vietnam.

Neville had warned me about Dave Glyde, the old machine gunner. A Queenslander like Ossie, Glydey is built like a bull, or a rugby front-rower, which he was. Unlike his gentle friend, Dave is a loud, abrasive self-proclaimed shit-stirrer and, like Neville, a practical joker. The other vets, including Neville, generally ignored Dave's provocations and did not rise to the bait of his political opinions, and enjoyed everything else about his company. It was an easy example to follow and over the next several years we got on famously.

Dave rolled his own cigarettes with Champion Ruby, the same tobacco his mother used to send him when was in Vietnam. He smoked his first cigarette on rising and his last before he went to sleep. In between he drank a dozen cups of instant coffee, and before retiring took a Stelazine for nightmares, and two Temazepam for sleep. He was seeing a shrink once a month: a psychologist, he insisted, not one of those psychiatrists who only want to put you on drugs.

He grew up at Bellingen, on the mid-north coast of New South Wales. In his childhood it was a dairying and logging district, but now it is advertised as a 'bohemian paradise'. Dave's father fought the Germans at Tobruk and the Japanese in New Guinea, and Dave was proud to follow his brave and honourable example in Vietnam. An old army mate of his father told Dave that after a battle in the Middle

East, Glyde senior had refused to let a group of Australian soldiers use their bayonets on Italian prisoners: he told them that they would have to fight him first, and none of them was game.

Barry Corse told Dave that 9 Platoon was the best bunch of soldiers he had ever led. Still proudly in uniform, when he got back to Australia, he took a train home from Sydney. As he recalls the moment, when he sat down in a compartment a young woman gathered up her daughter and left, telling the child as they went out the door that they would not travel in the company of a 'killer'.

Back in Bellingen, when Dave Glyde told the town barber where he'd been, the barber – a leading light in the local branch of the RSL – advised him that Vietnam was not a 'real war', more of a 'police action'. For years, the RSL kept Vietnam veterans out. The young men had marched in the footsteps of their fathers and grandfathers, they had been faithful to their precepts, accepted their instruction and kept their side of the patriarchal bargain: they had obeyed the elders of the tribe, honoured their traditions, proved themselves willing to die for them, only to find the elders busy reliving their own wars, hadn't noticed what their brave sons had done. This was probably the cruellest blow of all, the deepest betrayal, and they carried the injury long after the RSL decided to let them in.

The other vet remaining at Donydji was Dave ('Stretch') Bryan, who had been in the first draft and went to Vietnam in a different regiment, the 5th Royal Australian Regiment. He met Neville years later when they were living in the same Melbourne suburban street. Around the camp the difference between 5RAR and 2RAR was a theme of the daily racket. Being in the minority, Stretch was bound to find it trying at times. Had Dave Glyde followed through with his plan to put some dog turds in his tent, it might have been *too* trying.

David Bryan was born in the last year of World War II. Three of his mother's brothers has been killed in that war. He had been in the first call-up, and though sceptical about the war in Vietnam and the politics behind it, he went willingly enough. All through his training he felt sure that they would never send conscripts – 'nashos' – to Vietnam. Not on the flight to Saigon, not even in the helicopter taking them to Nui Dat did it seem real. Only when he was on the ground and heard the thump of guns did the truth sink in – 'Shit! I'm in a war!'

While training at Puckapunyal he met a bloke he'd been at school with. Their lives plotted the same course, until the bloke he had been at school with stepped on a mine in Vietnam. He wonders why it wasn't him who stepped on it. Next day the officer he had been working with the day before drove a steel picket into a Viet Cong booby trap and vanished before his eyes. It's the little things you remember, he says. He remembers the first time he got a Viet Cong in his sights and wondered if he could do it. He remembers thinking, 'This poor bastard's got a family, and he had no say in being here. He's like me.' He shot him. He'd always been a good shot; he used to go out shooting as a kid.

In the evenings, Christopher mowed the airstrip with the old Victa mower. The vets didn't like Christopher, the youngest of the Bidingal brothers. Where Tom wore a flicker of a grin, Christopher often wore a scowl. Tom's eyes were kind, Christopher's fierce. Christopher was short like Tom, but stockier. Twenty years earlier, he had strayed from the traditional path and become a fervent follower and a kind of lay pastor of the Christian Evangelical Fellowship. By the time I met him the phase had largely passed and, though Christianity remained an article of his faith, he was sticking to the clan songs in which he was expert.

While Christopher mowed, the bigger kids, from about six to sixteen, played Australian Rules football on the airstrip. The big kids somehow managed to show off their athletic skills while keeping the little kids in the game. One of them, Sammy Muparritj, grandson of the late Miliwurdu, a handsome, smiling six-foot-tall sixteen-year-old, who without coaching of any kind had competed in the Pan Pacific Games the previous year, played with majestic skill and verve. For two hours they kicked the ball and leapt for it, and weaved and chased without let-up. No one got hurt. No one complained. In that first week at Donydji I never saw a child hurt or one even tease another. The Donydji children are known for being gentle and well-mannered. The smaller children sat in circles on the ground and made each other laugh. The young women in brightly coloured frocks and tracksuits promenaded up the airstrip, and a couple of young men patrolled the fires they had set in the undergrowth on the other side. And Tom sat cross-legged in the dust watching the scene, breathing the scented twilight, content with the world. There was the faintest, softest breeze from the south-east; the 'nganda', the 'darling breeze'. Unmarried and without children, he had no hearth of his own, so boys and girls and dogs wandered over and sat down beside him.

And the vets, freshly washed and groomed, gathered by the fire at Neville's campsite, and with mugs of tea and coffee looked out at the tranquil scene, while Neville took his turn to cook the meal. Meat and dairy do not keep in the heat, so the staples were pasta, rice, root vegetables and anything that can be got in a tin. It all went into a big pot black with cypress soot. Ron, from Elcho Island, was not a vet but he was good with his hands and had volunteered to help. And Andrew, who worked at the organic vegetable stall in Melbourne's Victoria Market, where Neville started going when he got cancer, was another one of the volunteer crew.

Glydey had wept when Neville told him about the doctor's grim prognosis, but he didn't believe in this organic bullshit. 'Fuckin' organic sweet potatoes! How do you grow an inorganic one? Fuckin' Neville White bullshit is what it is!' he said, and when Neville served him from a pot full of white rice and tinned fish, he snarled, 'You fuckin' know I hate rice! And you know why I hate it.' All in good fun, of course. Vietnam was why.

I wondered if they would be talking so much about the war if I had not been there. They had been at Donydji for weeks, and it seemed possible that they had talked about it every night, as if within their heads they had not stopped talking about it for thirty-five years. The lines were not rehearsed, but as if fixed, predetermined. The Australians were well trained in guerrilla warfare, the Americans were not. The Australians patrolled on foot in silence. The Americans smoked cigars and wore aftershave and dangling jewellery, even when patrolling, as if they wanted the enemy to know they were there. The Americans went everywhere in armoured personnel carriers and never went anywhere without their music. Their idea of a patrol, Dave Bryan said, was to go out in armoured personnel carriers and 'start blazing away on both sides of the road. That was a clearing patrol.' Their night-scopes not only advertised their presence but created 'spooky green moving images' which only added to the general paranoia. The vets said they had never heard of Australian soldiers deliberately killing civilians, but it didn't surprise them when they heard American soldiers had.

On one thing they agreed. Australian and US soldiers alike thought the M16 rifle they had been issued was so unreliable, such 'lightweight shit,' as Glydey said, that giving it to them showed how the army and the government were either stupid or didn't care. The M16 was a 'betrayal'. For the Australians, so were the rations. Australian rations were 'crap'. American rations were ridiculously lavish, and they got four cigarettes with every meal.

I went with Neville and held a torch as he traipsed about dispensing what remained in the pot to the women's hearths, and then to the dark, mouldering interior of the single men's house where Neville scraped the pot into the plates the men held out. The single men needed new houses. Then we went back to the fire under the Milky Way – and Vietnam.

One of the conscripts in the platoon, Tom Donovan, had Aboriginal (Kalkadoon) ancestry. The platoon was walking in line one day, and Tom was at the back. A passing American officer said to the men at the front, 'What've you got him up the back for? We always put them up the front.'*

The Americans were something for the Australians to define themselves against. If the war had been fought as they fought it, the result might have been different. The war was not lost, but the Americans fought it too ineptly to stand a chance of winning. Dave Glyde was in no doubt – the Americans just threw in the towel. The Australians never lost a battle. Never. There is no arguing with the claim. Of course, American veterans also say they never lost.

There were no defeats until the end, but there were no victories to speak of either. Tet was a victory, but everyone thought it was a loss, which is what it ultimately became. Only rarely, if at all, were the vets' victories worthy of jubilation, and unlike Gallipoli or Dunkirk, no glory could be conjured from defeat when it came. There was only the final defeat and the enervating sense that it had all been for nothing, which had left them with a sort of stalemate of the soul.

On that night and the nights that followed, no one talked about the destruction the war inflicted on the Vietnamese. Two million civilian deaths, bombs equivalent in explosive force to 640 Hiroshimas, 350,000 tons of napalm. Hadn't the US general Westmoreland given the Vietnamese peasantry much the same choice as the invaders of

---

*   It might have been common policy. In the US army, Black and Hispanic soldiers 'were respectively 63 per cent and 43 per cent more likely to have experienced high combat exposure than whites.'

Arnhem Land gave the Yolngu when, in announcing an escalation
of the war, he said 'This will bring about a moment of decision for
the peasant farmer. He will have to choose if he stays alive.' Hadn't the
Viet Cong met Saint Augustine's measure of a just war? In truth,
the rightness or wrongness of a war is mainly a question for those who
are not fighting it. For the same reason, presumably, the conversation
at Donydji never went near any possible connection between the
destruction in Vietnam and the destruction that caused these few
dozen souls to be crammed in wretched huts in a far-flung homeland.
They were there – the connection was Neville. That was all.

The fire glowed. Every now and then a dog came looking for food.

Around eight o'clock the conversation faded. 'You taken your
pills, Neville? Take your fuckin' pills or I'm going home tomorrow,'
said Glydey, after he had taken *his* pills. He and Ossie plodded off to
their swags in the workshop. The rest of us took to our tents. Mine
had a roof I could see through. I lay there looking at the Saucepan
and listening to the dogs communing with departed ancestors on a
far-off star.

One night the new teacher at the school brought a little troupe of kids
to Neville's camp and they lined up and sang a couple of songs very
sweetly. The vets all clapped their brawny hands, and the children and
their teacher disappeared back into the dark, leaving the semi-circle of
white blokes touched and hopeful.

Another night one of the young men came over. That day a
hunting party had come back with a huge pig, some black bream
and a goanna, and the whole camp seemed energised by the success.
Everyone got some meat. The visitor with the lean and chiselled face
and neatly trimmed beard was the man who shot the animal, and he
began to tell us how he killed it. In a mixture of English and his own

language, but mainly with actions, he explained where the pig was
and where he was in relation to it, where it went, how he stalked and
shot it, where the bullet entered and where it emerged and how long it
took to die. One bullet had done the trick. It flopped into the mud.
Using his body as a model for the pig's, he showed us the parts they cut
off and those they left. He rubbed his hands along his limbs and down
his ribs, then pulled them away quickly to indicate the cut. It was an
impromptu mimetic dance.

They came home as their two years of service expired. Neville in
December 1967, Dave Glyde a month before him, Charlie Howe
late in May 1968, Alan Osborne and Tom Donovan three weeks after
that. In October 1987, the Australian government staged a mollifying
Welcome Home parade in Sydney. Neville did not march with his old
friends, but left an academic conference entitled 'Man the Hunter' to
meet them in a pub that evening. Thirty years later he choked when
describing described the moment Charlie Howe walked in. It was 'so
vivid . . . as if he'd stepped from a time capsule', as if they had parted
that morning. The stand-out soldier, the platoon's Ajax if not Achilles,
the one he admired above all, Charlie seemed unchanged – incredibly
so – until Neville heard his stammer.

He caught up with the others that night as well. They had shared
'the incommunicable experience of war', still felt 'the passion of life to
its top,' as the American Civil War veteran Oliver Wendell Holmes
described it. It is hard to say what the reunion meant to them after
twenty years, but Tom Donovan's wife, Robyn, said that when Neville
and Dave Glyde met Tom in Mount Isa for the first in the *thirty* years
since he got back from Vietnam, it probably saved her marriage and
possibly his life. Anxious and sleepless at night, prone to rage, he
would take himself into the bush for weeks at a time, and come back

wasted. In renewing his friendships from the army days, he finally saw something worthwhile in all the 'bullshit', as he calls Vietnam, the army and everything else he judges worthless.

What the psychologists who work with veterans generally say seems to be right: their ordinary lives and their traumatic experience – or even their army experience – cannot be pieced together. If not the sole source of meaning in their lives, their war experience is more intense than any other, and unique in that it never fades. They feel intensely and uniquely alive when they are united with the band. Probably this has always been true of returning soldiers, and why when they are not alone with their thoughts they are in clubs, at reunions or in gyms.

Through the 1990s the old platoon stayed in touch, on the phone mainly but with occasional meetings. Neville marched with them one Anzac Day. Their lives plotted different courses, except on one count. They all developed troubled minds.

Of the 60,000 Australians who served in Vietnam, 500 died and around 3000 suffered serious wounds. The casualty rate hardly compares with World War I. Seven hundred and fifty Australians lost their lives on the first day at Gallipoli; more than 1200 on a single day at Passchendaele. Deaths from illness took more than 10,000 Australian lives in World War II, most of them in the tropical climates of South-East Asia. In Vietnam three people died of illness. For this reason – and because the slaughter at Gallipoli and the Western Front and the ordeals of Australians in the Middle East and Asia were solemnised and carved into memory in ritual, song and ceremony – nothing that happened in Vietnam seemed to explain or justify the symptoms of mental collapse among the veterans of that war, or the compensation their advocates demanded.

DON WATSON

Albert Facey received no public welcome when he got back to Western Australia in 1915. He had been invalided from Gallipoli. In 1981, his memoir, *A Fortunate Life,* was published to universal acclaim and went immediately into the Australian canon. The book sold more than a million copies and, having been taught in schools and universities across the country, must have been read by several times that number. Facey, the self-educated bush worker, boxer and trade unionist, died nine months after his memoir was released. By then he was on the way to being a national hero, and a television series put the seal on it.

Bert Facey volunteered for World War I, left Australia in January 1915 and, though the book says he was in the first landing on 25 April, the record shows he landed at Gallipoli among reinforcements in May 1915. He recalled taking part in no less than eleven bayonet charges and reckoned no worse horror could be imagined. He believed he had killed 'hundreds of men'. He lost two brothers on that same battlefield, one blown to pieces by a shell, the other bayoneted. Bert wrote that he was wounded in the left shoulder, and a shell blast buried him under several sandbags. He was evacuated to a hospital in Egypt in August and shipped home to Fremantle. He was, he said, hurt 'badly inside'.

Back in Western Australia he recovered well enough to take up his life again, and battled on through all manner of hardships and frequent bouts of illness. His mother had deserted him as a child. As a youth he had been brutalised by stockmen. He had never had money, and, after the war, never good health. His readers were moved by his suffering, his stoic forebearance, his patient generosity and the sweetness of his tone.

Just when the Anzac legend might have faded, Bert Facey relit the flame. He was the paragon of modest and uncomplaining courage. How could any Vietnam veteran say his war was even half as bad as the war endured by men like Bert Facey? Much the same esteem was granted veterans of World War II: the generation of invincible faith and perseverance. Unbreakably tough. Men to fit the mould of General George Patton, who reckoned there was 'no such thing as shell shock'.

Yet, despite unprecedented measures to ease their passage back into civil society (including a plea to American women to give their returning husbands and sweethearts 'undemanding affection'), in the US in 1947 half a million veterans were receiving pensions for 'neuropsychiatric disorders', 50,000 were in hospitals for the condition, and twenty-five years after the war's end, there were still 44,000 returned soldiers in US psychiatric wards.

Homer recorded war's psychological wreckage in *The Iliad*; among the ruins, 'that gall of anger that swarms like smoke inside of a man's heart and becomes a thing sweeter to him by far than the dripping of honey.' The story of Achilles has much in common with the stories of Vietnam veterans who developed PTSD, as it does with 'shell-shocked' World War I soldiers and countless other veterans who broke down years after their return from twentieth-century battlefields. 'Post-war neurosis' and 'nerve sickness', 'effort fatigue' and 'battle fatigue' were among a dozen terms the medical profession came up with – though 'cowardice', 'weakness', 'character flaws' and 'compensationitis' remained popular in some quarters. But alone among all twentieth-century wars, if not all since the Trojan, Vietnam got its own syndrome. It was called Post-Vietnam syndrome in the 1970s, but when that term came to mean an aversion to protracted unwinnable wars and the humiliation of losing them, another name was needed. In 1980 it was entered in the third edition of the American Psychiatric Association's *Diagnostic and Statistical Manual of Mental Disorders* and was known thereafter as PTSD.

*

Anything shocking can trigger PTSD, but sexual assault, not war, is by far the most common cause. Of the 24 million US citizens diagnosed with the condition, two thirds are women. Fifty per cent of women who have been sexually assaulted develop the condition. The next most likely sufferers are combat veterans of Vietnam: roughly 20 per cent of them – American and Australian – developed the symptoms of PTSD.

No amount of screening would have kept the men of 9 Platoon away from combat. They were physically robust, resourceful, secure and patriotic. Most came from rural or working-class backgrounds; most were familiar with guns and, through their elders, with the concept of duty. Training had served as screening: they had self-selected. No one could say of 9 Platoon what used to be said of men who developed war neuroses, that they were 'not first-rate fighting material'. But their fitness for war did not protect them against PTSD.

The inward symptoms of the syndrome include intrusive, powerful memories of combat. Traumatic moments are as if 'engraved' on the memory at the time they occurred, and persistent recollection engraves them ever more deeply. The past constantly impinges on the present, imposing a state of 'timelessness'. Nightmares and flashbacks are common. More concrete signs include irritability, anxiety, rage, panic attacks, 'numbness' and depression. Sufferers often speak of a sense of betrayal, of having been deceived and used. They also speak of guilt. They exhibit various signs of maladjustment and dysfunction, including alcohol and drug dependence, failed relationships, episodes of violence, depression, alienation, loss of motivation and progressively more intense, almost exclusive identification with fellow veterans, especially those with whom they fought.

Dave Bryan served a year in Vietnam. The day after he got back, 'it was fairly eerie, I went for a drive and just thought, jeez, everything's just going on as normal, nothing's changed.

So I found this place at Kangaroo Ground on fifteen acres, bought that and I remember I used to get out of bed in the middle of the night, go and sit up under the bloody pine tree on top of the hill, thinking I'm going crazy, cos you couldn't sleep, there'd be all this shit going through my head . . . I'd be bawling my eyes out thinking I'm going nuts. And then I used to have little outbursts over the years and go troppo . . . just out of the blue, call it panic attacks, something like that. I'd just go to jelly, shaking.' He saw psychiatrists and went on to medication.

Charlie Howe says his wife, the teenage sweetheart he married before he left for Vietnam, was aware of the change long before he was. So were his friends. He thought he was all right, but they knew he was more aggressive, more often drunk, more prone to violent mood swings. He developed the stammer that shocked Neville when he saw him again. He was diagnosed with PTSD and saw a psychiatrist for years. What ate at Charlie Howe was that none of them ever planned to go into the army, much less to Vietnam. It was never going to be part of his life, but it became the biggest part of it. If he let it, the defining part.

Tom Donovan was working underground in the Mount Isa mines when he got his call-up papers. He could have exempted himself from National Service because of his Kalkadoon ancestry – curiously enough, men who were 'full-blooded aboriginal natives, half-caste aboriginal natives and persons with an admixture of aboriginal blood and live as aboriginal natives or amongst aborigines' were not required to register. It's likely Tom would have read that as an insult, or as what he would call 'bullshit'.

The tension of patrolling, the work and the lack of sleep – never more than two hours at a time. 'None of that shit got me until I got home, and then it got me.' Tom went out in the bush and burned his uniform, got on a horse and went ringing on a cattle station. Then he went mining on the West Australian goldfields. Always in the dry, deserted country, he wandered. He went back to Mount Isa and managed a cattle station, then set up as a mineral surveyor. Now in his seventies, he raises cattle on a farm near Rockhampton. Sleep is still his 'big trouble'. He'll just 'doze and doze'. And 'you think about some of the poor buggers you shot – you try and dig a hole and bung them in around the roots of the rainforest trees, you just dig a bit of a hole and get them in'. Fifty years later he still has the nightmares, still leaves his wife's side and spends half the night on the verandah with the lights on, or watching television in another room. A friend turned up and said, 'Look at you!' and got him checked out. They said it was PTSD and they gave him 'a lot of queer shit' that he threw away. His wife, Robyn, says it was after meeting Neville's wife, Alicia Polakiewicz, that she realised she was not the only one. Often, she had read the signs and backed out of rooms.

Vietnam was no less of a war for not being a 'declared' war, or a war that could not be won. It was no less of an ordeal for lacking the traditional lines of demarcation, no front or rear, nor an assured way to tell the enemy from the civilian population, or safe ground from ground containing mortal hazards. Tours of duty in Vietnam were not easier for being shorter than the average in the world wars. One Australian study showed that while soldiers in World War II went on much longer tours, on average they endured just 60 days of 'combat-like conditions': on a year's tour in Vietnam, 300 days or more was common.

'Patrolling, patrolling, patrolling,' Dave Bryan said. They patrolled for up to five weeks at a time. A psychologist who worked for many years with Vietnam vets says the silent hunts in shadowy forests and plantations persisted in the minds of the many PTSD cases she dealt with. By day, for hours walking in the footsteps of the man in front of you; at night, keeping a hand on him. Every minute expecting to stand on some death-dealing device of the evil spirits lurking in the shadows. 'Danger of death and mutilation,' the psychologists say, is a 'powerful corrosive that breaks down many fixed contours of perception and utterly dissolves others'.

The day after the incident with the sentry, 9 Platoon went looking for the forces they had run up against. Neville went forward scouting with one of the other men who had shot the VC. Fifty-four years later, he described the manoeuvre as if it happened a week ago, and as if the tension he felt then has never really subsided. Walking in open ground, wondering if the VC had them in their sights, or if there were mines or booby traps beneath their feet; pushing through screens of vegetation not knowing what waited on the other side. Eventually they found an encampment from which the enemy had departed. It was a substantial outfit the sentry had been guarding, possibly a company, a hundred or more soldiers. The VC had dug trenches. They had laid mines in the approaches to the camp. Had the sentry been more conscientious in his duty, or the Australians less observant of theirs, 9 Platoon might have been wiped out.

Albert Facey contrived a purpose for his war by refining the experience into a beguiling near-Homeric myth. Myth it largely was, and the more poignant because the 'war injuries' that 'caught up' with him persistently for the rest of his life were very likely to his mind. Four months on the Gallipoli peninsula had been all he could stand. The record shows that he was taken from the field to hospital with 'debility' and 'heart trouble' or 'tachycardia' – meaning rapid heart rate, a common symptom of trauma.

Just nine months after leaving for the war, he was repatriated to Australia as a 'special invalid', which was to say one with no physical wounds. The military and medical records do not mention physical

injury of any kind. Instead, they leave little doubt that, like countless
other veterans of that war, and all wars, his nerves were shot. That was
how he was hurt 'badly inside'. It seems very likely that Bert Facey had
shell shock or 'soldier's heart' or battle fatigue – or PTSD.

Bert Facey's story famously ends: 'I have lived a very good life,
it has been very rich and full. I have been very fortunate and I am
thrilled by it when I look back.' The words resounded around the
country like Reveille. Would that we were all as stalwart as Bert Facey.
But the last line in the first draft of the book had ended on a different
note. It read: 'I have often thought that going to War has caused my
life to be wasted.'

FOUR

The Yolngu's ancient habit of seasonal burning survives. As you head north on the red gravel road towards Buckingham Bay, gleaming lime-green cycads sprout in stretches of blackened savannah scrub. Patches burned months earlier burst with life in curiously formal arrangement, as if fashioned like Japanese gardens. The unburned is a miscellany of modest stringybarks, cypress, pandanus, silky oak and the termites' inscrutable plinths.

And then Gapuwiyak, slumbering, a town *like* a termite mound, hosting life but seeming lifeless. It's the hub-town, storehouse of European goods and services, marijuana and kava; repository of old grievances and new ones; last stop for the marginalised and dispossessed. The waterholes where the Wagilak Sisters were swallowed are a couple of kilometres away.

The boredom strikes you first, the aimlessness, the general fatigue. It is not unreasonable to call it battle fatigue: there are the same symptoms of dysfunction. And the town *was* born of battles, successive waves of them, from the invasion of the cattle stations, the frontier 'wartime'; the church missions that came to 'save' them from those brutalities and from themselves; governments, police, assimilationists; and, finally, the mining companies. Each wave dislodged them from their lands, jolted their beliefs, fractured their relationships. Gapuwiyak has streets and houses and a police station and school, like any town, but it is also a refugee camp, a permanent waystation for people from a dozen or more different clans uprooted from their lands.

At several houses, the familiar Aboriginal flag was flying, but there were unfamiliar ones as well. They have come down from the Makassans, who flew them on the boats they sailed to Arnhem Land, long before Europeans arrived. The Gapuwiyak clans have flags. Much else in the habits of the people, from the words they use to the rituals they practise, has Makassan traces. In the literature of colonialism, from the records of the colonisers themselves to the history and anthropology that came after them, the inevitability of conquest is generally assumed. At first sight Gapuwiyak is the sad embodiment of that notion – the clans' predictable defeat. But the story of the Makassans gives the lie to it. Conquest and removal might have been inevitable in the scheme of British thinking, but the Makassans thought differently. They came to trade not to settle, and from that experience the Yolngu learned their art of dealing with outsiders, to adapt their culture but not to cede it.

From about the middle of the eighteenth century – some say the seventeenth and some the sixteenth – squadrons of Makassan fisher-men came each year to the northern coasts of Australia, from the Kimberley to Cape York. They came for trepang (*bêche-de-mer*) to satisfy the appetite among Chinese who thought the sea slug both a delicacy and a sovereign remedy: 'The medical function of trepang is to invigorate the kidney, to benefit the essence of life, to strengthen the penis of man and to treat fistula,' a gourmand declared in 1757.

Most of the visitors were Muslims; their imams sailed with them and performed Islamic rituals, converted willing non-Muslims where they could, but not by force or bribery. Though there were as many

Bugis, Butonese and Bajau among them as men from Makassar, and Malays, Timorese, Javanese, and Filipino slaves as well, because most sailed from Makassar in south-west Sulawesi, 'Makassan' became the word for all of them.

To reach the trepang beds on the coast of Arnhem Land they sailed 1000 kilometres across the Arafura Sea. They came in praus, a style of vessel then common in the seas of the East Indies. They had two massive rectangular sails to catch the north-west winds of the monsoon, which blew in November and December and carried them to the northern coast of the country they called 'Marege' – 'wild country'. 'When the first lightning came, the Makassar men came too.' They stayed in camps along the coast, diving for the trepang, boiling them in cauldrons on the beach and drying them in the sun. They sailed home sometime between March and May the next year on the trade winds blowing from the south-east.

Along with the trepang, they took with them pearls and pearl shell, tortoise shell, herbs and sandalwood, most of it for sale to Chinese merchants. They brought to Arnhem Land iron axes, knives and tomahawks, molasses, cloth, arak and tobacco.

The Makassans grew rice and planted tamarind trees which still stand at Yirrkala, Milingimbi and other places along the coast where they regularly camped. From the Makassans, the coastal clans learned to make sturdy wooden dugout canoes capable of carrying six or more people. Known as 'lippa lippa', their superiority to the traditional kind made from bark very likely turned the economy and culture of the coastal clans towards the sea – though Warner observed most people went on using the easily made traditional variety.

The Makassans taught the Yolngu how to work the iron they brought and would later get from pastoralists and miners. The coastal people got the prototype of the death-dealing shovel-nosed spear from the Makassans, though in battle the inland clans preferred the flaked quartzite tips they quarried at Ngilipitji, which went 'deep into the bone', caused more bleeding and 'burned like fire'. Yolngu men grew beards in the Makassan style and learned the pleasures of tobacco smoked in the long-stemmed pipes made in the Makassan way. Tobacco went into Yolngu rites: the anthropologists Ronald and Catherine Berndt described female love magic in which a wad of tobacco stood as a wanted male.*

Some Yolngu sailed to Sulawesi on the praus. At the Wuramu ceremony conducted by Yolngu of the Yirritja moiety, the Berndts recorded songs that described scenes from life in Sulawesi: the wharves, the rice fields, cutting timber, working iron, making praus, women gathering lilies – 'all the colourful life in an East Indian town'.

Makassans may have abducted Yolngu women and taken them to Sulawesi. There must have been abuses, but in general it seems to have been the visitors' policy to leave Yolngu women alone, and Yolngu policy to keep them out of reach. The Yolngu custom of secluding women and hiding them behind portable bark screens might have evolved from the Makassan visits.

The early arrival of these strangers must have caused great alarm and upheaval in the clans, and there is evidence that on and off through all their annual stopovers violent clashes did occur. While circumnavigating Australia, Matthew Flinders came upon a Makassan prau off the coast at Nhulunbuy. The prau's captain, Pobasso, told him to 'beware of the natives'. Warner's great friend and

---

* Surely no commodity surpassed tobacco's seductive power in bringing about the transformation or demise of Indigenous societies, and even the abandonment of clan lands. Pastoralists used tobacco as a pacifier and as payment for work; the missions added it to the promise of salvation. It was a principal agent of negotiation and compromise. It greased the wheels of European conquest. And anthropologists, none more so than the great Bronisław Malinowski, used tobacco freely to melt hostility and reserve, win acceptance and get answers to their questions.

informant, Harry Mahkarolla of the Wannggurri clan, remembered the last arrivals, the joy and excitement they brought, and after wild sprees on Makassan liquor, fighting and much bloodshed.

Yet compared to subsequent invaders, the general pattern of the relationship was remarkably congenial. The trepangers left the Yolngu hunting and foraging economy and their cosmology and ceremonial life essentially unbroken, and the relationship at least approximated mutual respect and fair exchange. As Donald Thomson wrote, unlike the white trespassers, the Makassans did not impose their laws as if Yolngu law had no worth or meaning, did not take possession of Yolngu lands, did far less violence to the Yolngu and, unlike the men who succeeded them in the trepang and other industries, did not 'exploit [them] without any control or supervision'. It was a dynamic relationship and a model of what might have been, had Europeans been as willing to trade on equal terms.

The Makassan armada came for the last time in 1907. Thereafter their visits were prohibited by the fledgling Australian Commonwealth government, to protect the nation's racial and territorial integrity, and capture a profitable trade for white operators.

Neville went to Sulawesi in 1999 and 2002. He gave lectures at Hasanuddin University and the University of Indonesia in Jakarta. An anthropologist from Hasanuddin he brought to Donydji settled into the camp wearing a sarong and a traditional Makassan headdress. He was made welcome by the Yolngu men, among whom the professor noted the use of many Makassan words. It was while he was in Makassar that Neville heard the story of a Yolngu man who, like everyone else, was unaware that the trepangers would not be coming back, and sailed with them on what turned out to be the last voyage. Someone reported seeing him in about 1940. He was sweeping out a mosque.

Before they sailed away each year the Makassans raised their masts and fastened them to the decks of their praus. Seeing coastal

Yolngu of the Yirritja moiety following a similar procedure at their funerals, Warner concluded that as the raising of the masts signalled the Makassans were going 'that sundown way', the Mast Ceremony in mortuary rites signified the departure of the soul of the dead. This was one of many ritual borrowings: Makassan themes went into pole carvings and painting, and ceremonies involving swords, flags, boxing, smoking and alcohol. In the Wuramu ceremony participants intone 'Walitha'walitha' – a phonetic approximation of the words cried by the imams leading prayers, 'Allah ta'alla' ('God the exalted'): not Allah the one true God as understood in Islam, but Allah transformed into a Dreaming creation. Elsewhere in the ceremony, participants call, 'Ooo-ah-la! A-ha-la! A-ha-la!' *

Upwards of 200 words in the modern Yolngu vocabulary are loan words from Makassarese or the several other languages spoken on the praus. Many of the words entering the Yolngu vocabulary attached to items the Makassans introduced to north-east Arnhem Land: money, bread, spoon or shovel, bottle, house (in the European style), trousers, writing and paper, sugar or syrup, strong drink, coconut, pipe and tobacco are among them. In phonetically adjusted form, the Yolngu also took on Makassan words for father, tooth, work, moon, masturbate, few or some, enough or sufficient, greedy, okay or all right, and to care for. A Makassan word became the Yolngu word for nice or good or smooth; along with the words for west wind (or rainwind), north-east wind, south and south-east wind (also the word for year), white woman, drunk or stupefied or staggering, gamble, needy or

---

*   One writer concluded that at the beginning of the twentieth century the Yolngu were
      on 'a path of natural, unforced conversion' to Islam. That may exaggerate the influence
      of the creed or understate the length of the path, but it remains true that a century
      after the Makassans were excluded, the art, ceremonies and songs among the coastal
      Yolngu of north-east Arnhem Land remained 'all shot through with Makassarese
      influences'.

poor, prison, prayer and ringworm or ulcer or sore including those associated with yaws.*

The Yolngu word for a white person is 'balanda', a corruption of the Malay *orang belanda* for the Dutch colonists in the East Indies. Naturally, the clans on the coast adopted more of the words than those in the inland, and more of the visitors' habits and rituals. But all the clans, including those at Donydji, have Makassan words in their vocabulary, and all call white people balanda. All were keen to have the bounty the Makassans brought and made long treks to share in it. Makassan swords made their way inland, and rock and bark paintings in the inland, as well as those on the coast, depicted Makassan men and Makassan praus. The Makassans never came to Donydji, but their tobacco, rice and pipes and beards did. Dhulutarama sported a Makassan beard, used Makassan words and smoked a Makassan pipe. The old women at Donydji, some of whom like Rayguyun also smoked the pipes, told Neville that Dhulutarama regularly led the band on several days' walk to Roper River in the south and Milingimbi in the north to satisfy the craving for tobacco. It seems likely that the habit set in long before European cattlemen and missionaries.

It is the religious denomination of only 3.5 per cent of the Australian population, but at the most recent census more than 80 per cent of

---

* The Yolngu word for blistered skin is the Makassan word for smallpox. David Lindsay reported 'some of the tribes suffered from smallpox introduced they say by the Malays'. On this basis, and because no other theory is verifiable or wholly convincing, it seems possible that the Makassans were the source of the disease which devastated the tribes of south-eastern Australia soon after the arrival of the First Fleet in 1788. Yet the Makassan theory is also far from watertight, if only because there is no smallpox in the cultural memory of the Yolngu or any other Indigenous group in northern Australia.

the people in Gapuwiyak declared an affiliation with the Uniting Church. Their allegiance is not really to the Uniting Church – formed from a union of Methodists, Presbyterians and Congregationalists in 1977 – but to the Methodist Overseas Mission, whose first missionary arrived in north-east Arnhem Land in 1921. The census figure is a legacy of a century of Christian evangelism and European cultural influence.

'Gapuwiyak' means brackish or bitter water, the water being nearby Lake Evella, which is the other name the town goes by. The Reverend Harold Shepherdson, a plucky Methodist, saw the lake from his homemade plane in 1935 and, in the casual way of all colonisers, renamed it – after his wife Ella, and Eva Webb, the wife of his fellow missionary. The Methodist missionaries arrived in north-east Arnhem Land in the 1920s, twenty years after the Anglicans had established a mission on the Roper River. By the end of the 1930s the Methodists were running stations at Milingimbi, Yirrkala and Galiwinku on Elcho Island. Gapuwiyak became an extension of the Elcho mission.

In Arnhem Land as everywhere else in the world, Christian evangelism worked the same frontiers as settler colonialism. Sometimes the missions were a refuge from settlers careless of the fate of Indigenous people, if not actually bent on their destruction; sometimes the missions were as destructive as the settlers. In north-east Arnhem Land, they were to varying degrees both refuge and destroyer. In 1908 the Anglican Church Missionary Society set up below the southern boundary of Yolngu lands at Roper River, to minister to the 'poor degraded blacks' who had been coping with the invasion of their country by pastoralists, pearlers, Japanese and European trepangers, prospectors and poor degraded whites.

Whatever the limits of instruction they took from the missions' teaching, Christianity at least occupied a dimension with which the Yolngu were roughly familiar. 'But, beloved, be not ignorant of this one thing, with the Lord one day is as a thousand years, and a thousand years as one day.' They were surely not ignorant of that scheme and grasped just as readily the thing about Jesus being, as the Bible said, 'the same yesterday and today and forever'. The Christian God was a God of collapsed time; the past, present and future were all the same to Him, much as they were in Yolngu cosmology. And 'enlightened' as Protestant Christianity might pretend to be, the Bible remained the book of magical thinking and the cross was countless talismans distilled. Grace, salvation, mercy, atonement, love, refuge or tobacco; whatever comfort or lively hope the missions offered, the primary metaphysics were no barrier, and much of the missions' basic theology the Yolngu readily married to their own. Gardens were a different matter.

The arrival of the cattlemen meant dispossession, massacre, abuse and exploitation – it is hard to overstate the violence done.* The Roper River Anglicans called it 'the degrading influences of white settlement'. They concentrated on the children: they housed them in dormitories, there 'to educate them [and] eradicate their savage instincts'. The Anglicans adhered tenaciously to the tenets of their faith. The life and teachings of the dear Lord Jesus were principal among them, of course. Washing was another: washing the children until their 'little black bodies fairly shine'. And work. They rose at 5 am, worked till 7:15 am, when they got porridge, then the little children went to school and the older ones continued working. Work was the other gospel. The missionaries were determined to turn their hunter-gatherers into horticulturalists and impose the order

---

* Not only the cattlemen, apparently: in 1910 'many Yolngu' were killed at Trial Bay by a punitive force looking for a missing geologist. The geologist turned up after the massacre.

of an English village on the sweltering, fever-ridden, cyclone-prone, crocodile-infested wilds. Donald Thomson put it another way: the missions' 'dormitory system', he said, was designed 'deliberately to stamp out native culture'.

Roper River was traditionally occupied by clans whose several languages differed profoundly – and mysteriously – not only from those of the Yolngu to the north, but from the great majority of the 300 languages spoken on the Australian continent. Yolngu people, including Ritharrngu and Wagilak, came south to the cattle stations and the missions, to work at any tasks allotted them, from domestic service to shepherding goats, in return for tobacco, flour, metal, cloth and scraps. It was not that hunting and gathering failed to yield enough nutrition, but they knew hunger often enough for the prospect of a guaranteed supply of food, or a drug to take away the pangs – and the anxieties – all but irresistible. Dhiltjima, the senior Wagilak man in whose camp Neville lived at Donydji when he first went there, worked on the cattle stations for several years. He told Neville he had fallen off the back of a truck and had a revelation: he saw God, who told him that he must work for the white people. But he never lost his old beliefs. Dhulutarama told Neville that when he went to a cattle station he was given bones.

The Indigenous people took advantage of the missions' hospitality, but did not readily subscribe to the religion. 'They adhere tenaciously to their superstitions, and although they listen patiently to the Message which the Missionary bears, they appear to have no conception of Sin or its iniquity: much less any desire to be free from its tyranny,' one of the Anglicans complained. By way of poignant example, in church services 'some of the blacks sat with their hands over their eyes so that they might not see those of their relatives on the opposite benches whom they were forbidden by Aboriginal law ever to behold.'

Insofar as it might protect them from European abuse and exploitation, the evangelists' determined effort to quarantine the children from the rough habits of the frontier had more to recommend it than just the satisfaction of their moral doctrine. Yet families regularly frustrated these good intentions, and the progress of their children's education, by taking them away, often no doubt to fulfil the ceremonial requirements of their own religion. Upon their return to the mission, absconding children were confined alone in bathrooms, placed in stocks or chains, had their heads shaved, or were whipped. Like the Gospel of Work, the Gospel of Love had to be enforced. Even if they could suffer the heathen superstitions of traditional Aboriginal culture and believe that by education they could 'eradicate their savage instincts', when Yolngu met the requirements of their traditions by taking food from the mission and giving it to their kinfolk outside, the missionaries could only call it theft and see no remedy but punishment. Distressingly, for polygyny and 'the practice of "promising" young girls to old men', or the treatment of girls at the time of their marriage, there was no punishment and no consolation.

Not all the girls were going to old Yolngu men. In 1917 half the mission children were of mixed descent – 'half-caste' – and the missionaries reckoned that soon the 'pure black child' would be a 'novelty'. These Anglicans were a dogged bunch: malaria, sandflies, cyclones, floods, obdurate natives and ravenous termites, no torment or sin could deter them. The 'tendency of the half-caste is to sink to the level of the Aborigines', one of them wrote, so they set up a new mission at Emerald River on Groote Eylandt specifically for 'half-castes' – 'yella fellas', as the Yolngu came to call them and still do. There seems to be no evidence to show that by rubbing them with charcoal parents successfully disguised the genetic make-up of their children, but there is enough on the record to leave little doubt that they tried.

On Groote, the Anglicans fenced the children in and, forbidding any contact with the thousand or so Indigenous Warnindhilyagwa people, put them to work. Hard labour might be a more reasonable description, even 'a clear condition of slavery', as a 1930s police report called it, citing as criteria unpaid work seven days a week and 'complete deprivation of liberty under lock and key'. The punishments for disobedience included beatings, the stocks and chains. It is no exaggeration to say that the early missions were essentially concentration camps.*

Such had been their experience of Europeans, when the Methodists set up a mission on South Goulburn Island, off the Arafura coast, the people fled. But the missionaries lured them back with the promise of food and tobacco. The missionary Theodor Webb saw the problem *and* the solution to it. Unless the Yolngu gave up their nomadic food-gathering way of life, 'little if anything can be done for them', he said. He would 'allow them to congregate' at the mission stations. The longer they stayed and felt the benefits of a 'settled mode of life', the less likely was their return to the 'uncertainties' of the nomadic mode.

It was a game of give and take. The Yolngu wanted food, tobacco and medical care, the need for which grew the longer they lived at the missions. The missionaries gave them as much as would persuade them to hand over the children. The missionaries wanted the Yolngu to work as domestics, gardeners and labourers, and in gathering trepang, cypress milling or whatever cottage industries they set up. This, too, many Yolngu did, but for both sides these deals were always

---

*   Leprosy, brought to the territory by Chinese labourers in 1874, afflicted numbers of children at both missions and, in 1928, a separate compound for the lepers was set up at Roper River.

conditional: for the missionaries, on their charges' obedience to the Christian virtues, for the Yolngu, on the right to continue practising their own religion.

Some Yolngu thought the missionaries threatened their way of life no less than the cattle stations. Some regarded them as both a threat and an opportunity to be exploited. The conflict inherent in these arrangements became most evident and most destructive when Yolngu sought, and the missions invariably granted, refuge from traditional law. The art of ruling by dividing was not beyond the workings of Christian charity. If the missionaries intended to weaken authority and discipline in the clans, they could not have chosen a better way than colluding in breaches of Yolngu protocols; except perhaps by encouraging young men and women to break the rules relating to marriage. And this they did.

The Anglicans thought polygyny and child betrothals vile and an offence to God: the Yolngu thought that when the missionaries blessed marriages that were prohibited under Yolngu law they sanctioned incest, and by disrespecting Yolngu law broke the conditions of the agreement. As was ever the case on frontiers, ignorance (for which, very often, read 'indifference' or 'contempt') was the great blunt instrument, and the blows to clan society and governance were not less brutal for the absence of intent.

The 'wartime' of the 1930s might have been in part a consequence of tribal realignments after the Makassans stopped coming. But the missions made things worse for the inland clans by consolidating the power the coastal clans had gained from the Makassan fleets. There were promised women among the inland people who went to the missions, and their defection upset the clans' marriage system. With nothing except the vigour of their ceremonies to attract women, the inland clans concluded they had no choice but to capture them. Payback inevitably followed.

By the end of two decades, the missions designed to bring a new moral order to the region had created something more like mayhem, not only in and among the network of clans in north-east Arnhem Land, but in the inseparable realm of Yolngu cosmology, the web of their world's meaning. The divide between the mission Yolngu and those sticking to tradition was just one element in the strife. 'Traditional' Yolngu congregated at or near the mission settlements, on lands that were traditionally someone else's. In some cases, the country they left became the hunting grounds for people without rightful connection to it. More often the land was abandoned. The complex, intimate ties between land, kinship, marriage and authority were frayed and torn. Incessant squabbling and violence became part of daily existence.

In the 1930s at Caledon Bay, Wongu, a formidable leader of the coastal Djapu clan, had organised his people to collect trepang for Fred Gray, an English-born adventurer who plied the northern coast in his lugger. Wongu was hardly less adventurous. Thomson met Wongu when he was over fifty but seemed to be still in the prime of life: he was a 'tall powerful man' and 'frank and completely fearless'. He had twenty-three wives and at least sixty children, so we can presume he commanded around thirty warrior sons. He was widely known and feared. When Neville showed Tom a picture of him, Tom recognised him at once and grinned widely. With adjoining lands, Wongu's Djapu clan had strong ceremonial links with the Ritharrngu. Warner heard stories of a prolonged and bloody feud involving the Bidingal and Djapu clans.

When five Japanese men hunting for trepang and pearl shell were speared to death at Caledon Bay in 1932, and soon afterwards two white itinerants and a policeman were murdered, the unconnected events were rapidly connected and the Yolngu for the first time entered the consciousness of Australians in the southern states. They entered either as people more sinned against than sinning who were rightfully protecting their lands, or as 'wild natives' ('a cross between aborigines and Malays,' Lindsay's obituarist said) waging a 'Black War', with Wongu – 'Wongo, King of the Balamumu'– as the villainous mastermind.

The murdered five were almost certainly not the first Japanese among the hundreds working the coasts to be killed by Yolngu warriors. Sailing between the coastal settlements, Donald Thomson saw for himself that the Japanese pearlers corrupted Yolngu communities with contraband. The reserve was invaded, women and children were prostituted and violence with weapons constantly threatened. The government's failure to deal with 'a state of affairs inconceivable under Australian law' greatly diminished the 'prestige of the white man' in Yolngu eyes, he said.

The two itinerants had Yolngu women on their boat off Woodah Island when three Yolngu men – all sons of Wongu – and one called Tuckiar overpowered them and threw them into the sea. The policeman, McColl, had Tuckiar's wife with him when Tuckiar ambushed him. McColl appears to have got off two shots before his gun misfired and Tuckiar had time to hurl a spear into his chest. His wife was Japarri. Thirty-five years later, without knowing the story, Neville got to know her at Baniyala, a community near Blue Mud Bay. She was a small woman with great authority.

The missionary Webb warned against pursuing the guilty men. If an expedition must be undertaken, he said, missionaries should have no part in it. A year should be allowed to pass before starting, and then only with someone the Yolngu knew and trusted, such as Fred Gray. But an expedition was soon dispatched, and with the connivance of Anglican missionaries the culprits were persuaded to come forward.

In a Darwin court the three men were found guilty of murder and sentenced to twenty years' hard labour. Tuckiar was sentenced to death. Donald Thompson, the anthropologist and Anglican cleric A. P. Elkin, and many others in the Territory and the southern states pleaded for their release. The conservative Elkin argued that European law had not only failed but was unfit culturally to deal with the crimes alleged and native courts should be established to adjudicate in such cases. Four days before Tuckiar's scheduled hanging, the governor-general ordered a stay of execution, a right to appeal was granted and three months later, in faraway Melbourne, the High Court of Australia quashed the sentence.

Not everyone was pleased. Some folk demanded a punitive expedition that would finally teach the lawless Yolngu who was boss. An Anglican missionary said the natives needed 'a good beating', someone 'who goes among them like a Mussolini'. Someone must have gone after Tuckiar in the recommended way, for shortly after he won his appeal and was released from gaol he vanished and was never seen again. It is widely believed that the Territory police waylaid him in Darwin and threw his body in the bay.

In October 1935, having received official permission to enter the Arnhem Land Reserve, Thomson (always with his wolfhound, Tiger) and a small party including Raiwalla, a man from the lower Glyde River and two Ritharrngu men set out on a patrol to prove 'once and for all' that the region was safe for any European 'who understood the Aborigines and who treated them as fellow human beings'. They followed the Glyde River south from the Arafura Swamp and into the stony hills of the Mitchell Ranges. This was Ritharrngu-Wagilak Country, and as they went one or other of the Ritharrngu called out his personal name, and where he was from. 'I do not come to fight,' he would say. 'I bring a good white man to make quiet this Country.'

And from time to time, the Ritharrngu-Wagilak people, Tom's people 'appeared from nowhere'. Dhulutarama remembered Thomson and his big hound, and he and Bayman might have been among the hunter-gatherers of whom Thomson wrote: 'There is something indefinable, a quality, a permanence, about the nomadic hunters that abides with one. They are so much a part of the landscape; they fit in without a single note of discord, and I for one cannot bear to think of their passing, these lithe, splendid, unspoiled men, from their last stronghold in the oldest continent.'

When he returned from his journeys, Thomson persuaded the federal government to order the release of the three prisoners and allow them to return to their clans.

In 1934, the Reverend Edwin Smith, a missionary of the Primitive Methodist Church with long experience in Zambia, declared it a grave mistake of his vocation to confound Christianity with Western civilisation and impose on Indigenous people 'the whole gamut of our culture'. While he was convinced that there were 'fundamental needs of the human soul that Christ alone can satisfy', he recommended that all missionaries be trained in anthropology, the better to see things from the native point of view, for 'love there can hardly be without understanding'.

After a decade in Arnhem Land, the Methodists came to a similar conclusion. Founding a new mission at Yirrkala, the reverend Wilbur Chaseling believed the Yolngu had 'many fine customs and beliefs' and declared his intention to maintain them 'in every possible way'. One way of maintaining them was to purchase large quantities of traditional clan artefacts and objects for sale to museums, an operation that evolved into the core business of Yirrkala. Thus, tradition and commerce were united, and added to tobacco, food and medicine as inducements to the clans. Among those arriving was the famous Wongu and his family. He moved there around 1938 and stayed until his death in 1959.

Press coverage of the murders and trials may have enlivened popular prejudice, but the 'Black War' also generated sympathy for the Yolngu and brought national attention to questions of Aboriginal policy, including their land rights, as perhaps nothing else could. Donald Thomson told the government the 'casual interference of intruders' was the principal cause of serious trouble in Yolngu territory, and he recommended 'rigid segregation in the Arnhem Land Reserve and protection from all outside contact'. The Yolngu were entitled to live on their traditional lands as 'a stable, self-respecting, self-supporting, primitive community'.

Thomson's proposal had the support of the Territory's chief medical officer and 'Protector of Aborigines', the energetic Cecil 'Mick' Cook. Like Thompson, Cook believed the 'full blood' Yolngu should be left to their traditional lands to live in their traditional ways. He had little time for the Territory's pastoralists and even less for missions, which, he said, failed in their duty to educate the children they had enticed to their jurisdictions, and to provide decent standards of sanitation and nutrition. The missionised Aboriginal people were unhealthy, often seriously so with tuberculosis, venereal disease, hookworm, leprosy and yaws.*

When white Australians looked on misery among Black people, they did not see a social problem, much less a historical problem – they saw a colour problem. Like his fellow eugenicists – and doubtless a large part of the white population – Cook worried about 'the problem of our half-castes'. While the 'problem' had roots

---

*   At Yirrkala in 1948 medical examiners found more than one in five had yaws and/or tuberculosis and one in three had hookworm.

in racial prejudice and an unreasoning horror of miscegenation, it did have objective dimensions – the fact that many 'half-caste' children lived diseased and destitute with abandoned mothers, for instance.*

European opinion was divided on the 'full blood' Yolngu. The missionaries, to varying degrees, were assimilationists: they believed their missions would draw the clans into white society until in some inscrutable future they, or at least their offspring, would join the ranks of the Christian and the civilised. Governments supported the missions because it was the cheapest and most convenient way to manage the inconvenience of a non-white Indigenous population in a country defining itself by 'whiteness' and 'progress'. Pushing Aboriginal people out of sight bodily and bureaucratically was standard government procedure.

The separatists, Cook and Thomson, were united in believing the Yolngu should be granted exclusive land rights and protection against white encroachment, but for different reasons. While Cook believed in the Yolngu's right to good health and their way of life, he also believed that it was in the interests of the white race to keep them away from white towns. His motives were of a piece with his predecessor,

---

*   Unlike many of his contemporaries, not a few of whom thought sterilisation the best option (the Queensland 'Protector of Aborigines', for example), Cook believed Aboriginal people were capable of 'absorption' into European civilisation. In fact 'absorption', rigorously directed and managed, was his solution. '[T]he problem of our half-castes will be quickly eliminated by the complete disappearance of the black race and the swift submergence of their progeny in the white,' he wrote. To this end, he encouraged European men to choose 'half-caste' wives, sought the power to decide who among the European male population 'half-caste' women married, and had 'practically all' 'half-caste' children living in compounds or bush camps 'removed' to government run institutions. These steps would create what he – and before him Baldwin Spencer – called 'uplift', and would at once 'breed out the colour' and save 'half-caste' girls from poverty, prostitution and disease.

Baldwin Spencer, who was for isolating them and preventing them from 'coming into contact with other people'.

The history of European contact with Indigenous Australia showed the same results in every case, Thomson said – 'disorganisation of their social order, degradation and ultimate decay' – and until a policy had been tried and proved capable of preserving Indigenous 'life and culture' and preventing the 'prophesied extinction of the most ancient race among living humanity', the only way was 'absolute segregation'. It might have sounded like apartheid, but on the evidence of his writings at least, the integrity of the white race did not come into Thomson's calculations. Rather, he at once anticipated the land rights and homeland movement of the 1960s and echoed an Enlightenment voice from a century earlier. Seeing the Indigenous people everywhere 'treated with contempt and ridicule', Paul Strzelecki pleaded on their behalf: 'Leave us to our habits and our customs; do not embitter the days that are in store for us, by constraining us to obey yours; nor reproach us with apathy to that civilisation which is not destined for us.' He could have been speaking for Dhulutarama, Bayman or Tom.

Miners had been prospecting in Arnhem Land since well before World War II, but in the 1960s they crept across the land like a guerrilla army. That they were invading a reserve established by the Australian government in 1931 'for the exclusive use and benefit of Aborigines', and country occupied by the Yolngu for thousands of years, was a moral and legal irritant, but they had the doctrine of progress, the excitements of wealth and governments hungry for revenue behind them. Mining was a national tradition and govern-ments were loath to break with it. It was the economy's crutch. The miners' duties were to the nation's economic growth, the balance of payments, the integration of the Australian economy with the world economy, and the people of Australia 'as a whole'. Nothing that might be said in defence of the Great Serpent or the seasonal hunting of animals and birds would stand in their way.*

When the land at Nhulunbuy was excised for a bauxite mine, the Gumatj clan, whose traditional land it was, sent a petition to the House of Representatives in Canberra, written on bark and surrounded by paintings in the designs of Dhuwa and Yirritja. The Bark Petition was written in both English and Gupapuyngu, the language of the Gumatj: the 'land in question,' it said, 'has been hunting and food gathering land for the Yirrkala tribes from time immemorial', and it contained 'places sacred to the Yirrkala people and vital to their livelihood'.

The Australian government was unmoved by the Bark Petition and the protests of many lawyers, clerics, politicians and anthropologists in support of it. Mining also had traditions. 'It would be a pity,' the Northern Territory Crown law officer said, 'if natives who went . . . once a year to hunt turtles were protected at the cost of the nation's ability to supply aluminium for aeroplanes.'

When the Yolngu took their case to the Supreme Court of the Northern Territory in 1971, the judge found for the government and the mining company then known as Nabalco. The communal system of traditional Aboriginal society was not one recognised in British common law, he said, and even if some form of native title once existed, the assertion of British sovereignty must have extinguished it.

That failure aside, the Bark Petition and the Yirrkala campaign

---

* Nor was the reserve intended to conflict with 'assimilationist' doctrine or support the idea of land rights. The federal Labor member Kim Beazley Sr derided the government's position in these terms: 'We can now, if we wish, interpret the doctrine of assimilation to ensure that Aborigines lose everything. We can say to them – "We believe you should be equal to Europeans. Australian citizens of European descent do not have reserves. Therefore, Aborigines should not have reserves."'

roused a land rights movement that rewrote Australian law and added a new element to politics and public debate. In 1976, under an act of the Northern Territory parliament, the Yolngu were granted secure title to their lands, the Nabalco bit excepted. Fifteen years later, when the High Court decided that a native title *did* exist in Australia, and an act proclaiming it was passed in the national parliament, the Yolngu became the owners of all their traditional lands in north-east Arnhem Land.

But the Yolngu had no rights that overrode a miner's right to prospect. The government had excised a piece of their land at Nhulunbuy and no one doubted they would excise more if commercial lodes of uranium, gold or manganese were found. The miners scoured the land for signs. They hammered round it in their Toyotas, set up camps on it, gouged roads and airstrips with their dozers, drilled holes in any likely looking rocks, drew up geological maps which imposed their view of what was valuable in the land and what the relationship between land and men should be. They had no need, inclination or ability to see the land as the Yolngu saw it and no reason to think that it mattered.

It was John Wesley's view that in the beginning 'Man was made right', and it might have been a related notion that the Yolngu had not fallen far or irredeemably from grace, which made his Methodist descendants in Arnhem Land less punitive and judgemental than the Anglicans. Or it might have been only that Harold Shepherdson had more imagination.

Alarmed by the miners' unholy zeal, in the 1960s Shepherdson suggested to the local clans that they establish a settlement at Lake Evella and prove they were determined to stay on their land. The clans responded with enthusiasm. A cypress mill would provide timber to the outstations then being built, and skills and employment for the Yolngu. Extra cash, food, tobacco, tools and clothes would come the clans' way in exchange for crocodile skins, paintings and woven articles, all of which Shepherdson sold on their behalf. It was not the first time the Yolngu had been called on to provide labour for the missions. They had worked unpaid, or underpaid, to build and maintain all of them. With two tractors, a truck, a chainsaw and not much else, the missionaries and a couple of dozen Yolngu put up a church and a school with roofs of thatched reed and cleared an airstrip.

When Neville flew into Gapuwiyak with Harold Shepherdson in 1971, there was just one house and many bark huts, platforms and shades scattered in the nearby scrub. In 2005 the town was home to about a thousand people from surrounding clans, some permanent dwellers and many others who came and went between the town and their homelands.

In 2005, Toyotas populated the verges: some repaired, some under repair and some beyond repair. Under trees rustling in the languid breezes, groups of a dozen or more women sat on verandahs or the dry grass outside the houses, gambling in a card game that people say only the players understand. (The Makassans brought card games to the Yolngu, and it seems possible they brought the game the women play.) In oversized basketball singlets and shorts, loose-limbed youths moseyed barefoot in the dust, or gathered at the Arnhem Land Progress Association (ALPA) store. Each fortnight a barge from Darwin arrives at a landing on the Buckingham River 20 kilometres to the north, and unloads its bounty of flour, sugar and tobacco, bread, biscuits, sweets, Coca-Cola and some wretched-looking meat. Locals, mainly young, milled between the store, the café attached to it, the automatic teller machine and a concrete landing outside. Dogs hung about, hoping a scrap of anything would fall.

Ninety-six per cent of the 1000 or so people in Gapuwiyak are Aboriginal, the great majority from Yolngu clans. They live in a little over a hundred crowded dwellings. The town was built on Gupapuyngu land, but people from many clans live there, the largest of them Dhalwangu. The dominant dialect is Djambarrpuyngu, a clan whose traditional lands border the fringes of the Arafura Swamp in the north and, in the south, the Ritharrngu, with whom they have deep cultural connection.

The town's population is young – thirteen years younger than the national average. Forty-six per cent are under twenty; 60 per cent under thirty. Only 20 per cent are in full time employment, 18 per cent in part time work – the remaining 60 per cent are classified as either unemployed or 'away from work'.

Every essential indicator of wellbeing is dramatically inferior to that of non-Indigenous Australians, including rates of death, disability and avoidable injury. Diabetes requiring hospitalisation is four times the national average, bacterial and parasitic infections, respiratory disorders, cardiovascular disease several times the figure for the nation's non-Indigenous population; infant mortality and the proportion of low birthweight babies more than twice the national average; life expectancy in the order of seventeen years lower.

No reading of the statistics can hide the social disadvantage they imply, or the consequences of endemic drug use and gambling on a young and idle population. 'Gunydja' – marijuana – has also brought destruction. It stunts the lives of children and adults, impoverishes communities and guarantees endemic crime from theft to payback violence. Neville once told a senior Djambarrpuyngu man who lived in Gapuwiyak that it was not good for him to be smoking so much gunydja: 'Leave me alone,' the man replied. 'It's the only way I can live in this place.'

In the 1960s the Methodist Overseas Mission brought missionaries from Fiji and Tonga to north-east Arnhem Land to lead the Yolngu towards gardening and Christianity. It was hoped that growing bananas and sweet potatoes would help the homelands to something more like self-sufficiency, improve the diet and health of the people who lived on them, and instruct them in the rewards of work. It was common knowledge, after all, that the cultivation of the soils allied to a sedentary existence was the first great step on the path of civilisation. And to help the Yolngu take it, who better than Fijian Methodists with their faith and horticultural traditions? The word about gardens must have spread; when Neville came upon Dhulutarama, carrying a dead banana plant and asked him what he had in mind, Dhulutarama said he was going to plant it, because balandas reckoned if Yolngu did not plant things the land would be taken from them.

Alcohol is banned in Gapuwiyak, and there are police to enforce the ban. In Arnhem Land towns where it is not banned it ravages populations. Yolngu relationships depend very much on discretion. When alcohol breaks down that inhibition it sows discord and violence. Loathing alcohol's destructive curse and seeing the stress in Yolngu communities, and the simmering tension between the clans, in the early 1980s, Methodist missionaries from Fiji hit upon kava as a remedy. The root of *Piper methysticum*, from which kava is decocted relieves anxiety by depressing the central nervous system. In Fiji and other Pacific islands kava is essential to ceremonies and users freely enjoy the mild euphoria the drug induces. The missionaries believed it might create fellowship and cohesion among the Yolngu, as it does among Fijians and Tongans.

The World Health Organization considers the health risks of kava 'acceptably low'. But too much kava, especially if it is poor quality or combined with alcohol and other drugs, damages the cerebellum. It causes physical and mental fatigue, red eyes, skin rashes, and ataxia – slurred speech, uncoordinated movement, muscle weakness, staggering gait, inability to walk. Like alcohol, kava also damages the liver. Some residents of Arnhem Land returning from their homes in Tonga began bringing kava with them in their baggage and selling it to Yolngu who might otherwise have spent their money on food.

After a ceremony at Donydji became a farce because the young men were too intoxicated to perform their roles, Neville wrote to the authorities saying kava was causing great harm in Yolngu communities and should be a notifiable drug. A reply came to the effect that kava was not a drug and, though the supply is regulated, it was not illegal to import or use it, as Sydney's Pacific Islander communities do in their cultural ceremonies. The Aboriginal Affairs minister said police had 'pretty much broken the back' of the trade in Arnhem Land. Neither Yolngu elders nor the police agreed. The police said the trade was expanding, and the elders said kava was 'paralysing' their communities. 'Anything that's bad ends up in Arnhem Land,' one of them said.*

To get fuel in Gapuwiyak you go to a yard with a three-metre wire fence and after a rigmarole with locks you pump your own. The only petrol is Opal, a BP formulation that, instead of the 25 per cent in conventional fuel, contains only 5 per cent of the aromatics, toluene, ortho-xylene, and para-xylene that create a 'high' when inhaled. The government subsidises distribution of Opal in remote Aboriginal communities to deter young men and women from stealing the stuff and sniffing it from soft drink bottles. There is a theory that the Yolngu got the habit from white Air Force personnel when they were stationed at Milingimbi during World War II.

Petrol is one of several substances used by people – children aged twelve to sixteen are typical – known as 'volatile substance abusers'. Glues, solvents, insect spray, fire extinguisher propellants

---

* The drug was banned in the Northern Territory in 2007, but an illegal trade continues.

and aviation fuel are among the others. The consequences for health and wellbeing are catastrophic. Petrol sniffing has killed children as young as twelve. It's called a 'cheap drunk', but people who have studied the subject say sniffers more often tell them the high takes away the pains of hunger.

There is no better reason for the homelands than Gapuwiyak. Damien Guyula, from Donydji and until recently a police constable in Nhulunbuy, worked in a government job in the hub-town for ten years: 'I know what happens in the hubs,' he said. 'I never want to see you on a Gapuwiyak verandah,' Neville told his classifcatory 'daughter' and protégée Joanne, the assistant teacher at Donydji school. The older women at Donydji say they will never move there. Wanakiya, the flinty, dauntless sister of Tom and the Bidingal brothers, told a documentary maker who came to Donydji: 'You see that rock over there? That is our foundation. It's never been moved and never will be, and that's how it is.' They will spend all their days at Donydji and be buried there.

Post-war more and more Yolngu moved off their lands and to the missions. So did their neighbours to the west. When the Territory government established a settlement for trading and medical services at Maningrida on the coast west of Milingimbi, the Anbarra clans moved there in droves. The anthropologists Betty Meehan and Les Hiatt also moved there. When Hiatt arrived in the 1950s, he was shocked to see how few people were living in the bush. 'Everyone else,' the few remaining told him, 'was living at Maningrida, on a mission or in Darwin.' As ever, food, tobacco and medical care attracted them – and later, an education for their children at a school which Meehan started after she arrived in 1970. By 1969 the town had 1200 residents from at least eight clans, only one of which had proprietary rights to the land. The traditional lands of the others lay largely deserted while their owners squabbled in eight different languages.

By the early 1960s, the Ritharrngu–Wagilak clans that Thomson had encountered thirty years earlier were still living much as they always had, but with the missions, rich with food and tobacco, added to their migratory patterns. They were hunter-gatherers with an aspect of mendicancy.

But it remained Yolngu understanding that they lived in accord with Yolngu law and had no reason beyond avoiding punishment to recognise or heed another. Whether like some of the Ritharrngu–Wagilak clans they lived a substantially traditional life on their traditional lands, or in clusters of various clans and languages in the sedentary ways of the missions, the Yolngu insisted their law and religion still had force. Makassan religion and technology and European laws and beliefs they might add to their own, but they would not replace them.

They were adept at keeping their old ways intact. They maintained their culture not by driving out the new ways, but by incorporating them – 'syncretism', the anthropologists called it. The new technology, the new food, the new God of Islam and Christianity, new totems, new funeral rites and ceremonies – they moulded them all to suit. In Yirrkala, Galiwinku and Milingimbi in the 1940s and 1950s they debated weighty matters. Nothing less than the origins of life and the nature and meaning of existence were among the subjects. Did God make all things including the Dreaming, as the Christian missionaries said, or was the Christian and Muslim God another creation being, the Dreaming expressed in another form?

There was also the question of a civilisation's future. How much of their religion – which depended on secrets – should the Yolngu reveal to satisfy the Europeans to whom they were now inextricably bound? Would revealing them, demonstrating the depth and complexity of their religion, oblige Europeans to respect it? Would giving up some secrets assure its survival?

The Makassans had come to trade with them; the pastoralists to take their lands; the missionaries to convert them. The anthropologists and archaeologists came to study them. For the Yolngu they were one more crowd to be dealt with.

Arriving in 1948, a dozen scholars of the American-Australian Scientific Expedition to Arnhem Land, sponsored by the Smithsonian Institution and the National Geographic Society, spent eight months studying the people and the landscape, crudely excavating sites and collecting artefacts and human remains with shameless abandon. What were the Yolngu to do with these anthropologists and archaeologists, forever asking questions, sieving the soil for axe-heads and bones, and taking pictures of everything they found? They had accommodated Warner, Thompson and the Berndts, but rafts of them now came. '[W]hy do they come again and again to study us?' begged David Burrumarra.*

Burrumarra, an elder of the Warramirri, had spent time as a youth in the Methodist mission at Milingimbi, travelled with the reverends Chaseling and Shepherdson, worked on Japanese pearling boats and Fred Gray's trepanger, served in Thomson's Yolngu Reconnaissance outfit, and became an assistant teacher on Elcho Island where he

---

* In recent years the Smithsonian Institution has returned a few of the 35,000 skeletons of Indigenous people collected all over the world and stored in its collection. Two have been returned to Gunbalanya, in western Arnhem Land, from where they had been stolen by an American archaeologist on the 1948 expedition. Frank Setzler wrote in his diary that he deliberately showed no interest in the bones while he had company, but when 'the two native boys were asleep I gathered two skeletons which had been placed in crevices outside the caves.'

settled. He was fluent in English and eight Yolngu languages and became the Berndts' chief cultural informant. When he heard about the filming he protested. '[T]hey are taking away our possessions. Are we to lose all this? Our most precious possessions – our raŋgga! We have nothing else: this is really our only wealth.'

Clan elders found that beliefs which made sense of the world they had been born into made less sense as that world gave way. Caught between the two, Burrumarra and other mission elders decided the Yolngu must learn to live comfortably in both: to observe Yolngu *and* balanda laws; to practise Yolngu *and* balanda religion. To be hunters and foragers *and* sedentary householders living on mission rations, even gardeners, educated in Yolngu skills and rites *and* in reading and writing in balanda schools. They must take the best from the European culture to fortify their own.

So long as they observed Yolngu protocols and respected Yolngu law, they would accept the presence of the scholars, reveal to those they trusted the tenets of their cosmology, the ways of their lives, the knowledge of their land, and many of the secrets of their religion. And to underwrite this trust they would find places for them in their kinship system.

Burrumarra wanted to put Yolngu religion and Christianity on an equal footing, likewise the two cultures. He wanted a bicultural Australia, which, among other things, would mean Yolngu rights over the land and sea. It became known as the 'Adjustment Movement' and it began with a startlingly radical step. With the support of other elders, Burrumarra placed sacred objects on public display. It caused shock in the Yolngu community. Women and children fled thinking they would be killed for seeing the raŋgga. Things would never be the same again.

*

A Royal Commission into Aboriginal Land Rights, whose members had spent time in Arnhem Land, set in train a national political movement that gained momentum when a Commonwealth Labor government was elected in 1972. The conversations about land rights the commission triggered, and a perceived need to establish ownership through occupation, were among the reasons the Arnhem Land clans began moving back to their lands.

But the outstations they established also reflected dissatisfaction with their lives in and around the mission settlements and emerging hub-towns. There was 'too much trouble', including too much sickness and death and sorcery. Not only would there be less trouble on an outstation where everyone belonged and everyone spoke a language that the others understood, they would be healthier. They would supplement what they won from the land by hunting and gathering with food from the settlements. They could get the education and the medicine from the settlements without the debilitating dependence, and with their identity intact. They could have the best of both worlds – the world of the clans and the world of the Europeans.

What happened at Maningrida also happened in the Yolngu lands. Some of the southern clans at Yirrkala had begun semi-permanent outstations by the mid-1950s. By the late 1960s, the homeland – or 'outstation' – movement was in full swing. The missions were in decline and the lands were being repopulated. By regaining their lands they would regain their religion because land and religion were one. They would regain their health because that too depended on the land. By going back to the homelands they would regain their lives.

Donydji was born of this thinking and the general movement, but with this exception: the Donydji clans were not repopulating their lands – they had never left.

*

To finish the workshop, the vets needed building supplies and Dave Bryan was going to Nhulunbuy to pick them up. I went with him to catch a plane home the next morning.

Dave taught himself building and carpentry when he got back from Vietnam, and he made a living for a while as a handyman, before things went wrong. His wife gave birth to a stillborn child, their first. Their second one lived for only two days. He wonders about that.

He talked about the schoolfriend who was blown to bits by a mine. His name was Les. Dave wondered why he lived, and Les died. That was the thing: 'Everything would be quiet and then something would blow up.' His 'psych' wondered if years later his mind was still governed by the pattern of patrolling. Dave seemed to think that was right: 'The quiet and then the boom. I think sometimes you'd be like that, there are these periods of quiet and then suddenly you blow up.'

When they came back from patrolling, they worked, 'digging bloody pits' or 'putting up wire'. 'Work! We just worked the whole time,' he said. Except when they were drinking. And when they drank, it was 'as many as you can as quick as you can'. That was the rule, he said. 'I think I threw up on every rubber tree in the bloody camp.'

Then there was that time – the first time he got a Viet Cong in his sights and wondered if he could do it. It's the little things you remember, he says, the thoughts that cross your mind.

Dave Bryan was far from antisocial, and not as cynical as he sometimes sounded, or perhaps felt inclined to be. But he was an outlier just the same, with an edgy melancholy in his voice and laughter, as if on the verge of speaking like Job, 'in the bitterness of his soul', but holding the impulse at bay.

As we drove into Yirrkala, a teenage boy walked along the road towards us with a plastic juice bottle to his nose. The Buku-larrnggay Mulka Centre, which had put the town on the map was closed for the day. Yirrkala, with its school, and church, and well-kept lawns, nestled gently into the sea.

It had been a Christian mission *and* a centre of Yolngu culture. The mission gone, it remained a spectacular repository of Yolngu art, a living memorial to Yolngu culture *and* a means of extracting balanda dollars on unconditional terms. Over the next twenty or thirty years something like a Yolngu school of art developed; while the artists maintained the abstract clan designs, the paintings were more figurative, more often told stories and, breaking with tradition, were often the work of women.

Near the church a mountain of wreaths and flowers bedecked two graves, both with large crosses. I wondered if one of them was the grave of someone I knew. He had died recently and I knew he came from Yirrkala. He had wanted to talk about a speech he had to give. It was a good lunch and we parted like new-made friends.

Dave must have known more about the local politics than I did, or had a better instinct for danger, because he wasn't sure it was a good idea to look at the graves and stayed in the car while I walked to them a hundred metres across the grass. I suppose it was the crosses: the symbol of my civilisation. I had not got close enough to read what was written when a voice bellowed from a distance – 'What do you want there?' He was a tall, arresting figure, broad-shouldered and athletic, wearing a vivid yellow and green shirt. 'Where you from?' he roared.

I made straight towards him, telling myself that despite all appearances to the contrary, I could persuade him of my bona fides, prove that I was not some moronic tourist. But he kept coming, growing more splenetic with each stride. 'Get out of here! You fucking bastard!' There was no room between his curses. It was about when he called me 'filth' that I knew if I did not turn and walk away, the injury would be to more than my pride. 'You got no right! You fuckin' filth.'

I walked back to the car as abuse rained down on me, vanquished, driven off the land.

As I climbed into the car and Dave, who had watched my inglorious expulsion, said he had thought there might be a problem, I could only think to say that a person had to go looking if he wanted a story to tell. There *was* a story to the incident: White man blunders through invisible boundary, assumes goodwill must be magically revealed in his bearing, and when that fails, thinks reasoning will work. Doesn't realise until too late that the colonial arrangement had been reversed, right down to the lesson that cordiality is a false currency.

PART II

When we say 'No' in our language it should mean
'No' in English.

Tom Gunaminy Bidingal

FIVE

From the highest hills in Timor, the founding population of Australia might have seen smoke from bushfires lit by lightning 100 kilometres to the south: only 100 kilometres, not 500, because the Sahul Shelf, now 140 metres beneath the Timor Sea, was then exposed land. A small contingent might have deliberately set out for the land on bamboo rafts, perhaps with help from the same north-west winds that later filled the sails of the Makassan praus. It is also possible that they were accidental migrants, washed on to the Sahul coast clinging to logs or some other makeshift craft. Since DNA studies prove Australian Aboriginal people and the people of New Guinea have a common origin, it could be that the founders voyaged eastwards to the coast of the New Guinea Highlands when it was still part of Sahul. The founders were probably as few as fifty or a hundred, trickling ashore in small groups over many years. Whatever the manner of their arrival, the moment of it stirs the imagination; and whether the moment was 50,000, 60,000 or 70,000 years ago, it remains stirred whenever, like the archaeologists and anthropologists, we consider the bewildering epic of their civilisation and survival.

As they spread out across the continent, radically transforming the vegetation with their fires, they encountered – and, in time, rendered most extinct – kangaroos three metres high, land crocodiles seven metres long, wombats as big as rhinoceroses and 50-kilogram snakes. They lived through ice ages, thousand-year droughts, desertification, erupting volcanoes and sea levels rising 150 metres or more, submerging coastlines and vast expanses of land, and cutting New Guinea and Tasmania adrift. They adapted to every kind of environment from tropical to cool temperate rainforest, riverine to desert, to searing heat and glacial cold, to immense upheavals over time.

Recent genomic testing tends to confirm a view long held by prehistorians that the ancestors of Australian Aboriginal people were part of the migration of modern humans out of Africa, which is now thought to have occurred around 72,000 years ago. Current evidence suggests that the Australian Aboriginal population was isolated and 'relatively undisturbed' over the several hundred generations that separate the founders from the first Europeans. If there were later migrations from Asia, such as one associated with the arrival of dingoes and, just possibly, new tool technology about 5000 years ago, they have not revealed to science an appreciable genetic trace.

In any event, we do not need to posit later migrant groups arriving to explain the high degree of genetic variation in Australia. The exceedingly long history of Aboriginal Australians, their dispersal across great distances in the small bands typical of hunter-gatherers, and their exposure to natural calamities and upheavals in their environment resulted in isolated populations and inevitable genetic drift. Genetic drift, as geneticists explain it, is a microevolutionary mechanism that produces random gene changes, rather than the 'directional' macroevolutionary changes of natural selection. If, for example, a flood or famine wipes out many members of a group, the genetic composition of the survivors becomes that of the entire population. Geneticists call them 'bottlenecks', and the antecedents of the population that first arrived in Australia must have passed through any number of them. When a small group hives off from a larger one to establish a new community, as presumably the founders of the original Sahul community did, and countless others as they populated the continent, this 'founder effect', like genetic bottlenecks, limits genetic variation within each group, but creates it across the population.

In small populations such as Australian Aboriginal groups, polygyny enables males with many wives to make an outsize contribution to the gene pool and diminishes, often to zero, the influence of those without women. Topographical boundaries, marriage rules, religious taboos, ecologies and all manner of interrelated economic and cultural factors also determine the genetic structure of populations. The biological and the social are inseparable. Understanding human genetic variation needs more than biological inquiry – it needs anthropology.

Before the geneticists, the linguists Arthur Capell and Stephen Wurm uncovered great variation in the languages spoken by Australian Indigenous groups. At the same time, it was discovered that the languages spoken across 90 per cent of the continent belonged in a group – distinguished by suffixes – that Capell called 'Common Australian'.

By the late 1970s, Common Australian had become known to linguists and anthropologists as Pama-Nyungan – 'Pama' being the word for 'man' at the north-east extreme of the continent and 'Nyungan' the word in the far south-west. The prefixing languages that were spoken by the other 10 per cent of Aboriginal groups were categorised as non-Pama-Nyungan. By then it had been established that the suffixed language was much more recent than the prefixed. For reasons which can only be guessed at, Pama-Nyungan seems to have taken root in the lands at the southern end of the Gulf of the Carpentaria – the Gulf Country – somewhere between 5000 and 10,000 BP and migrated in 'a powerful and extensive spread across the continent'. Non-Pama-Nyungan languages continue to be spoken by clans located in a narrow band stretching through Arnhem Land and across to the Kimberley.

Bordering the lands of the prefixing non-Pama-Nyungan clans in the south and west of their territory, and thus isolated linguistically from the rest of the continent, are the suffixing Pama-Nyungun dialects of the Yolngu. How it came about that on the west bank of the Goyder River the people used prefixes, while on the east side they used suffixes, and the same was true north and south of the Roper, no one can say. It seems possible that the Yolngu moved into their present territory from the Gulf Country as rising sea levels turned Lake Carpentaria into the Gulf of Carpentaria. This has long been Neville's belief. And while it might have been only the language that migrated, his theory found support when DNA testing corroborated the results of his fingerprint research, showing the Yolngu's genetic affinities with people from south-west Cape York and the southern Gulf. The difference between the Yolngu and Central Australian groups is much more marked. This is one reason for thinking the Yolngu may have arrived from the south. Another might be found in the mythology. The Wagilak Sisters came from south of the Walker river. The Djanggawul Sisters came in a bark canoe from an island out in the Gulf south-east of the Gove Peninsula. And there is a place somewhere in the Gulf to which it is sometimes said the dead return.

Neville had been working on these questions for three years by the time he arrived at Donydji. In 1971, Peter Parsons, his professor of genetics at La Trobe, who had done some work at the Hermannsburg Lutheran mission in Central Australia, found a grant for him to go to the Northern Territory, and gave him his blessing. It was unusual to put such faith in an undergraduate, but Neville was probably hardier than the average.

He would need to be. He planned a 'survey investigating the extent of genetic variation and the genetic relationships among tribes in the Northern Territory ... especially among those in Arnhem Land'. Before he finished, he would collect raw biological data from eighteen communities and thirty 'tribes' or language groups, stretching from the deserts of Central Australia to islands off the northern coast and in the Gulf of Carpentaria. To the biological data he added biographical details: social affiliations of parents, birthplaces, details relating to marriage patterns, genealogies, territorial attachments. From all of this he hoped for nothing less than useful conclusions about the 'size, distribution, structure and genetic composition of the traditional Aboriginal population of northern Australia'. For an honours thesis, that was an unusually bold ambition.

He wanted to go with no preconceptions of what he might find, so he did not read the standard anthropological works by Warner or Ronald and Catherine Berndt, or much else of an anthropological kind. The Berndts and Neville's near contemporaries working in north-east Arnhem Land – Les Hiatt, Nicolas Peterson, Howard Morphy, Betty Meehan, Jon Altman and Nancy Williams, among others – were social anthropologists. They concentrated on social organisation, culture, belief, the cosmology. They tried to unravel the intricate kinship system, delved in the spiritual secrets. Neville would investigate genes.

Before he could visit the Aboriginal settlements, Neville had to apply for permission from the Department of Aboriginal Affairs. The department relayed his request by radio to the white superintendents of the communities for consideration by the Council of Elders at each outstation.* He asked permission to take fingerprints from residents in five communities and was granted it by four.

Our fingerprints begin to take shape ten weeks after conception: by the nineteenth week in the womb their formation is complete and their pattern will be ours, and only ours, for life. Our genes, just a few of them, perhaps twenty or twenty-five, decide the pattern. Being highly heritable, and less susceptible to environmental influences, age or genetic mixing, in the days before DNA testing, measuring 'total ridge counts' in fingerprints was the most effective way to find genetic affinities between populations. Collecting total ridge counts – the 'dermal ridge configuration of the digits' – involved little more than persuading volunteers to press each of their fingers in ink.

With help from Neville Scarlett, by then a botanist and plant ecologist, and funding from the Australian Institute of Aboriginal Studies, Neville visited Groote Eylandt, the Tiwi Islands, Oenpelli and Elcho Island. At each community he presented himself to the council members and thanked them for their cooperation. Members of the councils were keen to discover where links across clan boundaries existed and where they didn't. David Burrumarra was enthusiastic. So, later, were people at Donydji. They saw it as knowledge worth adding to their own – useful knowledge. While they gathered volunteers, he set up a table in the shade and seated himself with Scarlett on one side and the council-appointed translator on the other. Not everyone in the communities was prepared to come forward: among those who did not were people who, having been fingerprinted by police in the past, reckoned quite reasonably that Neville might be a policeman too.

---

* Most of the superintendents had been patrol officers under an earlier regime. For their new role, they had been trained in a program conducted by the anthropologist A. P. Elkin and the linguist Arthur Capell at Sydney University, and with one exception were sensible to the culture and mood of their communities.

But fingerprinting was less invasive than blood tests and much less likely to meet resistance. Neville took the impression and attached to it the name, the clan affiliation of the parents and, where it was known or could be estimated, the date of birth. Then he took the prints away and examined them, noting features that went by such names as tented arches, radial loops, ulnar loops, double loops and true whorls.

These were not the only tests he administered. The genetic basis of differences in skin pigmentation – as opposed to, say, environmental influences – is not well understood, and collecting data in the field is difficult. But with a portable reflectance spectrophotometer, Neville measured the amount of melanin in the skin of his subjects' upper arms. The ability to taste phenylthiocarbamide is an established single gene polymorphism used in university Genetics classes. Neville gave his volunteers strips of filter paper impregnated with a 0.5 per cent solution of PTC to see who could taste it and, of those who could, what it tasted like. Some said it tasted salty, some said bitter, others mentioned certain vegetables in their traditional diet; one said it was like hookworm medicine. At Donydji, where cycad bread was a staple, he saw Rayguyun and Gunbangul selecting cycad nuts by smelling them. The nuts they set aside, he found, contained the powerful toxin cycasin and needed leaching before they could be eaten. The ability to smell the poison was not shared by women at Yirrkala where food was more plentiful and cycad kernels rarely if ever eaten. The difference, it would seem, could be attributed to selection.

Neville was familiar with work of this kind carried out by the Americans Jonathan Friedlander and Eugene Giles in the Solomon Islands and New Guinea; and with research into population genetics under-taken as part of Australia's contribution to the ten-year International

Biological Programme. In time, he also looked to the work and advice of the Oxford biological anthropologist Geoffrey Harrison, a major influence on the profession of biological anthropology in the United States. Harrison became an influence, a supporter and a friend. And Neville became a biological anthropologist: which is to say, an anthropologist who studies the ways that social, cultural and environmental differences influence the biology of people – from individuals to populations.

Biological anthropology and anthropological genetics are closely related disciplines with a common interest in finding answers to big evolutionary questions, especially those concerning the human diaspora – the 'Out of Africa' thesis – and the reasons for human variation. It being the nearly universal view that the study of small groups of hunter-gatherers was the most likely means of understanding human evolutionary processes, scholars had scattered into deserts, jungles and savannahs around the world. Papuans, the Hadza of Tanzania, the Kayapo of the Amazon, the Aboriginal people of Australia – wherever hunters-gatherers went about their ancient business, bands of geneticists and anthropologists went with their ink and instruments, observing, questioning, measuring, recording, drawing their conclusions and, with laborious academic acknowledgement of sources, subjecting their findings to peer review in learned journals.

As Neville's focus shifted increasingly to north-east Arnhem Land, where genetic and linguistic differences were greatest, his research established a point of difference. The subjects of many other studies, such as the Kalahari Bushmen, the Amazon people or the Inuit of Baffin Island, lived in marginal or extreme environments, but the tropical savannah woodland of Arnhem Land was more typical of early human habitats. Neville's boyhood curiosity about 'why people are different' had become a study in microevolution. He would explore the extent of genetic variation within and between the hunter-gatherer clans of north-east Arnhem Land, and the causes of it. In particular, he would investigate the link between genetic and linguistic patterns of divergence.

As social anthropology approaches humanity from a social, cultural or ethnographic viewpoint, biological anthropology begins in science, and uses science to reach its conclusions. All the biological sciences, including genetics, are fundamental to the discipline. But to understand what modifies the genetic composition of populations – what makes them different – biological anthropologists must examine the complex interactions between their subjects understood biologically, and the culture and ecology they inhabit. Groups can only be understood in terms of their biological systems: where food is at different times of the year, when animals have the most fat, when mosquitoes are at their worst. Social structure, linguistics, nutrition, botany – the 'total ecology' – are all necessary avenues to understanding the human condition. Trying to comprehend the ecology and its place in the culture, Neville spent weeks in the bush with Neville Scarlett, and many hours listening to Yolngu describe the properties and uses of countless plant species.

They found some fruit was eaten ripe, and some raw. Some was eaten in the Wet, some in the Dry and some all year round. Some was 'emergency food', eaten only when regular food was scarce. The life cycle of plants determined the seasonal migrations of people. Some plants had one use, some were used for several things, from making rope to treating sore eyes. There were plants for fixatives and linement and medicines, for making weapons, coffins and clapsticks; a plant of which the fruit was eaten and the bark stripped and beaten, put in a dilly bag and dropped in a stream to stun fish. The life cycles of some plants were also linked to the cycles of birds and animals – when flowers of a certain plant are blue, the eggs of a certain bird are ready to be gathered. A certain grass helped to locate crocodile eggs. Some plants that were eaten by people at Yirrkala were despised as 'rubbish' at Donydji. The two men compiled a list of hundreds of plants: the Yolngu names, the Latin name, the common European name if it had one, the uses of the plant, the moiety it belonged to, the references to the plant in songs and ceremonies.

Neville wrote years later: 'Examining only cultural behaviour fails to consider our animal capabilities and limitations and concentrating on our biology omits the single most important attribute of humans: culture.' Thus, the geneticist who became a biological anthropologist in turn discovered that he also needed social anthropology. So Neville taught himself the discipline. He would be the first in Australia to combine a genetic study with comprehensive investigations of the social and cultural context. He came to call his approach 'biocultural'.

Scarlett, who joined Neville on many of these early adventures, remembered occasional arguments. His politics remained to the left of Neville's and, although generally taciturn and circumspect, once started he made his case in torrents. Scarlett knew better than most the quirks of Neville's character, his driven, uncompromising nature, and an occasionally abrasive controlling tendency. Privately, he still wondered if the example of his father fighting off all competitors on his way to the top left Neville with an odd mix of aggression and competitiveness, and an almost fanatical sympathy for underdogs.

He had been scrupulous in his dealings with the subjects of his investigations, none had been coerced or bribed into participating, and many had welcomed the research. But while it says nothing about intent, the image of a white man with a magnifying glass studiously examining black skin surfaces evokes uncomfortable precedents.

There were people in the 1970s, and many more since – including some teaching anthropology – who said the discipline was 'inherently racist'; that the relationship between researcher and subject was at best condescending, at worst humiliating and exploitative. Anthropology, according to this view, had never escaped its origins in white privilege and power, and was by its nature an exercise in cultural expropriation. True or not, if this could be said of anthropology, it might also be said of Neville's genetics inquiry.*

Excited by everything that was different in the New World and the bracing new faith of Evolution, late-nineteenth-century anthropologists came up with an evolutionary ladder. Anthropology, after all, relied on imperial patronage and protections, and for all its claims to science and objectivity, it could not escape imperial prejudice. And the discipline had practical applications in the colonial project. 'We now have definite schemes for anthropological instruction,' one anthropologist told a gathering of Anglican missionaries, 'courses of lectures specially adapted to the needs of those going out to work amongst races of lower culture, whether as missionaries or officials or in other ways.'

The late Victorian 'science of man' was essentially the study of civilisations whose capitulation and defeat by the destructive forces of 'more advanced civilisations' was proof of their inferiority. Studying these self-evidently 'backward' races offered a gratifying opportunity to investigate whence the more advanced had come, along with the comforting assurance that all the cruelty, suffering and theft inflicted by European conquests was nothing more or less than human progress.

---

* Curiosity about human differences appears to be common across our species: Franz Boas told Lévi-Strauss how, when he brought him to New York City, a Kwakiutl man from whom he had been learning in the Pacific North-west was much more interested in the dwarves and bearded ladies on show in Times Square than he was in the skyscrapers, the subway or any other wonder of the white man's industrial civilisation. In one of his articles, Neville noted that when he brought them to Melbourne, both Tom and Yilarama were much more interested in the people than the sights of the city.

The pattern was as clear in the United States and its westward march across native American territory as it was of the old European empires flung across the globe. Darwinism – or evolutionism at least – and imperialism were inseparable bedfellows. Proponents of both reckoned the different races of the world had different aptitudes for civilisation, and by this – the 'level of civilisation' – Indigenous peoples were judged.

In its imperial setting the science of anthropology became 'scientific racism', otherwise known as social Darwinism, and later, with disastrous consequences, as the pseudo-science of eugenics. The central edifice of scientific racism was a sort of racial ladder, the bottom rung of which was invariably occupied by hunter-gatherers – among them, also invariably, the Aboriginal people of Australia.*

For all their efforts over the last century to escape the discipline's colonial roots and disown connections, whether intended or not, to 'scientific racism', anthropology remains politically fraught, and Neville's field, biological anthropology, has been accused of lending support to racists by its concentration on the evolutionary basis of genetic variation.

In the late 1930s and again in the 1950s, the Harvard biological anthropologist Joseph Birdsell and the Australian Norman Tindale had toured Aboriginal communities from the east to the west coasts of southern Australia. With their wives alongside them as

---

* There are passages in Charles Darwin's *The Descent of Man* that needed little amendment to satisfy social Darwinist theory. At some time not too distant, Darwin wrote, 'the civilised races of man will almost certainly exterminate and replace throughout the world the savage races. At the same time, the anthropomorphous apes ... will no doubt be exterminated. The break will then be rendered wider, for it will intervene between man in a more civilised state as we may hope, than the Caucasian and some ape as low as a baboon, instead of as at present between the negro or Australian and the gorilla.'

assistants, Tindale made ethnographic studies and Birdsell gathered blood samples, hair and anthropomorphic statistics from more than 2000 people. He took full-face and profile photographs of each subject, measured noses, limbs and crania, and ticked off his findings on anthropomorphic data cards. Upon examining all his data, Birdsell concluded that Australian Aboriginal people were the genetic product of three different migrations of three different peoples, the second overwhelming the first, and the third the second. His thesis, 'The Trihybrid Origin of the Australian Aborigine', was widely accepted, both within the profession and outside it.

Well before he submitted his own thesis, Neville's research had persuaded him that Birdsell was wrong. Environment, mutation, distance, drift and selection explained most genetic variation in the Aboriginal population, and the remainder was no more than one would expect in a single racial group spread over a vast area. Few researchers now take Birdsell's 'Trihybrids' theory seriously.* But as much as his theory, Birdsell's invasive methods have fallen into disrepute. Some of his volunteers – and that word might not fit every case – later complained that they were treated 'like flora and fauna', or like 'guinea pigs'. Some said all the testing was only going to confirm what Aboriginal people already knew; others were concerned that it might reveal something different, with damaging consequences for people whose identity was consistently under attack. A student found a group that had been subjected to Birdsell's investigations refused to repeat the process, and Neville found a group in Central Australia that resisted his work after a geneticist had been there collecting blood.

If Birdsell's methods were objectionable, as Neville believes they were, it is also true that his research contains useful clues to the traditional movement and connections between groups. The hair

---

*   Both Tindale in his standard work, and Manning Clark in the first volume of his
       six-volume *History of Australia*, took it up as the accepted scientific view.

samples, which can now be DNA-tested, offer valuable information not only about the pre-European history of Australia but, with Tindale's genealogies and personal data recorded at the same time, evidence that might help people rediscover families with whom they lost connection in the chaos of European conquest. It might help people establish connection – and legal rights – to country. And genetic knowledge revealed by DNA testing might eventually raise levels of health and longevity.

Neville would insist that the consent of his volunteers was genuine and the knowledge he gained was valuable to science and useful to humanity. He would also say that far from believing in a hierarchy of races and cultures, he was convinced that by rejecting the lure of sedentary agriculture, the Yongu rejected lives of toil and exploitation, and escaped epidemic disease, slavery, genocidal warfare, for the most part famine, and ruin of the physical environment.

After working for years among Inuit people on Baffin Island within the Arctic Circle, Franz Boas, a German Jewish anthropologist, concluded that the Darwinian notion of racial hierarchies or a ladder of cultural development was 'dangerous fiction' with no basis in science. In the early decades of the twentieth century, he wrote that the Inuit people had taught him civilisation is not absolute but relative. One of his disciples, Ruth Benedict, put it simply: 'The crucial differences which distinguish human societies and human beings are not biological. They are cultural.' That was the point of Neville's research. Why did human populations differ? Mainly because of adaptations to climate and environment, and because of culture.

In the last decades of the century, the results of mind-boggling developments in scientific research tended in Boas' direction. The new research, including everything learned from the DNA analyses of genomes – mitochondrial and nuclear – lends scientific weight to the view that race is socially and politically constructed. The popular notion of 'race' describes the geographical distribution of humanity, but 99.9 per cent of human DNA is shared, and even the distinctions between groups in the remaining 0.1 per cent are blurred and far outnumber the differences within them. Among experts, if not humanity at large, the idea of distinct races is not regarded as 'scientifically meaningful'.

Neville had not read Boas and knew little about him. Yet Boas – who had immersed himself in the life of the Inuit, endured the isolation and hardship, diligently observed, questioned, measured and recorded – might have been a model. As Michel de Montaigne (who had himself once met a Tupi tribesman in Rouen) did through travel and observation three centuries before him, Boas came to believe that anthropology demanded 'training one's heart to see the humanity of another'.

This, as far we can tell, went close to Darwin's other sentiment, when he insisted that humanity's success and survival depended less on the capacity for cruel indifference it shared with all of nature, than on its heritable 'social instincts'. A century earlier, Rousseau called it pity. For David Hume it was 'certain instincts originally implanted in our natures . . . the love of life, and kindness to children, or the general appetite to good, and aversion to evil.'*

And what was the good if it did not include sympathy, reciprocity, concord. Duty. Mateship.

On Elcho Island, where Neville began his research on the Yolngu in 1971, he was met on the airstrip by David Burrumarra. Fluent in

---

*   Darwin wrote: 'Even when we are quite alone, how often do we think with pleasure or pain of what others think of us, of their imagined approbation or disapprobation; and this all follows from sympathy, a fundamental element of the social instincts. A man who possessed no trace of such instincts would be an unnatural monster.'

nine languages, Burrumarra had been the Berndts' principal source of cultural knowledge. Smoking a pipe like Ronald Berndt's and tamping it with his thumb as Berndt did, he said to Neville, 'I suppose you want to learn about sub-sections and moieties.' Neville did.

When he moved to Yirrkala a year later, the young and charismatic Mandawuy Yunupingu and his sister Margaret (Djuwandangu) helped him to understand the intricacies of kinship and translate his interviews with Yolngu individuals. In Yirrkala he also found a friend in Bakali Gurrawiwi – with Tom, the best natural historian he ever met – who gave him a start in ethno-botany. At this stage, Neville was interested in developing a 'human ecology project' that would show how the Yolngu interacted with the physical and natural environment. It was during this work that he learned the Yolngu did not distinguish between the natural and the cultural, that they had no word for 'nature' – or, for that matter, 'culture'. Everything in the landscape was in some sense spiritual or sacred, and within the spiritual overlay there were sites where sacredness was concentrated. He also got to know Mandawuy's no less impressive brother, Galarrwuy, who was then leading a momentous campaign against the mining companies' exploitation of traditional Yolngu lands at Gove. Mandawuy later became principal of the Yirrkala school, and soon after – some say at great expense to Yolngu education – lead singer for the transformative rock band Yothu Yindi. Galarrwuy would become chairman of the Northern Land Council, chief negotiator with the mining companies, and the most powerful Aboriginal leader in Arnhem Land.

The Yunupingus were one of two important friendships Neville made in Yirrkala. The other was the Austrian-born, Sorbonne-trained linguist Bernhard Schebeck. Schebeck wrote his PhD on the languages of the Caucasus, perhaps one of the few subjects that might make the languages of north-east Arnhem Land seem readily comprehensible. He came to Australia in the early 1960s and made the beach at Yirrkala his base for travelling through Yolngu lands – often on foot – recording the different dialects and studying their relationship to social organisation. He returned to Paris in time for the strikes and demonstrations of 1968 and, escaping the consequences of his involvement on the streets, arrived back in Australia the following year. He became a crucial source of information for Neville when he met him in Yirrkala and remained a sounding board through all the years after that.*

It was Schebeck, in 1968, who suggested the word Yolngu might be the most suitable collective name for the dialect groups of north-east Arnhem Land. None of the four terms – Murngin (used by Warner), Wulamba and Malag (by Berndt) and Miwatj (a rarely used 'warname', Schebeck said) – could be convincingly applied to the clans in total. '[I]f there must be a common name,' he wrote, 'the most suitable term would be the term Yolngu . . . human being': human beings of one culture as opposed to any other self-identifying group including balanda. Calling themselves by the word for human was not to say that other groups were not. It established identity, not superiority. It meant 'we are what we take human to mean'.

Schebeck knew Lévi-Strauss, and much of what Lévi-Strauss knew about the Yolngu he learned from Schebeck. Schebeck acknowledged the 'high explanatory power' of structural anthropology, but he found that close observation over long periods and command of the language, often led to different conclusions. 'I learned about these things,' he wrote, 'as I went about my business of recording texts in the native tongues of many Yolngus – old and young, but preferably

---

* Forty years later, Bernhard Schebeck was living alone in a modest flat in an outer suburb of Melbourne with very little money, and working every day in the local library.

old – and, by doing so, learned about their perceived linguistic and social affiliations.' He also learned about rule breaking.

Neville came to share Schebeck's doubts about the tendency to imagine a coherent and unchanging body of rules, at the expense of recognising the changes wrought by random forces through many generations: by the vagaries of life, nature and reproduction, all manner of accidents, and the varieties of human character, including such rule-breaking alpha individuals as Wongu of the twenty-three wives and sixty children. While it is true that Yolngu society differed most profoundly from agricultural societies, or modernity in general, in being constitutionally indifferent to progress and linear time, change does occur. There is the ideal and there is what really happens. Yolngu law – known as 'Rhum' – is indeed fixed and unassailable, but like other laws, Mosaic law for instance, there are apostasies. There is the universe as conceived in religion, and there is also the universe of human beings and big and small catastrophes – Albert Camus' 'universe of jealousy, of ambition, of selfishness, or of generosity'. Such changes in the 'superficial structure' wrought by personality and chance events lead to changes in the 'deep structure,' Schebeck said.

In any event, anthropologists, however scientific their methods, do not record life as it's been lived through millennia, but as it is being lived while they are recording it in their notebooks, cameras and tape recorders. To be sure, they might find clues to human society in an earlier stage of development, but they cannot assume the mirror they hold up reflects a culture 1000, 10,000 or 50,000 years ago.

Sometime in the 1930s the complex Yolngu kinship system had been adjusted to ingeniously accommodate increasing numbers of outsiders by making them 'malk', or 'skin' relatives. The Yolngu social world was extended by dividing each of the two moieties into four subsections. This widened the range of marriage choices to more distant groups, and made it possible to create kin relationships for people – such as Neville – who were not actual kin. Nothing could make these skin relatives Yolngu, but under the system of subsections they were given a place in the Yolngu universe, a privilege that came with certain rules and obligations. Bakali made Neville a member of her Galpu clan, and made Gurruwiwi – effectively – his surname. He would be Manduwuy's mother's brother, known as 'Balang' – brother. As no one exists except in relation to someone else, this was how Neville existed when he arrived at Donydji. Since his early days in Dhawugari's Wagilak camp at Donydji, he has been affiliated with the Marrlarrmirri Wagilak, but he is still known there as Balang, and he exists in various formal relationships with individuals there, most enduringly perhaps with his 'daughter', Joanne (Yindiri) Guyula.

The Guyulas are a Dhuwa clan within the Djambarrpuyngu, and Joanne is one of the very few who can write both the Djambarrpuyngu dialect and her mother's very different Ritharrngu dialect, the language of Donydji's owning clans. Joanne shares Tom's desire to teach the traditional language and customs as well as English, reading, writing and numeracy at the school. Neville had worked closely with Joanne's father, Burrukala, and stood to him as brother: Joanne and her sister Sonya then became Neville's classificatory daughters, and their brother Damien his classificatory son. He calls the young women 'daughter'; they call him 'father': or, to be precise, 'malu' in their father's dialect, 'bapa' in their mother's. Joanne and Sonya's mother is also Ricky (Ngambit) Guyula's mother. Ricky's father is Burrukala's brother.

Burrukala was a senior Guyula man. He would not let his daughters be promised. If they are to marry it must be to a Ritharrngu or Gupapuyngu man, but no one will be forced on them. He lives in Gapuwiyak, but as a young man, when he was living on his clan lands on the fringes of the swamp at Mirrngatja, he was the anthropologist Nicolas Peterson's main cultural informant.

On Elcho Island, David Burrumarra talked to Neville about his vision of a bicultural and bilingual Australia, and his belief in 'both ways'. If Neville wished to meet people living in the nearest thing to traditional Yolngu ways, Donydji was the place, he said. There were people at Donydji who had never left their country. They were the most nomadic of the Yolngu. Their cultural knowledge was intact and alive. He would meet the Bidingal men, Bayman and his brother Dhulutarama, and the sons. They would help him with his research, and Neville in return would help them make maps to keep the mining companies away from important sites, including some linked to Burrumarra's people, and prove that the clans owned and used the land.

The Donydji clans had a ceremonial link with Elcho Island through the story of the black duck that laid its eggs there. Neville would see the rocks there, the 'Djawk', the eggs. He said he would radio the people there and tell them that Neville was coming. And he did. And that was how Neville arrived there.

Bronisław Malinowski, along with Arthur Radcliffe-Brown, was one of the great influences on twentieth-century Australian anthropology. Malinowski was convinced that in all human societies every custom, belief, ritual, relationship and material object, had a function indispensable to the group's biological needs. Hence the term arising from his works – structural functionalism. To understand a society – *any* society, but the 'primitive' kind was preferred – Malinowski's anthropologist had to comprehend the 'totality of all social, cultural and psychological aspects of the community, for they are so interwoven that not one can be understood without taking into consideration all the others'.

This immense task could only be undertaken by a practice known as 'participant observation'. The 'participant observer', generally an anthropologist or ethnographer, immerses himself or herself in the society under study, makes friends, earns trust and takes part in the daily life of the community. (To immerse himself among the Trobriand Islanders, who wore next to nothing, Malinowski chose a pale safari suit, pith helmet and leggings.) The researcher gleans knowledge through close observation and diligent recording of everything seen and heard. Establishing a close relationship with a knowledgeable and trusted informant is all but essential.

By these means the participant observer hopes to approach perfect understanding. Taking human society as 'organic', and therefore capable of scientific understanding in the same way as other 'organic' things, Malinowski believed that not only the society under study but the 'universal motivations' of *all* societies could thus be understood.

In Yolngu society, the religious and the physical, the organisation of the cosmos and the organisation of society, were interwoven to an extent that perhaps only a fanatic could hope to unravel – or at least one for whom finishing a PhD (finishing *anything*) was a matter of life and death.

Lévi-Strauss, who disputed many of Malinowski's claims, reckoned anthropological fieldwork had therapeutic values – at least for the field worker. It was transformative, rather like training in psychoanalysis. One could not become an anthropologist by theory alone, and one's work could not be judged by tests. As no one can became an analyst without undergoing analysis, only someone who has been through the rigours of fieldwork and 'accomplished that inner revolution that will really make him into a new man' can be vouched an anthropologist.*

The rigours are considerable: loneliness, fatigue, hunger, illness, isolation, helplessness. Anthropologists have only themselves to deal with the hardship, but it is the same selves that they must give up in order to see through the alien culture and language and find the other – their subjects. Lucretius urged dispassionate scientific study to overcome emotional anxiety and look upon the world, however bizarre or horror-filled, with equanimity: as if to say that, with the right training, surveying humanity like a participant observer could be useful psychotherapy – 'a way of learning to let go'. He was on to something. In these first years of fieldwork Neville's relentless habits of industry and his instinct for persevering took hold. He had both his father's ambition and his willingness to absorb punishment. But it also seems possible that, consciously or not, he was in a kind of therapy.

For the next half-century of 'participant observation', Neville would teach himself to look at pain, loss, life and death with the kind of sangfroid and control he could not always manage when he thought about Vietnam. He would make himself write down everything he saw, heard and wondered about, everything the Yolngu said to him, everything that happened – and, however inconvenient the circumstances, on the day it happened. He would join in, observe and record, but not interfere. With a capacity for self-denial bordering on masochism, Neville was well suited.

Neville believed that his skills as a 'participant observer' owed something to the time he spent as a teenager with the Bracken family, where he had learned to keep out of the way and be 'respectful in his interactions'. Tom added more demands. If Neville wanted to really take part in an oral culture, he had to develop the quality of memory

---

* Forgetting of course that Ruth Benedict and Margaret Mead, among other leading anthropologists of the day, were women – as were many psychoanalysts.

on which the culture depended. Whenever he forgot something he'd been told, Tom chided him sternly. He *must* remember. He'd point to the notebooks – what was the good of writing it down if he didn't remember?

It was not unlike the challenge Simone Weil set her students: to look away from their own consciousness and outward to others; to pay scrupulous *attention* to others; to receive the world others were observing – or 'attending to' – in the way of scrupulous translators, adding nothing of their own. Neville did not share Weil's mysticism or religious conviction, but he had a healthy dose of the same self-denying fervour, which helped to keep his roiling angst submerged. The conscientious observance of the rules of fieldwork satisfied a personality that bordered on obsessive and went willingly into an unbreakable embrace with the intellectual, ethical and physical demands of the discipline.

It was not the first time he had forfeited his self to the 'other' and to the trials the 'other' endured. There was no privation to which he would not submit if the 'other' suffered it; no risk he would not take if the 'other' took it. If theirs was a mood of assent, it would be his also. There was no hardship in surrendering the self if it was a way to see the world anew, through different eyes and senses, what was like and what unlike his own. Self-surrender gave him more than a view onto the stuff he could record and analyse; in visceral, sensuous and sometimes painful ways, it heightened his experience of what it is to be human. Surrendering the self was a means of knowing the self. Nor was it unpleasurable to immerse himself in the strangeness, complexities and ambivalences of the clans' world, and in their stories and their memories, especially when it meant stepping away from his own. Then there was the most agreeable of all immersions: the natural world in which he pitched his tent.

*

In the time before the homeland, about 100–150 Ritharrngu ranged over the clan lands stretching between the Arafura Swamp in the north and the head of the Walker River in the south. Including Wagilak, the number might have been closer to 250. They moved in small bands, Ritharrngu, Wagilak and smaller numbers of Djambarrpuyngu, whose lands lay north of Donydji, all related by descent or marriage. In the 1970s Neville found 75 per cent of all marriages were between Ritharrngu and Wagilak, the great majority arranged at clan ceremonies held along the paths of the mythical ancestors that the bands followed. The bands were essentially extended families or households: senior men and their wives, their children and their spouses, grandchildren and often old grandparents. The numbers in each varied, as all families do.

'Mobility and property are in contradiction,' as Marshall Sahlins put it: it made no sense to carry more than the little that they needed, the few implements, bags and woven baskets of various kinds, some items of ritual often in a little 'power bag' called a 'bathi', and sacred objects, including sometimes bones of deceased relatives. Women carried all these things and children as well, men having decided somewhere in deep time that to effectively thwart ambushes or procure game they should not be burdened with anything more than their spears.

Sometimes, for big hunts or ceremonies, regular bands came together into much larger groups. When the effort to feed everyone became too taxing and strained resources, or when relations grew tense, the bands broke up again. Broadly speaking, bands were the economic units of Yolngu society, the hunting and foraging units. Donydji was in essence a cluster of these bands, made up of the different clans ('mala' or 'barrupa') or dialect units (matha).

In 1971, in north-east Arnhem Land for the first time, trying to work out the biological relationships among the people he was studying, Neville heard the young people referred to each other as siblings, and was repeatedly told that they were all one family. He wrote much later, 'What a remarkably large family, I mused . . . It wasn't until four of the women and two of the men were acknowledged as mother and father, respectively, that I became aware of the complexity of kinship and the difficulties it poses for human genetics.'

According to Warner and the Berndts, the ideal Yolngu marriage is that of a man to his mother's brother's daughter – a matrilateral first cousin. Other anthropologists report that a second cousin is the ideal – a mother's mother's brother's daughter's daughter. The belief appears to vary from clan to clan. Some senior people at Yirrkala told Neville that first-cousin marriages should be avoided. But at Donydji both kinds were acceptable, though first-cousin marriages were uncommon. Whatever the rule may be, there are 'wrong marriages'. Some of Wongu's twenty-three were certainly 'wrong'. Many other men, keen to consolidate their power – and deepen the gerontocracy – no doubt broke the rules and did so long before the missions. The frequency with which men chose to 'take' wives by force or deception is reflected in Warner's reckoning that 10 of the 72 male homicides he recorded were retribution for stolen women. If powerful men with many wives crossed clan lines to steal women or obtain them by other 'illegal means', the motive to do the same was likely just as strong for young men denied wives by their elders' appetites.

Infractions of the marriage laws required what the Yolngu call 'straightening out business'. But straightening out marriages so they fit the cross-cousin ideal makes life difficult for geneticists trying to construct genealogies. Failures of memory make it even harder. With the passing of generations, it can't be said for certain that a right marriage was not a wrong one that had been 'straightened out', or if cousins were biological kin or classificatory. Polygyny, including both levirate and sororate marriages, adds to the difficulty: how is the geneticist to confidently establish lines of paternity when it is common practice for a surviving brother or brothers of a recently deceased man to adopt his children and take his widows as their wives, and when it is just as common for men to take biological sisters as co-wives?

The clans were the landowning groups, and the war-making groups. Like the Greeks they fought over women. Wars – or blood feuds – were more frequent and lasted longer among clans of the same moiety because they competed for women of the opposite moiety. Warfare made polygyny possible, Warner said; and polygyny provoked warfare by limiting the number of available women.

The boundaries of the lands they roamed were determined by traditional entitlements. Ownership came by way of patrilineal descent. On the lands of each owning clan were sites with which the clan identified, and many with which other clans had spiritual connection: 'sacred sites' created by or associated with the spirit beings of creation. Each member of the clan had totemic ties to at least some of these sites, and it was the duty of each to protect them and perform the ceremonies and rituals associated with them. The spiritual and the temporal, sacred myth and practical land management, were thus intertwined, if not indivisible.

Clans and dialect units are exogamous – they marry 'out'. The Bidingal Ritharrngu are the landowners at Donydji. It is their 'Father's Country'. The men take Wagilak and Djambarrpuyngu wives. When Neville first went to Donydji there was a Ritharrngu camp and a Wagilak camp further up the airstrip. Roy (Wuyngambi) Ashley, a great painter like his father, lived with his Ritharrngu wife in the Wagilak camp; Miliwurdu, a Djambarrpuyngu man, lived with his Ritharrngu wife in a camp next to the site Neville chose by the airstrip. Because they marry out, the borders of clan lands overlap, and for this reason, and because of trade and ceremonial exchange, up to 60 per cent of vocabulary is common to most of the clans and virtually everyone is multilingual. The sacred sites of the landowning clan are generally shared with other clans, even clans whose lands are not adjacent. Despite this co-mingling – or rather, because of it – each clan has its own dialect. As clan members cannot marry each other, nor can speakers of the same dialect. The differences between these dialects are often so minor as to suggest they exist primarily to delineate and reinforce the separate identities of clans and clan boundaries. Tom put it in concrete terms to Neville when he told him: 'A man should be able to understand his father-in-law.'

Insofar as they can be separated from the ceremonial and religious, or from the imperative of exogamy, the boundaries' origins lie in concerns of an entirely practical nature, namely food and water. The Ritharrngu and Wagilak clans' intense relationship with their riverine habitat is reflected in a rich and evocative vocabulary of the natural environment. A single word – 'damburmur' – denotes 'black soil country with razorgrass'; and 'wayala' does for 'flat country prone to flooding.' The human body is metaphorically embedded in the landscape: a creek is 'mayang', which literally means neck or throat; a creek junction 'lukubaltharr', meaning literally foot + joint = the ankle; a billabong translates as 'eye' or 'belly' surrounded by dry land. The word for a point in a stream where the direction of the flow changes is a combination of 'joined' and 'head'.

The life of the Yolngu clans, including their ceremonies and their language, were patterned on the land's physiography, especially its rivers and watersheds. Coming to understand this was a breakthrough for Neville. The clans were distributed around drainage basins to maximise the resources for each group. In time he would uncover the relationship of the dialects to the drainage basins: how, working as an 'isolating mechanism' (and a barrier to gene flow), language served the interests of each clan, policing access to food and water, and to women. And in a revelatory moment when, to explain, Dhulutarama drew a kind of hub and spokes diagram or cobweb map in the dust, Neville realised that a map of the dialect groups mirrored a topographical map, the dialect boundaries reinforcing the natural boundaries of the clan lands. The concentration of populations in the drainage basins, isolated by linguistic and religious attachments to their lands, and marrying within the basins, explained the greater genetic diversity in north-east Arnhem Land, and why the pattern of genetic diversity correlated to the linguistic pattern.

Donald Thomson wrote of his 'intense loneliness' while living among the Yolngu before he learned to speak their language. Neville surely felt the same in the first couple of years at Donydji. Until they could understand his questions, and he their answers, his work was painfully slow and often speculative. To learn, he had to push boundaries, but so long as he did not know the language, he could not accumulate the knowledge he needed to judge which ones to push and which to avoid, or how far he could go before he gave offence. He had to read intonations, facial expressions, body language, signs – literally sometimes, when the Yolngu communicated in sign language.

He had been coached in the language for many months by the men, yet when it happened it was sudden and surprising. He was sitting with them as usual, listening to them talk, and not aware of any difference between this day and all the others he had spent with them – until he realised that he understood much of what they were saying. All at once the world of Donydji became a different place.

In October 1976, Tom's older brother Yilarama set off with Neville to walk in country whose traditional owners, the Madarrpa or

Malabarritjarray Ritharrngu, had left long ago. Neville had grown close to Yilarama, much closer than he was to Tom in those days.

Some of the Madarrpa clan had been early residents of Donydji, including Cowyboy's father, Munuma. Munuma grew up on the Roper cattle stations where his family had gone when he was a boy, one of the many migrations that left clan lands unmanaged. Despite their own ancient connection to the place, it had been years since any Donydji Ritharrngu had been there. It lay in the hardest of the stone country, high in the Mitchell Ranges, a formidable place at any time of the year, but in October so parched and blisteringly hot it is barely fit for human beings. That was why, once they had moved away, the Madarrpa Malabarritjarray did not go back: to live in such country, you could not afford to lose contact with it.

Neville had often heard the men talk about the place and wanted to see it and map it. October was not the ideal time, but Yilarama agreed to go with him. He had been there as a boy and felt confident that once he saw it again, he would know where he was going. The senior men were not so sure. Even if Yilarama remembered the country, the country might not remember him. As the two young men set off, they passed Bayman, Yilarama's father, who was cooling off in the creek with one of his wives. He told them it was perilous territory, especially at this time of the year, when there might be no water. And higher up in the ranges there were black dingoes: real or mythic animals Neville never discovered.

Yilarama took his pipe and tobacco, a hunting spear and a spear thrower. Neville took a sleeping sheet, his mapping essentials, very little food, his army water bottle and some tea leaves. They went up the steep western slopes, over a ridge, down into a narrow, scrubby valley, then on to the next ridge. High up, they came upon a stone arrangement, a Wagilak site, representing the different clans and their relationship to the Evening Star. The site faced west and must have given a marvellous view of Venus. Neville's thermometer recorded a shade temperature of 40 degrees, but the glare and the heat contained in the baking rocks made it much hotter.

Just as he predicted, Yilarama's memory of the land returned. He remembered the way over the ridges, and where the water was. They were making for a place where a stream ran down a rock face and into a pool. In the mid-afternoon they came to the place. The rock was stained black by running water. But it was dry. Neville's army water bottle was empty. They walked following the blackened rocks that marked the path of the missing water. They felt their tongues swelling.

This was a bit of biology that Neville had wrong. In the early stages of extreme dehydration, your tongue feels swollen, but only because it is sticking to your palate. The rest of it he knew. In favourable conditions a person might survive three days to a week without water, but in this country, in blazing heat, two days would do it. Their kidneys would fail, their blood would thicken, their cells – including their brain cells – would shrink. In another day they might not have the strength to look for water, or the necessary cognitive function.

If thirst is a primary human drive, panic is a primary human response. But they subdued it. As if the unique misery of death from thirst were not enough to contemplate, Neville could not escape the thought that he was responsible for the calamity enveloping them. It was for him that Yilarama had agreed to make the trip, even when the senior men had warned against it. Yilarama remained stoic and good-humoured. He reckoned there was water on the other side of the ridge, but the ridge was a long way off. They walked on, and when they couldn't walk any more, they sat down and rested.

What at first Neville took for a shadow at the foot of a massive granite boulder turned out to be a little soak. For all they knew it might have been the only one in all the ranges. Fifty years later he can still see the patch of darkness. They managed to get two inches of murky black water into a quart pot and boiled it with tea leaves.

They slept the night on the hot rocks. Next day they trudged up the ridge. There was water on the other side, Yilarama said. And there was. A spring-fed pool, probably the headwaters of the Koolatong river, which flows north from the ranges, then east into Blue Mud Bay.

They toiled back to Donydji. The signs of their ordeal were clear, especially in Neville. He spent three days in his tent, only coming out to vomit. There was disquiet in the camp. One of Bayman's wives came to him, saying she believed he had been ensorcelled in country that did not know him. Neville thought it likely that others were thinking along the same lines. He was 'buggered for a long while'. Months later, when he was out in the bush, he found himself in such pain he thought he might die. The doctor who found the oversized kidney stone thought extreme dehydration was probably the cause of it.

While Neville was back in Melbourne, Yilarama wrote a song about their adventure.

> The white cockatoo is screeching
> It's crying out high above the stone country
> He watches the two men below returning home
> He is crying
> Their shadows wander among the rocks
> Their shadows tell him something is wrong
> He cries from worry.

> (Neville's translation)

The song spread around the homelands, and was so popular that one of the Rembarrnga clans asked Yilarama if they could make it their own, and Yilarama agreed.

In 1979 while mapping the country with Yilarama, Neville found some stone flake fragments and points. Back at Donydji, the old men told him the best stone points – the 'richest' – were to be found several days walk south of Donydji, at Ngilipitji. Dhulutarama offered to take Neville there. He would also take three of his sons, so they could learn to find the stones and work them. In Canberra, Neville told the archaeologist Rhys Jones about the idea. Jones agreed to join them. With money they raised from the Institute of Aboriginal Studies, they arranged to make a professional film of the expedition. It would be called *The Spear in the Stone*.

In 1981 Neville, Dhulutarama and the sons, Yilarama, Jimmy, and Tom, Neville Scarlett and Rhys Jones set off for Ngilipitji, the quarry – of 'legendary renown', Thomson said – near the Walker River in the southern reaches of Ritharrngu–Wagilak lands. Dhiltjima, the Wagilak traditional owner of the land around Ngilipitji, went with them. Neville translated. Jones narrated. Scarlett, still working on the ethno-botany project, scouted for plants.

Neville wore skimpy football shorts. Jimmy added to his shorts a bright orange shirt and matching socks and a massive afro hairdo. Young Tom, shy, always in the background and never speaking, sported a clipped black moustache and the sort of pipe usually seen between the teeth of tweedy academics. His face even then was deeply lined, as if creased by worry. Like the other men, he was short and lean and perfectly muscled.

In a cave on a Kakadu plateau Jones had found blades and spear points with items he had dated at 3500–4000 years old. It is possible that the points had come from Ngilipitji. The same quartzite blades mined and manufactured at Ngilipitji were traded over great distances. They have been found in western Arnhem Land, the northern and eastern coasts, including Groote Eylandt. The blades were an essential commodity and vital items of ceremonial exchange.

They made knives ('larr') used mainly for butchering animals, but also for circumcision and cutting the cicatrices on the chests of young men; but they were most prized as 'ngambi', spearheads. Glued with ironwood resin and hafted with string onto spear tips, they made deadly weapons. Archaeologists consider the blades significant because their appearance 5000 years ago marks a change in Aboriginal technology. With the stone heads, spears were too light to be effective, and the spear thrower may have been invented to overcome the problem.

The men drove some of the 150 kilometres, then, instead of the old path through the ranges, walked a mining survey track, a 'short cut' which took them away from the quarry and close to some dangerous religious sites. They moved on. The men forbade any more filming until they reached the quarry. But where was the quarry? Dhulutarama was confounded, and to everyone's alarm he said they should return to Donydji and start again on the old route. But next day, after Neville and Yilamara walked 25 kilometres, they found the quarry.

The young men shot a wild bull, butchered it and baked great slabs beneath paperbark. The old men told them to be careful, there would be buffalo about. 'Don't worry, old men,' Yilarama said. 'We young men can deal with any buffalo.'

'If a buffalo comes,' said old Dhulutarama, 'I will beat it to death with my shoe.' And he demonstrated with his shoe.

Bayman had died and Dhuluturama was now the boss at Donydji and Dhiltjima was the senior man of his Wagilak clan. The two of them were probably the last men alive who knew how to extract and fashion the blades. Dhulutarama was very likely the last man to have been speared with one in battle.

The phlegmatic Dhiltjima was not much younger than Dhulutarama, but he had long since given up hunting and he was not as lean and lithe. They were both half-blind with cataracts, and Neville's doctor friend, Kel Semmens, had recently found an ulcer in Dhulutarama's eye that he said must have felt like a hot coal.

Squatting on the ground at Ngilipitji, with the director, Kim McKenzie's camera trained on him, Dhulutarama took a large oblong stone – a hammerstone – and whacked the edge of a quartzite rock with it. A sliver of quartz fell off. 'I was taught this is a baby stone . . . it has baby stones inside it,' he said. 'It must be put back in the earth and left to grow . . . as all things do, men, animals, everything.' He rolled it back where it came from. It must be left where it is, 'only here, it cannot be taken away,' he said. As Jimmy began hammering a rock, Dhulutarama told him bluntly to 'sit correctly, or it will cut you'. The stone was 'old and must be respected. Do it properly,' he said, 'as we used to before.'

He had to get inside 'to the fat,' Dhulutarama said. Some rocks he declared 'too lean' but this one was 'fat'. Dhiltjima held a rock and exclaimed, 'My spirit is one with that of the stone. My spirit comes here when I die!'

'Such sad talk! We'll cry!' someone off-camera called, and everyone laughed. Dhiltjima smiled at the teasing. 'My father and my grandfather did this. My own spirit. All this is true. Every word,' he said solemnly. 'Tears flow,' someone said sardonically. Dhiltjima was not put off. His grandfathers and uncles had all gone and left him this land to look after, he said.

The stones yielded plenty of points. While the old men knocked them out, the young men refined the edges. Neville and Jones measured them. The finest of them, fat and alive with spirit and power, were wrapped in a paperback bundle – just as Thomson had observed when he was taken there forty years earlier – and presented to Neville. Emu fat, also powerful and held in high regard, was traditionally wrapped in the same way.

Seated cross-legged, Dhulutarama held up a point, jagged and about three inches long, and told the camera it was one like this that wounded him long ago. He put the pointed end in his mouth and wet it all over. 'We do this before throwing a spear,' he said. 'It makes it sharp. The blood flows, and death comes quickly. My enemy used such a spear,' he said, swinging a long, sinewy and remarkably elastic arm back as if about to throw an imaginary spear. 'He threw his spear. I threw mine. We both ducked. He too was a man of this stone country.' Someone out of shot asked where the man, a member of the Garrawuti clan, died, and he replied: 'At the top of this river.' Then, sotto voce, he asked Dhiltjima, 'Should I say more?'

When Dhiltjima didn't object, he went on: 'He died there by sorcery. He was poisoned inside because he had speared me.' He tapped the scar, a little wider than the spear point, on his left shoulder, three or four inches from his heart, two from his jugular. 'My relative, my "partner", did it to him.' After a brief but well-judged pause, Dhulutarama threw his arm back to the throwing position: 'The fight went on,' he said.

'My shovel-nosed spear went close. His stone spear flew past me,' he said, indicating how it went under his right arm. 'I missed again as he threw, and close to my heart I was hit.' He told the gathering how he got up and threw his last spear at him – missed again – but drove him away, hitting him repeatedly with his spear thrower. There followed a vigorous re-enactment of his journey back to camp. He tried to walk 'but heard the voices of spirits call to me. My forebears, my kin.' He sang their voices, for only a few moments but with striking effect. 'I felt weak,' he said. 'One moment I was staggering . . .' (He staggered) '. . . the next I passed out.' He fell down and lay on his back, arms akimbo.

Sitting up, he told how people from the camp found him, bit his fingers to wake him and kept biting them to keep him conscious while they dug up the roots that would heal him. 'How that wound burned!' he said. 'You can't imagine.' In the foreground of the shot, Dhiltjima looked into the distance and seemed decidedly uninterested in the performance. It is customary not to look at the person declaiming, even to turn one's back. But it also seemed possible that Dhiltjima had disengaged from a story he had heard many times before.

Before the party left, Dhiltjima solemnly played clapsticks and sang in a resounding voice. When he finished, he turned to the camera revealing the fiery red and yellow colouring of his cataract-filled eyes. Off-camera someone played yidaki. A caption on the film reported that, 'as a result of the trip,' Dhiltjima took his family from Numbulwar to live permanently near the quarry, 'to protect it from the incursions of mining companies and others.'

Because of the reference to sorcery and his fear of retribution, Tom insisted that the film never be shown in north-east Arnhem Land. Neville put a note to that effect on all copies. But some years later, *The Spear in the Stone* was shown in Gapuwiyak. An older man complained that Dhulutarama's account of the sorcery that did for his enemy – the moment when he asked Dhiltjima if he should go on – might reignite a blood feud.

Jimmy emerged from the film as the livewire, the joker; Tom watched from the fringes. The charismatic and commanding figure was the garrulous, theatrical, sometimes comical Dhulutarama. It was also possible to see his natural successor in Yilarama. Bright, funny and beguiling, in his few brief appearances on the screen, the young man shone. He had the traditional knowledge and through Neville he was gaining English. He could be the bridge. Yilarama was the great hope for Donydji and the future of the clan.

*

With several scholarly articles published, Neville was deep in academia well before he finished his doctorate. A PhD would cement him in it. He became a lecturer in the Department of Genetics and Human Variation at La Trobe University and delivered a steady stream of papers to academic journals, books and conferences. He enjoyed the mixture of intellectual effort and the physical demands of fieldwork – he was made for it – and he liked teaching well enough. But he got little pleasure from campus and departmental life and loathed the pettiness and spite. He would return from the vast horizons of Arnhem Land and the intricate mysteries and existential trials of Donydji, to hear people complaining about the quality of the carpet in their offices.

But he had joined the company of anthropologists, ethnographers, prehistorians, geneticists and archaeologists following the paths of those who forged a grand tradition: the likes of Howitt, Roth, Thomson, Strehlow, Baldwin Spencer, Pink, McConnell, Elkin, Tindale, the Berndts, Mountford, Meggitt and Stanner, men and women of an insatiably curious and intrepid cast who had devoted their lives to uncovering the intricate and often startling facts about Indigenous Australia.

Most startling of all, perhaps, in the late 1960s the geologist Jim Bowler discovered the skeletons of a man and woman who had lived on the shores of Lake Mungo, in south-west New South Wales, 30,000 years ago. This was remarkable enough: the oldest evidence of Homo sapiens yet found in Australia; proof of human occupation spanning not 10,000 years, as most had thought, but three times that figure; the world's oldest example of ritualised cremation and funerary practices; evidence of a Late Pleistocene people with the same thin skulls as modern humans, and akin in culture and religion to Indigenous Australians immediately before European conquest.

She lived 'a long, long, long time ago,' said Alan Thorne, the anthropologist who reconstructed the skeleton, 'and she was just like us.' But thirty years later, improved dating technology showed Mungo Man and Mungo Woman were not 30,000 but 42,000 years old, and that people had been living at Lake Mungo – 'Australia's Eden', Jim Bowler called it – for at least 8000 years before that. Now it is all but universally acknowledged that there has been a human population in Australia for 55,000–60,000 years, and some insist much longer than that.

The findings of anthropological and archaeological research rarely reached the public mind, much less excited a substantial portion of it in the way the Lake Mungo discoveries did. But for the men and women in the field, these were heady times. They scouted at the edges of immensity: explored deep time for patterns in the disorder, the familiar in the mysterious, the profound in the mundane. And like explorers of the conventional kind, their intellectual curiosity took them to places that tested character as well as intellect and skill; that demanded equal measures of physical hardihood and the kind of unrelenting devotion that alone made possible scholarly rigour in a leaky tent or a cloud of hungry sandflies.

The examiners of Neville's thesis, a geneticist from the University of Illinois, a professor of Biological Anthropology from Cambridge, and a Genetics professor from Newcastle Upon Tyne, thought it worthy of a doctorate. They were even impressed. The American anthropologist, though not persuaded by Neville's (tentative) suggestion that selection may have played some part in the genetic variation he described, thought his work 'remarkable in its integration of biological and sociocultural anthropological data'. The biological anthropologist praised what he said was 'the first genetic study of Australian Aboriginal populations ... to take full note of the importance of ecological factors'. He also observed that in detailing 'inter-tribal differentiation of a genetic trait', Mr White with only a little help from his friends had completed a task normally undertaken by 'large teams of workers'. It was indeed some sort of accomplishment to collect biological data on 3260 Indigenous people of the Northern Territory, from thirty-six different groups, including a third of all the people living in Arnhem Land, and 35 per cent of the Yolngu. The geneticist declared the work a substantial original contribution to knowledge not only of Aboriginal genetics but to 'the theory of population genetics as a whole'. He also commended Neville for his 'highly sensitive' and 'sympathetic approach to the tribes chosen for investigation'.

Between them, Neville's generation of hardy, conscientious scholars wrote hundreds of articles and a great many books, if few for the general market. In print and in seminars they refined their ideas, contested those of others and argued a good deal. For all their prodigious scholarship, their heroic effort, the wonders they uncovered, the gaps in knowledge they filled and the misconceptions they corrected, they talked mainly among and to themselves, and as the end of their long careers approached, Australians knew as little about the wonders as they had half a century earlier.*

Meanwhile, at Donydji and Gapuwiyak and countless other places in Australia, the subjects of so much anthropological study were poor, uneducated, unhealthy and, for the most part, at the mercy of people who had not read a word of anthropology or spent a night in a homeland or hub-town.

---

* Among Neville's contemporaries and near contemporaries were the archaeologists Jack Mulvaney, Rhys Jones and Jim Allen, and the anthropologists and ethnographers Les Hiatt, Betty Meehan, Josephine Flood, Nicolas Peterson, Jon Altman, Alan Thorne, Diane Barwick, Diane Bell, Nancy Williams, Kenneth Maddock, Bob and Myrna Tonkinson, Peter Sutton, Marcia Langton, Ian Keen, Howard Morphy and David Trigger.

'Cobweb' map

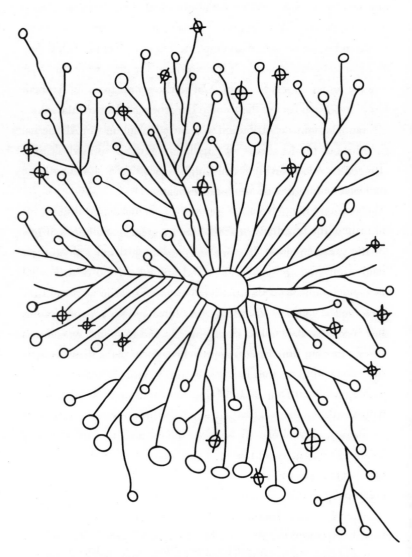

Donydji's traditional owners' representation of how their principal sites,
including sacred sites, are connected to their spiritual centre.

SIX

The difference between the marvellous structures built by spiders and bees and those built by human architects, Karl Marx said, is that 'the architect raises his structure in imagination before he erects it in reality.' The imagination is what led humans from the satisfaction of the primary needs of eating, drinking, clothing, constructing habitations and the like to 'self-activities', the satisfaction of which demanded new methods and new implements, and these in turn led on to newer methods and newer structures, and so on to ever 'higher stages of civilisation', and ever greater detachment from nature.

There were days at Donydji when even Marx, had he camped there for a while, might have understood why some people chose to pass up 'self-activities' and put their imagination into living in the natural world – like a spider or a bee, in a web or a hive.

Jimmy, third-born of Bayman's sons, had less of the older Yilarama's magnetism and self-possession, less of the younger Tom's earnestness. He was the light-hearted one, the merry-maker, and everyone's favourite. In most photographs his long, deeply lined face has a big grin on it. Jimmy had always wanted to see Melbourne, and Neville promised to take him. In 1987, when Neville was about to go home after a long stint in the homeland, Jimmy became strangely quiet. Puzzled by a mood so out of character, Neville went and sat with him. Jimmy said, 'I'll never leave my country.' One evening about two weeks later, when Neville was back in Melbourne, Jimmy returned from hunting and said he felt unwell. In the morning he was dead. He was about forty years old.

His body went to Nhulunbuy, where an autopsy revealed a blockage to his heart. Neville and Alicia Polakiewicz, who worked with him on health and nutrition in the community, suspected *Strongyloides* or some other parasites might have caused it. The pathologist thought it possible. When Neville passed on this assessment to Jimmy's brothers and other senior men, they respectfully disagreed. They had traced Jimmy's footsteps back to his last campfire, where they found the burnt remains of six fruit bats. He would never have eaten all of them, they said. He would have brought some back and shared them. At the camp they found footprints which were not Jimmy's, or those of anyone known to them. Their various inquiries had left them in no doubt that his death had been the work of sorcery or Galka. When the body was returned to Donydji for burial, the scars of the pathologist's incisions near the heart were just as the men expected, the entry point of a killing stick, the evidence of sorcery. As far as Neville could discover, Jimmy's life was believed to have been taken in retribution for a breach of protocols in totemic rituals.

Sorcery and magic are dynamic parts of the Yolngu world. Life and death cannot be understood without knowing the magic at work in them. At Donydji, troublesome spirits ('mukuys') presented in natural phenomena: a willy-willy was one of the mischievous kind, and the women would make a racket to drive it away. A still, silent stick insect might be an ancestor, keeping an eye on his descendants. Magic was the key to the underlying reality, the poetic truth in things.

Warner noted that it was in the south and west of Yolngu country – the parts where the Donydji clans lived – that the most powerful sorcery was believed to be practised. Here, he said, 'magicians, both evil and good, are found everywhere'. Death – even sometimes the death of old people – physical or mental illness, any variety of personal or social maladjustment and misfortune of all kinds were put down routinely to sorcery: either to the work of magicians in other clans, or mukuy. Warner also observed the work of 'good' magicians who healed by various means, including the removal of 'killing sticks' from the bodies of the ensorcelled. Many of these magical powers – good and bad – were unique to the stone country people. It seems possible that other clans feared and disliked the Ritharrngu-Wagilak clans for their sorcery and magic, and this, along with the hard country in which they lived, was why the Bidingal brothers could not attract wives.

'Every dogma religion has hitherto produced is probably false,' Jane Harrison wrote, 'but for all that the religious or mystical spirit may be the only way of apprehending some things, and these of enormous importance.' These things of 'mystical apprehension', she said, defied analysis and linguistic expression: 'they have rather to be felt and lived than uttered and intellectually analysed; yet they are somehow true and necessary to life.' But Harrison's contemporary James G. Frazer had little time for the idea. He reckoned human society progressed in an upwards direction from magic to religion to science. Belief in magic was the province of the world's benighted. The enlightened West made myth and superstition – a sphere of the human imagination alive and ineradicable in all cultures – the stuff only of the unenlightened. In imperial ideology few conceits were more influential than this: few made a greater contribution to the invaders' invincible self-regard, or so effectively insulated them from curiosity or enlightenment about the cultures they were trampling.

If one believes that the soul lives on past death, it is all but given that souls have effect in the world, and that other unseen agents and shapeshifters are active. If in little else, the Yolngu had this much in common with both ancient Sumerian farmers and modern suburban

Pentecostalists, and many other varieties of religion wedged in the years between them. Like the streets of London when Madame Blavatsky and Theosophists walked them, the bush was interpenetrated with spirits sensed and often seen by people who believed in them. They spared themselves bleak visions of a hellish afterlife, but the Yolngu considered it essential to respect the spirits by scrupulously observing funerary rites and giving them, and the devilish mukuys, no reason for anger and revenge. Washing and smoking purification ceremonies are carried out for this reason. After every major ceremony, the participants spend anxious days wondering if they or others had made mistakes for which the spirit ancestors will exact an awful price. As life brings body and spirit together, death separates them: the body perishes, but the spirit – provided the right procedures are followed – returns to the place whence it came to re-enter the mother's womb. What separates the body and the spirit, and what makes sense of illness and death, are human breaches of the rules.

A few years before Neville arrived at Donydji, one of Bayman's sons attended Gunabibi, a great totemic ceremony that spread into Yolngu Country from south of the Roper.* The son went despite protests from

---

*   Gunabibi is a totemic ceremony that lasts months and sometimes even years. It originated south of the Yolngu clan lands in the Roper River region. Warner reported that when it was not held in north-east Arnhem Land, men from there would travel south to take part. Now held in Yolngu Country, it is attended by Yolngu from all over north-east Arnhem Land. It is one of two great Dhuwa ceremonies associated with the founding myth of the Wagilak sisters and Yurlungurr. People of the Yirritja moiety take part in Gunabibi in roles as specific to them as others are to Dhuwa. It is both an increase cult and an 'age grading' ceremony – a rite of passage for boys entering the secret religious world of adult males. In recent years it has become more overtly related to the power of clan leaders, whose traditional authority has been eroded by social breakdown in the hub-towns and the steady waning of customary knowledge. These days male youths are all but compelled to participate in Gunabibi, one might say 'conscripted', to learn the secrets they must know if they are to become men, to learn discipline and accept the authority of Yolngu law.

some of the Ritharrngu elders, who thought the rites were dangerous. It is not clear how or why, but soon after leaving the ceremony Bayman's son died. In his grief and rage Bayman savaged a sacred rock, cleaving a piece from it with a machete. Bayman had yaws, a common disease among the Yolngu long after it became treatable. In 1936, Donald Thomson injected children at Blue Mud bay with *neoarsphenamine* and got great satisfaction from the results. Bayman was not treated. By the time Neville met him his nose had been eaten away. A tropical disease closely related to syphilis, though not venereal, the yaws bacterium (*Treponema pallidum pertenue*) is spread by skin contact. But as his symptoms worsened, Neville found Bayman's affliction was discreetly held to be a consequence of his attack on the rock.

Galka is a fearsome and inscrutable personage, at once a shocking creature of the imagination and probably a real-life hitman. Warner heard from men claiming to be Galka the secret methods of their vocation: how they opened the left side of the victim, slit the skin between two ribs, bent the ribs back far enough to allow a hand to enter and, reaching up inside the body, plunged a small 'killing stick' (a sort of magic sword) into the heart. How, when the heart had stopped beating and the blood had been drained into a paperbark bowl, the wound was healed up by rubbing it with a heated spear thrower and the juice of green ants mashed up with a lizard. His soul gone, the victim would go about for two or three days after the procedure, and then die.

Warner said there were 'a number of these soul stealers in the southern and western parts' of Yolngu Country, which would include the Ritharrngu-Wagilak parts. He knew some of them. They lived like any other men in their communities, but they had all been taught by their fathers or another near-relative 'how to kill a man and make him alive to die'. They were taught other equally grotesque procedures for killing women. One assassin told Warner that while living at the

Milingimbi Mission, he captured a woman who had given another man an axe that had been promised to his brother; he and the brother had taken turns to bleed and all but eviscerate the woman while they ate some freshly cooked bandicoots.

For all their horror, the fantastical elements in the procedures Warner described leave some doubt about their authenticity, whereas hanging, drawing and quartering, and incinerating troublemakers' entrails before their eyes, were horribly real, as were setting folk on piles of wood and burning them alive, breaking their bones on a wheel, starving them to death in dungeons, nailing them to crosses, garrotting and so on. Probably the worst that can be said of the grisly accounts Warner recorded is that they issue from the same dismal mental realms, and the same wish to incite the profoundest fear, as all the other tortures devised by men.

Warner was in no doubt that, if not by the appalling means described to him, brutal assassinations of men and women were not uncommon. He knew of one 'soul-stealer' who was credited with the deaths of seven men and one woman. Another, 'not very different from the ordinary man in the tribe', 'nothing sinister, peculiar or psychopathic about him', had killed many men and women, and he gave Warner detailed accounts of the various ways in which he did it. A Wagilak man told Neville Scarlett that a poison extracted from the bark of the ironwood tree was used by assassins to cause fatal heart attacks.

Bernhard Schebeck concluded it likely the assassins were real and were still operating while he was there. Neville also believes that in his own time in the region, deaths have occurred that might be put down to Galka.

In common with fundamentalist religious communities, the clans were as if battlegrounds for the rival forces of good and evil. Neville said that, when camping, the men would often sit with their backs to the fire and their heads lowered almost to the ground to scan the area around them and listen for the approach of enemies corporeal and less so. At night he would hear them grinding their teeth as they slept. He has examined skulls in the National Museum of Victoria, collected by Thomson, that showed signs of a lifetime's grinding. It was the same fear of Galka that drove Cowboy to train a bright light on the bush and have his wife stand guard through the night. Neville has also observed that when there is division and strife among the families the fear of Galka prowls in the collective mind, which the functionalists might say means the avenger is there to maintain order.

From conversations with Yolngu, Warner estimated that in the two decades before he arrived, almost 200 men under the age of twenty-five had been killed in blood feuds. The seventy-two deaths he counted while he was in north-east Arnhem Land was of course nothing compared to the slaughter he had seen just a few years before as a nineteen-year-old soldier on the Western Front, but it far exceeded the homicide rate per capita anywhere in the United States. Feuds, like wars, tend to have a life of their own and to continue long after the antagonists have forgotten what first antagonised them. But polygyny had a role in it insofar as it made women chattels and rewarded successful males not only in sexual satisfaction and domestic convenience, but in the power and influence accruing to a man with numerous warrior sons to protect his interests and infant daughters to bestow. A man's several wives were, as Lévi-Strauss found among the Nambikwarra of the Amazon, 'at one and the same time, the reward of power and its instrument'. And an incitement to jealousy, frustration, cuckolding and strife.

When the Methodist missionary Keith Cole visited Donydji in 1979, he reported finding 'a happy integrated group, hunting and living largely off the bush'. Theirs was the only homeland where people stayed through the wet season. That was the thing about those Ritharrngu men – they stayed. They stayed through the war with the cattle stations, and through the internecine fighting in the 'wartime'; they stayed when others were going into the missions. The men were 'strong and stayed', the women said. 'That's what we think about them.' For the missionary to find the Donydji people resolute, 'happy' and 'integrated' was not surprising: there were plenty of days thirty years later when the same words applied. But Cole added a description, passed on by a 'local aboriginal church worker', of 'a good and faithful people, part of God's family, and sharing the gospel with each other'. Good and faithful to be sure, but thirty years after Cole's visit I never saw a gospel or more than a glimmer of the Christian God's influence.

The Methodist mission had an old connection with the Donydji people. To the extent that it had been serviced at all in the 1970s, it was the mission on Elcho Island that did it. Harold Shepherdson flew in from time to time with supplies, and sometimes tracts they couldn't read. In the shade of his plane's wings, he conducted Christian services to which, according to Neville, who witnessed them, the people were respectfully inattentive. 'Bapa Sheppy' had been doing it for fifty years: bringing food, medicine and materials, fixing engines, building houses, repairing boats, wirelesses and plumbing, keeping the communities in touch by means of a plane he bought out of a catalogue, assembled at the mission and taught himself to fly. As long ago as 1938, the general secretary of the Methodist Church said that he couldn't imagine how they would manage in Arnhem Land without him. A decade after his death, it was impossible to avoid comparing what he and his wife did in a home-made plane on a minister's stipend with what an army of paid employees and contractors failed to do with millions. In their isolation, the Donydji people needed Shepherdson and held him in fond regard. But if they were part of God's family, it was a passive part at most, and their attachment owed more to the mission's supplies of tobacco than the promise of salvation.

But Jesus came as never before around 1980. His sudden arrival took Neville by surprise and over the next ten years he watched with a mixture of proper anthropological detachment and personal frustration and alarm.

It was known as the Fellowship and it began on Elcho Island, stirred into existence by the visit of Ralph Bell, a Black American evangelist from the Billy Graham crusade, and sustained by the weekly radio broadcasts of legendary crusader, the Reverend Garner Ted Armstrong.

The 'Church Council' of the Fellowship issued pamphlets in simple words and simpler drawings to 'enable even illiterates to "read" about worship, baptism, witness, etc.' and find the path to a happier life, even an everlasting one, through renouncing sin and following Jesus. Baptism, the pamphlets declared, was 'not the same as the Yolngu cleansing ceremony'. Baptism was not magic, they said. Water was not magic. They did not say if the Holy Spirit was magic; or if the Cross, the resurrection or the devil – represented by a snake – were magic; or if prayer, or shouting, 'Praise the Lord!' and 'Hallelujah!' were. But they all had enough magic about them to lend the Fellowship magical power.

Sufficient power, it seemed, to resist Yolngu magic. One young man told Neville that singing the hymns and crying 'Praise the Lord!' cleared the headaches he attributed to mukuys doing the work of his recently deceased classificatory mother, who came to him in his sleep and hit him with her digging stick. The movement gathered intensity, Neville wrote, when Jimmy died suddenly.

Every night for two hours or more, prayers were uttered, invocations chanted and 'born again' hymns were sung. The single men were the most fervent. All believed that turning to God and away from

Yolngu religion would ease tensions in and between homelands. Most of the meetings were held at the young men's hearths, but they sometimes moved to other fires, and on at least one occasion to a camp of young Wagilak women a little distance from the main settlement. Neville had never seen it before: young men and women grooming themselves, brushing their hair, rubbing their bodies with oil.

The older men and women were not moved in the same way, and some disapproved of both the new religion and the intermingling of the sexes, but they did not try to stop it. Perhaps they were moved by the happiness and energy of young men and women to whom Jesus had granted permission to hold hands, gaze upon each other, dance and sing together, and on a tractor-drawn trailer travel for hours to the deserted Dhunganda outstation together, where, by the baptismal brook, they sang and danced around a cross and fell backwards into each other's arms. And came home together, bouncing along on the trailer in the dark. It was not Yolngu law, but it was pleasurable.

Tom was one of the Fellowship converts for a while, but the most fervent was Christopher. As a self-appointed lay preacher, he earned status and influence within the homeland and among the missionaries and service bureaucracies. There was no doubting his sincerity or his fitness for the task. A crucifix hung from his neck and bounced off his cicatrice. He got hold of a battery-operated portable organ and he took it wherever he went: not only to the evening prayer meetings, but when out in the bush after game, as dawn crept across the sky his fellow hunters woke to hear, not the rustling of the leaves or the echo of millennia in the call of the koel, but Christopher in a Uniting Church T-shirt, belting out a din on the keyboard and crying 'Hallelujah!' 'Praise the Lord!' He preached sermons and led hymns in an 'unintelligible' English, and he conducted holy communion with 'red cordial in a cut down plastic bottle and pieces of damper as the sacrament.' Neville arrived at the homeland one day to find

Christopher had cut up the aluminium frames for a kit house and made them into crosses.

The Fellowship disciples at Donydji began to call Yolngu law the 'wrong way' or the 'Old Testament'. Once, Neville told the elders as tactfully as he could that he was sorry there were so many Christian 'manikay' (songs) and so few of the Yolngu kind. They agreed with him, and soon after performed a 'bunggul' (ceremony). But when they came to do it, some of the young people first sang hymns and apologised to 'God Jesus' for the 'Old Testament business' they were about to perform, but they were doing it for Balang.

To seek solutions to the problems of their isolation, and in non-traditional rituals find relief from the tensions of traditional life, made it a typically utilitarian measure as much as a religious conversion. Neville became convinced it was a kind of cargo cult, driven in the main by young men who saw the ecstatic rites of the faith as a path to material comforts and easier lives. In a little tin shed, adjacent to a tall aerial in a tree, the pedal radio picked up messages from the Department of Aboriginal Affairs in Darwin, and prayer services in the coastal homelands. When the prayers were on, the men crowded into the shed and while one pedalled in the sweltering air the others joined in the prayers. 'Tell Him to send tobacco!' 'Cordial!' 'Sugar!' 'Torch batteries!' 'Buffalo bullets!' They didn't say 'Women', but Neville wondered if they thought the Fellowship might over-come that chronic shortage as well.

If not immediately, sooner or later a plane did fly in with supplies. And judging that the Fellowship had made life better in the homelands than it was in the hub-towns, several women did return to Donydji. They brought children with them – which added to the need for a school.

The Fellowship cut into the traditional culture, with consequences that went beyond ceremonial life. Faith healing, including the 'laying on of hands', for a time held sway over both traditional and Western medicine. The women continued to gather food, but Neville estimated Christian prayer and ritual reduced the time men spent hunting by 60 per cent. The old men complained that the young men were not bringing them meat, and they were growing weak for want of it. The women went on making baskets and mats to sell at the mission stores, but the men gave up their painting and craft work, partly because they reckoned it belonged to the 'old way', and partly because, like the hunting, the effort was pointless when prayer could bring them all they needed.

It was an odd amalgam of symbols and rituals, but Christopher's message was consistent, and consistently Christian. Stop fighting and follow Jesus, come together in His name and He will provide. He will heal the sick and drive out the devils – the mukuys and Galka. Neville thought that despite the message in the evangelical propaganda, it was not the prospect of a Christian life everlasting that attracted them at Donydji, but the calm and order it brought to the homeland. That was why Tom joined in for a while. The communitarian revivalist style of the Fellowship touched something the old missions had not, and it went some way to vindicating Edwin Smith's Primitive Methodist vision of a missionary Christianity in tune with the Indigenous people, and without such 'accretions' of Western religion and culture as work and gardening.

Yet the new faith in the powers of the invisible 'God Jesus', and the words and symbols by which He could be reached, did not strip the old meanings from the land or stop the Yolngu talking to it. The senior men and women, including the Fellowship followers, did not ask the mining companies for Christian charity or threaten them with eternal damnation. Mangay from Mirrngatja held up his Djambarrpuyngu New Testament and said to them, 'You tell us to take the right path, but why then do you push us off it?' But that was more of a debating point. They opposed the miners on strictly traditional grounds.

The Great Awakening at Donydji was not sparked by disenchantment with traditional religion but by frustration at the failure of secular authority, and the clans' inability to make the modern work for them in the ways it worked for white people. The old rituals to encourage fecundity in nature did not work for flour, tobacco and medicine. Some new magic was required. It was a product, too, of the revolutionary shift to sedentism. Living permanently in one place heightened old hostilities and created new ones. At the same time the custom of hiving off to escape tension became progressively more dependent on a vehicle, and vehicles added to the tension as often as they relieved it.

Yet the evangelical movement marked no profound change in Yolngu ontology and no sudden belief in the resurrection of the dead, or the hell or heaven the Fellowship promised. Christian ministers took part in the movement and Christian hymns were played on tape-decks, but in funeral ceremonies the clans still sang and danced the spirits of the dead to their ancestral homes.

Songs were part art, part religion, and part mnemonic devices interweaving myth – the Wagilak stories for instance – with practical knowledge of the land and the seasons. So, when women sang as their ancestors sang, of the plants that were ready for harvesting at a certain time in a certain place, they knitted myth and tradition into lessons in survival. Elders led children on the Dreaming paths, telling the ancestral stories and singing the songs that attached to sites both venerated and, in season, bountiful. Songs were a cryptic record of the natural and mythical world within the clan's boundaries. If they did not speak to the land and maintain an active, reverent relationship with it; if the land thought them neglectful or disrespectful; if the land forgot them, did not recognise their voice, or smell, the land was bound to punish them. Nature being the living and conscious cosmos, and human life inseparable from it, this was no more than one would expect.

All in the world, including humankind, was fixed in the Creation. All relationships, human and non-human, were resolved. The Earth, the stars, the seasons, were fixed. All that could be understood, was understood. What could not be seen, magic dealt with. The Yolngu cosmos was dynamic but ageless: dynamic in the sense that events remained open to human interpretation and expression in songs and ceremonies, many of which originated in human dreams; ageless in that Creation was beyond argument or manipulation, as unchanging and unchangeable as the law and religion to which it gave rise – like this, Yilarama said, squeezing a rock in his hand. 'You can hit it, but it won't break.' Europeans still acquainted with Ecclesiastes, the Old Testament poem often recited at funerals, might find something familiar in this world view; and an echo of that poem – 'One generation goeth, and another generation cometh; but the earth abideth forever' – might have led Bill Stanner to choose the word 'abidingness' for Aboriginal philosophy.

The Yolngu did not worship nature, but rather spoke to it, coaxed it, paid it attention, avoided giving offence, begged recognition and welcome. The relationship was intimate and critical. If they knew the land and made themselves known to it, and in ritual, ceremony, dance and song paid respect to its transcendent power, the land would be more inclined to provide, less inclined to deny them, or destroy them.

In the early 1990s the Fellowship lost its hold, possibly because it had lost its apparent efficacy. The supplies seemed to arrive or fail to, with or without praying for them. The same day-to-day imperatives applied. The same squabbles broke out and went away. Things seemed to be much the same with or without the Fellowship. The world leaned towards continuity. There were old rituals to encourage this

Neville White, Vietnam 1967.

Charlie Howe, Vietnam 1967.

From left to right: John Millstead,
Neville, David Glyde in Vietnam.

Donydji when Neville first arrived in 1974.

Bark huts in the Dry season of 1974.

Bark hut with sleeping platform, Donydji, 1975.

Jimmy (Ngarriwaanga) and Ronnie (Malapar) with three brolgas. Adam (Wupatha) and Tom in the background.

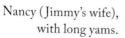

Nancy (Jimmy's wife), with long yams.

Neville's tent at the Wagilak camp at Donydji, 1975.

Bayman (in striped shirt) with some of his family. His wife Gunbangal is beside him, and Rayguyun is second from the left. The men, from left to right, are: Jimmy, Yilarama, Christopher, Leslie, Ronnie and Tom.

Yilarama with Neville's Super 8.

Neville filming Rayguyun in the 1970s.

Jimmy with fighting spear probably traded in from Groote or Numbulwar.
Dhiltjima beside Neville, Dhulutarama sitting. Behind them, a house built by
Gapuwiyak Council for Dhulutarama.

Banbalmiya (Tom's sister), cooking in an earth oven.

Tom stripping bark for a painting.

Women returning to Donydji from the lower stone country with buffalo meat.

Neville administering Dettol and bandaids.

Roy (Wuyngambi) Ashley painting clan designs.

Dhulutarama and David, 1975.

Rayguyun, 1975.

Women and girls in pipe clay, dancing during a ceremony in 1975.

Miliwurdu with hunting spear and spear thrower.

Yilarama, 1976.

Neville receives his bathi in 1981. Beside him: Jimmy, Dhiltjima and Dhulutarama.

Yilarama on the fringes of a hunting fire (wurrk), 1981.

Tom with fish and water monitor, early 1980s.

On the edge of the Ngilipitji quarry, 1981. From left to right: Jimmy, Neville Scarlett, sound recordist Wayne Barker, cameraman Kim McKenzie, Tom, Dhiltjima, Dhulutarama. Sitting: Yilarama with camera, Rhys Jones.

Ceremony, 1976.

Dhulutarama with
Makassan-style pipe.

Judy (Miliwurdu's wife and Djikambur's mother),
cracking cycad nuts and removing the kernels to
make damper.

Tom in seasonal swamp
(wayala) in late Dry.
Recently burned grass
in foreground.

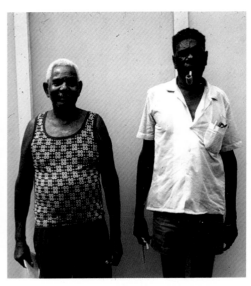

Bakali, the great botanist and Neville's Galpu tutor, with bunbun roots at Yirrkala, c. 1973.

David Burrumarra (right), the Yolngu (Warramirri) leader who told Neville to go to Donydji, and Willy Golumala, son of possibly the last Makassan prau captain to visit north-east Arnhem Land, c. 1974.

Crossing the Donydji creek downstream from the homeland at Dhupuwamirri, where the Wagilak established a camp. Yilarama paddling.

Bringing firewood, 1980s.

Tom with an emu he had speared and butchered in the stone country and carried back to Donydji, 1980s.

Dr Kel Semmens conducting health checks in 1982. Tom and Dhulutarama in the background.

Donydji, 1982.

A bunggul performed during a major ceremony at Donydji.

Jimmy tutoring Neville in the Ritharrngu dialect, early 1980s.

With Rhys Jones on an archaelogical survey, west of Donydji, c. 1997.

Tom with a catfish (garlki). Southern Arafura Swamp, 1990s.

Ricky (Ngambit) with baby, c. 1993.

The bathing pool in Donydji creek.

Neville and Tom (in ranger uniform) at La Trobe University in 2001, with a men's fighting club (balatha) that Jimmy made and painted in Bidingal clan designs. It was almost identical to one collected by Donald Thomson in 1936 and now in the Melbourne Museum.

Detail from painting by Yilarama showing a number of species that feature in Bidingal songs (manikay).

Two baskets woven from pandanus, and a necklace of seeds and shells made by Joanne; a bag for collecting honey made by Nancy; and a snail-shell rattle made by Rayguyun.

The vets' tents around Neville's fire in the early morning.

From left to right: Andrew Sharp, Dave Bryan, Tom, Neville, Dave Glyde and Alan Osborne in the newly constructed workshop, 2005.

Work in the garden that Charlie Howe got started in 2005.

Tom, 2005.

Joanne teaching at the Donydji school.

Sharon (back left), an outstanding teacher, with some of her pupils at the first Donydji school, in 2003. The school was built with funding from the Rotary club and other philanthropic organisations.

Vets and Yolngu trainees building a house for David and his family in 2008.

David renovating.

Joanne and Sonya outside their new home in 2010.

Wanakiya (sitting) with Joanne's sister Julie and a catch of freshwater turtles dug from the mud of a lagoon near Donydji, 2008.

Damien with a freshwater crocodile he caught in a river north of Donydji in 2010.

Ceremony to 'clear' the area around sacred trees, prior to the construction of a bridge over Donydji Creek, on the Central Arnhem Road, 2015.

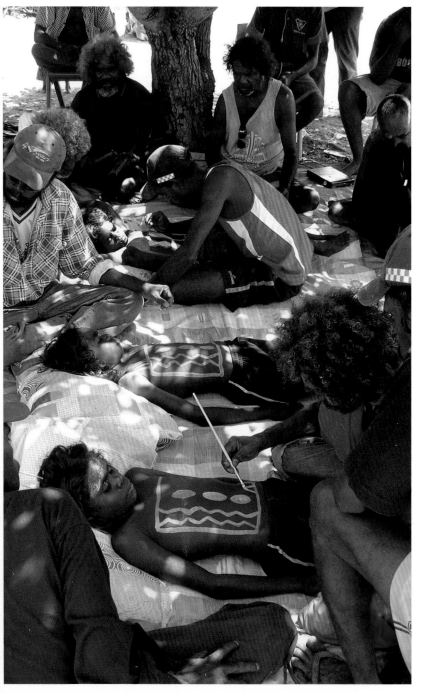

Dhapi being painted in clan designs in 2011. Ronnie and Dick at the back,
singing.

Donydji, 2022.

Neville with Tom on his last return to
Donydji, 2012.

Tom's grave, with Warramiri and
Geelong FC flags.

favourable tendency. The seasons inclined to stability and plenty. There were rituals for this as well. The serpent and the ancestral heroes, like the earth, abided forever. The clans would abide too.

Around 2000, Neville walked with Tom, Christopher, Mangay and Roy Ashley to Bungurrunydji, the heart of the stone country. The land belonged to a Ritharrngu clan, the Malabarritjaray Madarrpa whose most senior man, Munuma, had died a few months earlier. Being Ritharrngu, it was Father's Country for Tom and Christopher. For Mangay (Djambarrpuyngu) and Roy (Wagilak) the connection came through their grandfather.

On the ground beneath a rock overhang, they saw a grinding stone. A departing band had left it there, overturned against the weather, ready for use when their seasonal journeying brought them back. But they hadn't come back. No one had lived in this country for many years: probably not since Munuma's father took his family to the Roper half a century ago. Across all empires in history, that walk from traditional lands to the mendicant fringes of the frontier was made countless times, and a more melancholy sight is hard to imagine.

The men walked to a place high up on a hill and looked down over a waterfall, a significant site for the clan. They stood in a line holding hands and called out to the land. 'We're back. We're sorry we've been away.' On a branch just a metre or two from where they stood, a huge stick insect appeared, the biggest Neville had ever seen. The men saw it. 'He's here,' they said. 'He's happy. He's pleased to see us.' They meant Munuma, of course. No one really leaves the world.

SEVEN

Passive, introverted, peace-loving Tom was the boss at Donydji, the eldest surviving son of the landowning fathers, with Christopher next in line. But it wasn't always meant to be that way.

A year or two older than Tom, Yilarama was the magnetic one, the most resourceful and articulate of the Bidingal brothers. Not Tom but Yilarama was the one destined to be the leader at the homeland.

Most of the English language that Yilarama mastered he learned from Neville, and Neville's command of Ritharrngu-Wagilak owed much to Yilarama's coaching. He was the closest of Neville's Yolngu friends. When Neville married Alicia in Geelong in 1986, Yilarama, in Leo White's tuxedo, was his groomsman.

The Yolngu had had secure title to their lands since 1976, but the mining companies were a constant presence in their lives. The 'sandstones and bimodal volcanics known as the Donidjy [*sic*] Group' were a 'potential uranium target', and half a dozen companies had their sights on them. When the miners arrived in the mid-1960s and began carrying out ground and aerial surveys, Donydji men carried supplies and cleared trees in exchange for food and tobacco. But a decade later the miners were not welcome. By then, exploration licences were pending on nearly all the Donydji lands. For the miners' benefit, the track from the Stuart Highway to Nhulunbuy was upgraded to an all-weather road. Later, when the mine in Nhulunbuy decided to install a gas pipeline parallel to the road, the inland clans said no.

At a public meeting in Gapuwiyak protesting the mining applications and the proposed pipeline, Yilarama addressed the mining companies: 'We are the landowners here. The trees are ours. The water, the rocks, the turtles and all the animals in the bush – all are ours.' The companies kept asking for the land, but they wouldn't get it – 'You will not destroy us,' Yilarama said. 'We are not going to change our law the way you white people keep changing yours.'

The following year, 1984, Yilarama was in Darwin hospital for a minor operation when he saw television reports of the Bhopal chemical spill which killed thousands of people and left thousands more permanently disabled. The news persuaded him that something like this could happen if Donydji lands fell into the miners' hands. Once out of hospital, Yilarama told Neville that since the companies took no notice of their written submissions, the people should make a tape recording and let them hear their voices. Neville recorded several Ritharrngu-Wagilak people saying they did not want mining on their land, but the tape drew no response.

Yilarama said, 'They need to see our faces. We need to make a film.' Neville hired a cameraman. Several clan leaders gathered near Ngilipitji, and one after another they spoke into the camera.

No screen actor ever looked more at home in front of a camera. The Wagilak elder, Dhiltjima, of the grey whiskers and towering forehead, with a wound over his left eye, looked fiercely down the lens as if there was nothing between him and a mining executive. He spoke in Wagilak: 'I'm telling you, you won't shift me away from here, or my father's land. I own this land, which is my home and my Dreaming. I own it and I'll hang on to it, this land with its ceremonies and customs. Here I'm going to live and die – here on my land – and then my kids are going to take over.'*

'This is my grandfather's country,' Nimbaliman said. 'We've been here from the beginning. And yet you come to argue with us . . . What are you going to give us? You can offer us nothing! And still you keep asking, asking and pushing all the time. Thinking we'll crack and give you our land. Then you'd come to get rich, and we'd be poor. What rubbish! We don't long for your stuff – keep it, we don't want it. We'd rather be poor.'

Judy Gulungurr, whose home country was Dhunganda, said shyly: 'I am from that place. I'm responsible for that country. I must look after it. I say to you white people, you are not to come here. With mining we'd get sick – children too.' The companies were 'too ignorant' to know the dangers, Nimbaliman said: the 'spirits would settle us all'.

They did have a point. Perhaps the ground did not contain 'dangerous sickness', 'boils and leprosy', but uranium mining does come with menaces. In western Arnhem Land, despite company assurances that their procedures would cause no harm to the environment, radioactive and other contaminants spilled into creeks and waterholes from the Ranger uranium mine. Europeans had been digging in those parts since the late nineteenth century. Some of the old shafts are marked 'radioactive', and the surrounding clans have long regarded it as 'sick country'.

The miners decided that persuading the Yolngu depended on establishing the location of certain sacred sites and guaranteeing their protection. The Yolngu said there was much more to it than this. It was not possible to isolate the sacred sites and mine 'around' them. The clan lands were crisscrossed with the tracks of the ancestral beings,

---

* Neville and Bernhard Schebeck translated the speeches.

as they were with the clan boundaries. No one could fence them off. The sites were significant for more groups than the clan owners of the land. The spiritual relationship with the land was inseparable from the material relationship. All the land was 'significant' for hunting and gathering, for seasonal movement, and the traditional practice of large groups breaking up into smaller ones. There were many sites of no great ceremonial importance that were nevertheless significant in the clan's day-to-day life: sites that served as resting places on the way to other sites, places where water could be got, where food was available at certain times of the year were no less 'significant' than sacred sites. Even if the clans no longer lived that way, all sites served the cultural memory of the tribe – all the land did. It was inscribed in the collective mind through song, dance, ceremony and art – in the weave of the culture. 'You're too ignorant to know this,' Nimbaliman said. 'You're white people and we're Aborigines.'

Yilarama – like his brothers barely 165 centimetres tall, lean and muscular, with an open, confident face – began in English: 'Listen to us. Leave us lonely. We need to stay same our law. I'm a bit worried this one, and I think big stink.' The rest he spoke in the Ritharrngu dialect. 'We will not give in to you,' he said. 'You will not destroy us.' The land they wanted to mine was 'Waanga Ngaraka – the home of our bones.' He brought a boy before the camera. The boy was David, Dhulutarama and Betty's youngest. 'I want you to meet our children,' Yilarama said. 'I would like to teach them our culture and our law . . . our law as it has always been. The law that says he can't get drunk or go to the gaols or make any other problems . . . They would learn properly like before . . . When I die this boy will take my place on this land, following the same path and the same law. He can't change the law, he can't . . . become like a European.'

*

Yilarama would never sit and tell his children about a spear fight he had been in. He would never have the spear fight. There would only be the memory of Dhulutarama's tale, and even that fading into legend. Dhulutarama had six wives, but there was no wife for Yilarama at the homeland. There were young women there, but they were the 'wrong' women for a Ritharrngu man. He would know the country better than anyone who came after him, but not in the way Dhulutarama or his natural father, Bayman, knew it, because there would be no going back to the nomadic life. When rivalries and tension ran too high in Dhulutarama's pre-Donydji days, he could take his family and head off in another direction, until the trouble eased. When it got too much for Yilarama, the only place to go was another homeland, perhaps in his mother's country, where the tension was likely to be as bad, or to Gapuwiyak, where it was incomparably worse, or to Nhulunbuy, Yirrkala or Katherine, where there were as many tensions, and drugs, booze and illness as well.

When he thought about the future at Donydji, Yilarama surely saw these problems. There would still be hunting, but not hunting in the way the old men had hunted. There would still be ceremonies and songs, but with fading memory of the places they concerned. There would still be the clan, and still jealousies and spite. There would still be sorcery. But the unrivalled thrill of combat, the enjoyment of warfare – so obvious in Dhulutarama's tale, and as well known to military psychologists as the after-effects – he would be denied.

Whatever the social or psychological origins, and whether in satisfaction of a grudge or to procure women, the abolition of warfare drained something essential from the lives of the men. Warfare reinforced the kinship structure and tribal laws. It was essential to the culture of the clans. War was the ultimate test of manhood, part of life's pattern, a logical extension of customary belief. A man who shirked a fight was 'called a woman and held in extreme contempt,' Warner said.

Yilarama might not have yearned for mortal combat, but without it, traditional life was unfulfilled and made less sense.

There would still be country: nothing inhered in Yolngu hearts and Yolngu minds like country. But country was not everything. If it were everything, as Bill Stanner wrote, no one would leave it. Yet for tobacco, tea, flour and sugar, for marriage, medicine, convenience and safety the owners had been coming and going – and often just going – ever since Europeans arrived. There are many clan lands in Arnhem Land from which the people migrated long ago. Country is important, but so is a wife. And children. And food. Freedom is important. Keeping one's zest for life is important.*

Yilarama took a job liaising between the Gapuwiyak council and the homelands. He had some of the necessary qualifications: deep traditional knowledge, the personality to persuade and appease, and competence in spoken English. But the job was stressful. He was a Ritharrngu man, heir apparent at one homeland, dealing with other homelands competing for funds and services. Friction and resentment were inevitable. The job meant time amid the incessant squabbling at Gapuwiyak. After a year in the job, he told Neville he couldn't take it anymore. What he didn't tell him was that he was also quitting Donydji. The tensions there had also got too much for him. He saw trouble ahead, and very likely too many responsibilities falling on his shoulders when Dhulutarama was gone.

Without telling Neville, Yilarama left. Neville heard that he'd said the spirits were after him. He didn't return for twelve years. He went to Darwin and got on the grog. He moved to Oenpelli in western Arnhem Land, where a Rembarrnga woman became his wife.

---

* In the novelist Pat Barker's hands, William Halse Rivers, the ethnographer and celebrated World War I psychiatrist to the shell-shocked, wondered if the prohibition on head-hunting imposed by missionaries deprived his subjects, the men of Simbo Island, of their zest for life, and left them 'a people perishing from the absence of war'.

He took up painting barks in the artists' community at Gunbalanya. Tom reckoned 'clan business' should not be depicted outside the clan, and objected to selling secret religious knowledge in the Yolngu art market. But in paintings such as 'Water Dreaming of My Father's Country' (in 2022, for sale on the internet), the Bidingal clan design, though disguised, can be seen by those who know it.

Neville's disappointment at Yilarama's leaving was profound. He loved him and it was on him that his hopes for the homeland largely rested. He had lost a friend. That was the worst of it: when Yilarama abandoned Donydji, he abandoned Neville.

Neville Scarlett saw Yilarama's defection as a disaster for the homeland, but also as a symptom of its central problem: the Ritharrngu men could not find wives. It was impossible at Donydji, and when they went looking elsewhere, they found that women, including the preferred Wagilak women, were unwilling to live in such an isolated place and among people who were deeply conservative and notorious for magic. Tom had a 'fiancée' on Elcho Island for a while. Neville wrote letters to her on his behalf. But she couldn't be persuaded to come.

Tom was passive but he was also resolute. With Yilarama gone, he was senior man when some mining honchos came to Donydji with Northern Land Council (NLC) officials. They wanted to survey the Ritharrngu–Wagilak lands. Tom and some other men stood with their backs to them, listening in silence to the miners, and the arguments of Yolngu men who were prepared to bargain with them. At last, satis- fied they had agreement to go ahead with their survey, the visitors made to go. But Tom, who until now had said nothing, stepped up on a nearby verandah and pointed in three directions: 'There is our land, there is our land, there is our land,' he said. The land and everything that grew on it, and moved on it, visible and invisible. What was under the surface, and in the air above. He cast around – the air, the earth, the trees, the creek, the hillsides – everything in this direction and that direction, *all this*. We do not want you here, he said. The miners had brought rocks with numbers on them to show the Yolngu what they were looking for. 'Take those rocks,' Tom said, 'and put them back where you found them. Go – and don't come back.'

Tom was making the point that every anthropologist since Warner and Thompson had been trying to make: that the difference between a Yolngu and a balanda was not a matter of skin colour or race, but one of being.

It was in part to give the difference continuing expression that the homelands were established. Until they understood that land could not be separated from its human use and occupation, and *all this* was what the traditional owners owned, they understood nothing, and their acknowledgement of Yolngu ownership was phoney and meaningless.

It was this that the clans hoped to establish when, at Neville's suggestion, they applied to the Australian Heritage Commission for inclusion of their lands on the Register of National Estates. Neville, with Tom, Mangay and other clan owners, spent three years preparing an application to register the Arafura Wetlands and Surrounds as a 'cultural landscape'. This meant documenting in detail the flora and fauna, mapping the topography and geography, charting the seasonal variations of 900 square kilometres – a freshwater ecosystem stretching from the margins of the Arafura Swamp in the north to the Walker River in the south. The project demanded a great deal of walking, bush bashing, river crossing and rough sleeping. In addition to the gruelling physical demands, and much mapping, measuring, studying, identifying and recording, the application depended on long discussions and long walks with the elders from six Yolngu groups whose tradi-tional lands the area encompassed, and several other groups beyond the boundaries but with links to the clans and sites within.

Neville's nomination to the commission noted more than 700 'sites of cultural significance': campsites, quarries, rock art, fish traps, stone arrangements, shell mounds, artefact scatters, religious sites, named places. In effect the survey filled in Dhulutarama's 'cobweb map', identifying campsites within reach of water and resources that were regarded as significant by all the overlapping descent groups that shared them. Research for the application swelled knowledge of the lands and their plant and animal life, including the refuges and breeding rookeries of several species of waterfowl and other birds, fish and crocodiles. Read now, even in summary form, the case for protection and preservation of such a 'complex mosaic of plant communities' seems unarguable on environmental grounds alone – the more so because buffalo, pigs and cane toads were a permanent threat. So were invasive plant species, which choke waterways, and mission and gamba grass, which overwhelm native plants and, by adding tonnes of highly flammable material to the fuel load, make 'cool' burning at best a problematic art.

But the point of the survey was to demonstrate that the integrity of the environment could not be separated from a continued presence of the clans who found in the landscape the means and the meaning of existence. It had in equal parts material, spiritual and aesthetic value. Maintaining such a 'cultural landscape' and protecting it from incursions by mining companies and unsupervised tourism was consistent with any definition of a 'national heritage' worth conserving. It was not a 'wilderness', but an inhabited cosmos.

The wetlands certainly met the criteria laid out by the present Australian Heritage Council: 'exceptional natural and cultural places that contribute to Australia's national identity. National heritage defines the critical moments in our development as a nation and reflects achievements, joys and sorrows in the lives of Australians. It also encompasses those places that reveal the richness of Australia's extraordinarily diverse natural heritage.' The lands also provided 'insight' into the human occupation of Australia, and the ancient and continuing interaction of the Yolngu and their environment, the application said. It was the inspiration and the home for some of Australia's foremost Indigenous artists, musicians, actors and community leaders, and some of Australia's greatest art. It had been the scene of a violent European invasion and violent Aboriginal resistance – a scene of 'sorrows' by any measure. The application also made the point that by observing the ongoing practices of the Yolngu, much could be learned about managing the Australian environment, including the crucial element of low-level burning. In every facet the application assumed continuing active Yolngu occupation of the lands. The application was therefore also consistent with the continuation of the homelands and, it followed, government support for them.

When the mining companies objected to the nomination, a meeting was organised in Melbourne. Neville brought Tom. He displayed the maps and translated as Tom told the assembled commissioners and miners that he and other clan elders were the owners of the land and responsible for its care, and how everything within the mapped area was connected. When he had finished no one spoke. No one asked a question. The commission accepted the nomination. The miners took no notice of it.

The nomination was given interim listing in 1993. The decision seemed to mean that the clans would be recognised nationally and internationally as the custodians of the land and the lands would be protected from environmental damage. Despite Neville's misgivings, a ceremony was held in Yirrkala to acknowledge the listing. Members of the Heritage Commission flew in from the south to join the clan leaders in celebration of a great moment, and issue each of them with a certificate indicating that their custodianship was beyond question and their lands were safe from encroachment.

The battle, however, had another eight years to run. Full recognition required more field research and more argument with opponents, including the mining companies, the Northern Territory Chamber of Mines and the Northern Land Council, the last of which had long ago lost the Donydji clans' allegiance. Finally, in 2001, the Arafura Wetlands and Surrounds was officially placed on the Register of the National Estate.

But it was all a mirage. The certificates were worthless, as the irascible Djambarrpuyngu elder Mangay learned years later when he flourished his at the men pegging out a route for an internet cable. None of the protection implied by the listing came to pass. For Neville, whose labours had been monumental, it was a bitter defeat. He could not help but suspect the clans felt he had misled them or broken his promise to them. Twenty years later it still tormented him. 'The promises that have been made to me,' he said despairingly as we drove out to Donydji in 2019. He meant the promises made to him on which his promises to the clans depended, and when dishonoured, dishonoured him.*

Some good did come of the exercise. In 1996, under the umbrella of an Arafura Catchment Ranger program, five homelands appointed

---

* What was more exasperating, a decade and a half later he discovered that the Arafura Wetlands and Surrounds listing had been transferred to the Non-Statutory Archive of the Register of the National Estate which, a telephone call revealed, 'provided recognition but not protection'. Neither he nor anyone else had been consulted or even notified of this decision, and no one at the Australian Heritage Council knows where the supporting documents for the application have gone.

rangers to work with scientists from La Trobe University and the
Territory's Parks and Wildlife Service. Each ranger sported an outfit
with a logo specially designed by the clan elders of each homeland
to represent their connection to the country. Their work, most of it
involving cool burning, helps control exotic plants and animals which,
since Neville's survey in the early 1990s, have invaded the catchment.

The scheme provided useful and generally satisfying employment
for young Yolngu men and women, and by keeping them connected
to the land old knowledge is retained. The younger men tell Neville
they want to know the country as their fathers did. That alone makes
the Ranger Program worthwhile, even if it remains true that only
those who were raised walking on the lands have deep knowledge
of them, and as one by one they die, in Neville's words, we lose
'forever an irreplaceable fragment of a deep intellectual tradition and
understanding of our world'.*

---

*   The scheme worked well until funds from the National Heritage Trust were cut off in
       2002. In 2011 the program was partially revived at Ramingining, a hub-town on the
       edge of the Arafura Swamp and subsequently took in young men from Donydji.

EIGHT

On patrol with Yolngu companions in 1936, Donald Thomson lived well on what they found in the bush and the waterways: mud-filled shipworms cut out of sodden logs, lace lizards, snakes and snake eggs, birds and bird's eggs, tortoises and honey, a few items in the hundreds that the country afforded. In the Ritharrangu-Wagilak diet Neville counted twelve varieties of native mammal and three introduced species, eight varieties of reptile, eighteen types of bird, thirteen of fish, three tortoises and all four of the four types of honey, along with dozens of different roots, seeds and fruits. Much of their food was gathered along the watercourses, in the streams and the pandanus and paperbark forest or jungle on the margins.

Fish were by far the major source of protein, and after fish, reptiles, birds and mammals. Though meat was the food most craved, it made up less than 30 per cent of the traditional diet – and by the 1980s the greater part of that was not wallaby, kangaroo or even buffalo, but feral cats shot by the men or dragged out of trees and clubbed to death by the women. Neville found (as did other anthropologists in Arnhem Land) that the Yolngu knew well the relationship between diet and health. Their awareness of the virtues of a balanced diet affected the pattern of their nomadism. Too much vegetable food, they told Neville, could give them diarrhoea; or, if it was too dry, headaches and coughs. Too much meat gave them 'heavy heads'. Travelling and camping with the Yolngu men, Neville recorded 'a continual cycle of food crises . . . based on food cravings'. Too much of one and a craving for the other, and they would shift camp. Their movements were determined by the seasons, but also, he concluded, by 'a desire for variety in the diet'.

Beginning in 1980, when he dragged in the caravan fitted out as a laboratory, Neville made an intensive study of nutrition and health at Donydji. After the 3500-kilometre trip from Melbourne to Katherine, it took another ten days to get the caravan up the 450 kilometres of track from Katherine to Donydji, and they burned out two winches on the Land Cruiser hauling it across creeks. He parked it next to the little shade and his tent by the airstrip and there it remained. His findings fed into the academic debate about Indigenous diet, social organisation, nutritional standards, hunting practices and so on, but they also had two practical purposes. One was to discover what in the people's biological make-up and post-European diet and lifestyle put them at risk of developing diabetes mellitus and cardiovascular disease. In this the project would contribute to scientific understanding of the near epidemic of those 'Western lifestyle diseases' in Aboriginal communities across the country. The second, related purpose was to find ways to help the Donydji people adjust to their growing dependence on Western food, medicine, and technology without harming their health.

The hunting and gathering range of the Ritharrngu-Wagilak clans before the homeland was 3000 to 4000 square kilometres. It is now a fraction of that. Less hunting and foraging over a much smaller area to feed a permanent population that in earlier times would have broken into smaller bands has guaranteed increasing dependence on, and a growing preference for, store-bought food. In his first decade at the homeland Neville counted 106 species of roots, fruits and seeds regularly collected and eaten. By 2000 he could only count twenty. At the same time, he saw a 30 per cent decline in ecological knowledge among the young men, who hunted less frequently and in four-wheel drives, and a similar decline among young women who, relying on store food, had less need to know the vast range of bush foods that their mothers did.

For much of the year the Donydji people were healthy, and the more they relied on food they hunted and gathered, the healthier they were. They looked healthier, the older people said they felt healthier, and Neville contrived to prove that they *were* healthier when they lived off the land. It was in the late 1970s, when about 80 per cent of the Donydji diet was still bush food, that he brought Kel Semmens and Alicia to the homeland. The two doctors conducted medical checks on every individual at Donydji. They found there was more than enough of everything needed in the diet, and their health overall was good, certainly much better than the people eating only store food in the hub-towns, or for that matter Indigenous people living in or on the fringes of towns across the continent. There was little obesity: in fact, their 'extreme leanness' was their 'most striking characteristic'.

With the doctors Neville took bloods from twenty-four people whose diets had been monitored over the seven days preceding: the meat intake was higher than usual because 'one wild Hereford heifer' had been shot and eaten, but the rest was typically varied – small freshwater fish, mussels, bustard, crayfish, file snake, agile wallaby, fork-tailed kite, goanna, snails, water lily roots and buds, honey, pollen, a variety of other roots and tubers, powdered milk, sugar and flour. After the bloods were analysed in laboratories in Melbourne, Neville said he believed the Donydji people had the best nutritional profile of any Aboriginal group in Australia, and it was for one reason – they lived substantially on what the bush provided them. He showed the people the bloods they had taken, pointing out that while Gapuwiyak blood was cloudy, Donydji blood was clear. There was just one concern: their triglyceride and fasting insulin levels were 'inappropriately high for their very low body mass', which suggested they were at heightened risk of type 2 diabetes as their diet became more westernised.

The missionary Wilbur Chaseling noted in 1934 that Yolngu food was 'mainly of vegetable origin', and suggested that the term 'Man the Hunter' did not in truth apply. He might have added that 'Woman the Gatherer' was much nearer to reality: if catching fish, file snakes, feral cats and goannas is not hunting. Thomson said the same: 'contrary to the general idea, the main food supply among Aborigines [Yolngu], except at certain restricted times of the year, is not animal but vegetable'. Decades later, Rhys Jones and Jim Bowler disputed the vegetable thesis. 'Some two thirds of the gross weight' of food eaten by the Indigenous people of the tropical savannah was meat, they said, and meat made up half of it 'in calorific terms'.

Neville's observations tended to align with those of Thomson and Chaseling, though he made the unsurprising observation that, given the vast differences in climate and environment, and therefore in food resources, there was no typical diet among Australian hunter-gatherers.

Bernhard Schebeck found a clue in the language: 'ngatha', the Yolngu word for vegetable foods, is also the word for food in general: whereas the words 'wayin' and 'dhaanggu' or 'warrakan' apply only to game and meat. Neville believed the desire for meat weighed more heavily than the amount in fact eaten, and he found that the men's stories of the hunt and the importance they attached to kill sites belied the number of animals in fact killed. In other words, 'Man the Hunter' had a streak of 'Man the Fantasist' about him, an inevitable tendency probably when proof of manhood depended heavily on hunting successes, and hunters, like other men, were inclined to make fetishes of what they most desired.

Caring for children, collecting firewood and preparing food, much of it for the men to eat, probably doubled the women's hours of labour. Their days were spent in semi-servitude and the men's, relatively speaking, in the idleness of gentry, sitting under a tree sharpening their spears, or gathered under a ceremonial shade (a 'gurrngannara') made of boughs or bark, crafting ceremonial objects, talking about the secret things or introducing boys to some of them – attending to matters spiritual and temporal.

Observing the Ritharrngu-Wagilak on the fringes of the Arafura swamp in 1966–67, Nicolas Peterson found at least 60 per cent of the community's food was provided by women, and at certain times of the year the figure approached 90 per cent. This included much of the animal protein, from fish, tortoises, birds, eggs, and reptiles. Neville's calculations were similar. The women spent about 30 hours a week 'gathering', which was substantially more than the men spent 'hunting', and the women returned with food 95 per cent of the time while the men came back as often as not with nothing. The women's share dropped to 20 per cent in the Wet and the late Dry, the 'hungry times', when very likely, the women, and children still dependent on them, suffered most.

In all, the traditional seasonal movement of the bands provided an adequate diet for everyone, but in the hungry times they depended on the men. The hunters were only sometimes up to the task. At one point in the early 1980s, when the whole camp at Donydji was hungry, the men went hunting and returned with one kookaburra.

Returning empty-handed did not always mean the men had not had some success. The notion that everything was shared is true; that it was shared *scrupulously* is fiction. Often they ate some of it – and no doubt all of it on occasion – 'on site' and said nothing upon their return. Rhys Jones called the 'sharing' obligation 'reluctant reciprocity', Nicolas Peterson said it was 'demand sharing', and Bernhard Schebeck used the term 'mutual taking'.

Nevertheless, the protein, iron and polyunsaturated fats in the meat the hunters brought back was as vital to the general good as it was to the hunters' self-esteem and status. Everyone in the community got some, even if they did not get some of everything the men caught, and the men, especially the old men, got the best of it, and the older women the worst. In a scholarly article, Neville included a diagram of a kangaroo showing the various cuts and their recipients. The fat and the liver, the pieces with the highest load of carbohydrates, B vitamins, vitamins A and C and iron, went by right to the men. The men's defences against anaemia were bolstered, while women, served the less nutritious portions, were denied what they needed as much as men did, and more than men when they were pregnant, lactating or menstruating – at which times they were also subject to food taboos. Their compensation might have been that eating more plant food provided some benefits that the meat-eating men missed out on.

From the beginning Neville had been determined not to intervene in the health of the Donydji people. He was there to study the community and to participate, when invited, in their secular and religious lives. He was not there, as the missionaries had been, to convert them or redirect them, much less to save them. He 'observed' their health, as he observed their habits and rituals. He 'observed' what they ate, and 'participated' in it to the extent of sharing the parasites. He measured and observed every detail, but even when he could see the connection between what they ate and what they suffered, he did not interfere.

The explorer David Lindsay noted that the young Yolngu women 'always [had] good teeth'. But at Donydji just about everyone, from early teenage on, had bad teeth. In the early 1980s, Neville estimated each person at Donydji was eating 2 kilograms of sugar a week. As an undoubted consequence of their greater reliance on sugary store-bought food and drink, Neville saw more decaying teeth, ulcers and abscesses. The doctor he had brought from Melbourne said their bad teeth were having a detrimental effect on their general health. What was more, many of them were in constant pain.

None suffered more than Miliwurdu, the Djambarrpuyngu man whose camp was next to Neville's. He often had blood and pus running down his chin. One morning Neville saw him lying on his back on the ground while his wife, Judy, whose teeth were not much better, sat on his chest and poked in his mouth with a sharpened, fire-hardened stick, trying to puncture an abscess on his gums. When Neville politely asked what she was doing, Judy said she was digging out the grub that had burrowed into her husband's tooth. The sight broke Neville's resolve. He had a course of antibiotics in his shed, and he gave them to Miliwurdu. The abscess went quickly. Judy congratulated him on his good medicine. She opened a tobacco tin and there, amid globs of pus, was a large wood grub. She had found it beside their bed that morning. 'Your medicine drove it out,' she said.

This was a turning point. There wasn't an adult in the place with decent teeth. In 1990 Neville had a van fitted out as a dental surgery and found a dentist willing to travel to Donydji to treat the whole community. The Northern Territory government office in Nhulunbuy refused to support the project and told Neville to keep his nose out of government business. When Neville asked why, he was told, 'Because if you do one place all the others will want it too.' As for the toothache and abscesses, 'These people have a higher tolerance of pain [than Europeans].'

The health problems went to housing and plumbing and education and employment. No longer a mere participant observer, a host of other roles soon fell Neville's way – project manager, facilitator, money raiser, go-between, advocate, patron, benefactor, urger – altruist. He would exercise those 'instincts for benevolence'.

There had always been an understanding that the ethnographic information provided by the clans came with an obligation to help them in their dealings with balanda authorities and interests. Dhulutarama had long ago urged Neville to come and live with them permanently. That was more than he could do, but he was now offering the material benefits that a white man with connections and energy could bring. In return they granted him as much status as it was possible to grant an uninitiated man and gave him access to many secrets.

Dhulutarama called him 'son-in-law'. Years before, he'd said to a camera: 'Sit there, my son-in-law, and I'll tell you. This is not a rubbish man. He's not Black. He's not even a yella fella. But a proper white man.' And he'd given Neville a big kiss. He was part of the family. The implied understanding that the relationship was one of mutual benefit was made formal and explicit when Dhulutarama presented him with a bathi – one of the small woven 'power bags' containing 'secret objects that relate to the person's being', carried by men in battle and in ceremonies grasped between the teeth. His adoption and the granting of the name Balang had come with the expectation that he would open the way to the white world, help Yolngu people deal with it, and be an advocate for Yolngu tradition. But the bathi went beyond this. It came 'from the belly of the clan ... from the law on top and deep below'. It was not only proof of his rank and the esteem in which he was held, it was a symbol of unity between the clans, and it bound him, at least by implication, to work to maintain that unity. As its owner, Neville was required to protect the country and the social order. Neville accepted the bathi with pride. But it tied him firmly to Donydji and to what the clans expected of him. Being a conscript to duty was not a new experience.

The formal requirements of the discipline detach the anthropologist's sympathy from whatever suffering he witnesses, and demand an impassive non-judgemental view of belief and customary practices.

Yet if Lévi-Strauss was right to say anthropology is a redemptive calling that owes its existence to 'strong feelings of remorse' in the Western societies where it evolved, perhaps the shift in Neville's self-described role was not so radical. The feelings might have been all the stronger because he had fought in a postcolonial war and found it eminently agreeable to be disengaged from the 'home' society which, in the name of false gods, had sent him there. He could be a 'critic at home' and a 'conformist' abroad; in Sontag's words, 'the very model of twentieth century consciousness'.

'That grub was after sugar,' Neville told Judy and Miliwurdu. 'If you don't want grubs boring into your gums, you should eat less sugar. And when you do eat it, afterwards rinse it out of your mouth and clean it off your teeth.' He gave everyone the same advice, and for a while they did eat less sugar.

Seeing how underweight some children were, a visiting social worker concluded the parents were neglecting them. But Neville and the doctors believed parasitic worms were the cause of it, and that it was likely the entire community was infested with them. The people brought their stools to Neville on pieces of bark. They came at all hours. When Alicia examined them in the caravan, her assessment was confirmed. Nearly everyone in the camp had worms. The adults seemed able to tolerate them, but the immune response was not as strong in the children. The doctors' treatment raised their haemoglobin levels immediately. Nearly half the population had *Strongyloides*, a common tropical and subtropical parasitic worm, which causes few symptoms in healthy people but is potentially deadly in those with compromised immunity. Untreated, the parasites can live in the body for decades and have severe consequences later in life. Veterans of wars in tropical climates are particularly vulnerable.

Over the next two decades Neville recorded a steady erosion of the traditional diet and increasing dependence on processed, store-bought food: not only the staple flour and sugar, but cordial, soft drinks, sweets and snack foods. The effects of the change could be measured in triglyceride and insulin levels, which soon enough would manifest in heart disease and type 2 diabetes. He wrote articles on the health of the Donydji people with Semmens and Polakiewicz, and on botany and the Indigenous pharmacopoeia with Neville Scarlett. Thus, among scores of species similarly described, pandanus: '*Pandanus spiralis*, Moiety Yirritja, Fruit (baluk) used in the dry season: cooked in large fire until blackened, then put on a stone and endosperms extracted and eaten . . . Leaves used to make mats, dilly bags and baskets. The pith is extracted, put in water bashed up and placed on sores on the genitals. Pith called dulpurru. The baby teeth of children are hidden in pandanus: believed to make the next set grow more quickly. Employed in a ceremony to cure snake bite . . .'

Yolngu medicine was based on an extensive pharmacopoeia and an overriding belief, familiar to Western practitioners, that health and social and domestic harmony are entwined. With Neville Scarlett, Neville identified dozens of plants, along with types of clay and earth and insects, with specific medicinal uses. Some of them the Yolngu had shared with the Makassans. Some were used for the same purposes by the Indigenous people of Cape York. Some, no doubt, were more effectual than others, and none were less so than bleeding a person with a headache or diphtheria or giving brandy to an ailing infant. Some also, no doubt, had a placebo effect – which is to say they worked, as placebos in all medicine do, because the people receiving the treatment thought they would. Human suggestibility is both a cause of illness and a cure in all cultures.

Magic – like calling a priest to the bedside or urging optimism when there is no cause for it – was another essential part of Yolngu medicine. 'Good' magicians were called to cure injury and illness, including, it would seem, mental illness: recently a good magic practitioner appears to have banished the symptoms of dementia that Dolly, an old Donydji woman, had been displaying for years. More generally, sickness and injury, even when the cause is clear and unmistakable, are interpreted 'magically'.

One day in 1976 word came to the camp that a young man had 'cut his foot off' and was dying. Hurrying to the scene in the bush, Neville found that the wound was a minor one caused by a splinter and needed nothing more than antiseptic and a bandaid. But was it a splinter or a sorcerer's killing stick? The hunters felt it prudent to treat him as if he had cut his foot off, and they pushed him three kilometres back to Donydji in a wheelbarrow. The night following, he took part in purification rituals, and he stayed close to the camp for several days.

There had been a clan dispute and much tension in the camp. At such times, as other communities might expect retribution for offences again God, the state or the market, the Ritharrngu expected sorcery and so sorcery was judged to be the cause. As Neville wrote, the exaggeration of the wound was proportionate to what was expected, and this in turn reflected the level of anxiety in the community. Looked at this way, the lesson of the splinter in the foot amounts to the clans' first principle of medicine: good health depends on social concord.

No person or thing did more to bring about a decline in health and communality than the four-wheel drive. Toyotas closed the gap between the hub-town and their problems and the core of tradition still alive in the homelands. The drinking towns of Nhulunbuy and Katherine, even Darwin, were brought within the boundaries of the clans' extended range. The lands the hunters once walked they now traversed in Toyotas. The world's greatest pedestrians, the males at least, began showing symptoms arising from a lack of exercise. In Toyotas they went after buffalo and cattle, big feral animals which, unlike the lean kangaroos, wallabies and emus of tradition (the original 'paleolithic diet'), were full of saturated fat. They left unburned places they could not get to in a vehicle, and their cool burns often failed to cross the wheel tracks they left. The traditional mosaic pattern established by burning on foot fell away. Toyotas brought wonderful convenience, and debilitating anxiety, envy, frustration and disharmony. They brought violence, injury and death. They shrank distance, and devoured money. They symbolised and accentuated the old settler colonialist gap between white bureaucrats and tourists and – in their broken, unreliable cast-offs – the Indigenous people.

Neville saw the vehicles deplete not only the diet of the Donydji people, but their cultural knowledge. Where once it was the custom to take them hunting, now boys were left behind because the combination of guns and four-wheel drives made the chase too dangerous. While they continued to be instructed in ceremonial knowledge, they learned progressively less about the art of hunting and the land to which they were heirs, and on which the ceremonies were based. They shared in neither the exhilaration of the chase nor the bonding with older males that went with it. Instead of sharing the meat eaten on site, they stayed at the homeland and ate store food. In 1989, Neville and his friend and fellow anthropologist Betty Meehan observed a 'marked increase' in iron deficiency among the boys, especially in comparison to girls of the same age who still went with the women to look for food. The effect was on more than their iron levels: their attachment to the homeland and the 'traditional' ways it preserved became more and more a hollow one.

Betty Meehan, who had established a school at Maningrida on the coast of central Arnhem Land, spent July 1972 to July 1973 with a group of about a hundred Gidjingali-speaking Anbarra people at their new outstation near the mouth of the Blyth River. The place was called Kopanga, which suggests Koepang in Timor and Makassan era origins. With Rhys Jones she lived with a band of thirty-five or so as they moved from one camp to another with the seasons. Their estate was a fraction of the size of the Doyndji clans', but with the river and the coast, it was so richly endowed that little effort was required to harvest 'an excess' of energy and protein. And, unlike the inland clans, they suffered no 'hungry time': food was abundant all year round. They were, Meehan said, 'affluent hunters with high gastronomic standards' and 'a clear idea of what constitutes a good diet'.

With the use of Western commodities such as guns, metal and nylon, and a 'minimal' degree of reliance on Western foodstuffs, the anthropologists could not pretend they were observing hunter-gatherers living as they had before European (or Makassan) contact. But in that year, the Anbarra were 'almost entirely' supporting themselves by hunting and gathering, and the researchers felt that their experience had 'profound resonances' of past tradition. Their hosts, clearly, saw it the same way. Aware that time was running out for the old ways, and that hunting and foraging would be soon a very occasional pastime, a senior man who was their chief cultural informant insisted that Meehan and Jones get it all down, and accurately: 'more better you bookim down straight,' he said.

When she joined Neville at Donydji for a few days in 1989, Betty Meehan marvelled at the time and effort needed to get a day's food compared to the ease with which the Anbarra people gathered their elegant sufficiencies. For all the difference, the same story was unfolding in both places: the people still hunting and gathering were much healthier than the people in the large settlements – Maningrida in the Anbarra case, Gapuwiyak in Donydji's. They both knew there was no going back to the traditional diet, or even the modified version prevailing when they began their fieldwork in the early 1970s. The clans would never live as they once did. And just as certainly, the extensive field research that she and Neville had carried out in Arnhem Land would never be done again. Their journals, she wrote, 'document a passing phase, half frozen . . . in the lens of history'.

Neville knew it, but he was bound by a solemn promise. To repay the knowledge and status granted him, he must try to make Donydji a successful homeland. Some would call it resisting history: not just post colonial history, in which Indigenous populations must always surrender their lives, land and culture, but the clan history. The clans had never lived as one large sedentary group, and everything in their culture was opposed to it. Donydji had been a seasonal camp and a ceremonial site; it was not a place of unlimited food resources like those on the coast or the fringes of the swamp. Isolation made it an even more unlikely venue for a homeland: isolation from the source of European food, medicine and services, from the tourist centres where other homelands sold their artworks, and from the mainstream of Yolngu politics, through which more powerful and worldly clans and individuals could wring concessions. The Ritharrngu-Wagilak had always been isolated. As Tom said many times, nothing useful could be learned about the inland clans from the clans on the coast: the stone country people were different.

I have sometimes wondered if Neville knew he was fighting the tide of history, and if that was what attracted him. Anything less than impossible was not a worthy adversary. Then again, as he saw it, you have to fight the tide if you want to save folk from drowning.

In 1997 a sore appeared on Neville's back. Both Alicia and Tom told him that it looked dangerous. He took their advice. It was a melanoma.

After it was cut out, the doctors told him if it did not resurface within a year, he should be alright. He was about a week short of a year when, while swimming in the Goyder River, he felt a lump in his armpit. Back in Melbourne, he learned it was metastatic. They told him there was nothing they could do and reckoned his chances of surviving at 5 per cent.

His two small children would have been left without a father. That aroused memories of Vietnam – the photo that had fallen from the Vietnamese sentry's tunic. The image of the woman and two children gave him 'a lot of trouble,' he said. His nightmares were intense, always in or on the brink of combat, and always in colour. He took up meditation and twenty-five years later he is convinced it saved him.

In 2002 Yilarama came back to Donydji. Dhulutarama had died, and it was the general hope that Yilarama would stay and lead the homeland as his stepfather had. But he had not come back to replace Tom – not immediately anyway. He was working as a consultant for the Northern Land Council, helping them and the Nhulunbuy bauxite mine to reach an agreement with the Ritharrngu-Wagilak clans over a gas pipeline the company intended to build.

The man who had told the mining companies that the clans would never allow them on their land was now showing them around. When he told them he intended to go with NLC and mining company representatives in a helicopter and show them the way through the maze of sites on the clan's land, his brothers thought he had lost his mind: literally lost it, in the sense that someone had taken possession of it.

Yilarama might have argued that nothing was going to stop the pipeline, and he was merely making sure the damage to the land was minimal. It was a line of reasoning as old as human conquest. For Tom it was not only a betrayal, it was also madness. Something bad was bound to happen. It invited disaster. Mangay phoned Neville, who was not long home from Donydji: Yilarama must not do this, he said. He had been away too long. The country had forgotten him. It wouldn't recognise his smell. Like Tom, Mangay was convinced something terrible was about to happen.

But the Laynhapuy Aviation helicopter picked up Yilarama at Donydji just before noon on 5 June. After surveying a site near the Goyder River, they were only a few kilometres from Donydji when a member of the party – Yilarama very likely – said there was a site below that they needed to survey. Flying above the treetops as the pilot was looking for a place to land, the helicopter plunged to the ground, landed on its side and burst into flames. The pilot, an NLC representative, a mining company representative, and Yilarama were killed. The newspaper report said Yilarama was forty-four, but Neville thinks he was fifty-one or fifty-two.

An air search found the burned-out wreckage and a severely injured survivor the following day. The 'meticulous and safety conscious' pilot, Adrian Wagg, had more than 5000 hours' experience flying the same Bell 206 helicopters in Arnhem Land. Neville knew him well. An anthropologist himself, he had flown Neville around on his environmental surveys.* The helicopter had been serviced three weeks before the accident. It was in perfect condition and had plenty of fuel. The survivor recalled hearing beeping in his headphones, then the pilot said, 'Hang on, boys, this is going down.'

---

*   Adrian Wagg was much admired and respected by the Yolngu as a founder of Laynhapuy Aviation and friend of the homeland movement. An adopted member of the Mangalili clan, he was accorded the rare honour of a ten-day 'hollow log' ('Dhakhandjali') funeral, which had not been performed in Yirrkala since the foundation of the mission.

An alarmingly perfunctory one-page report of an investigation by the Australian Transport Safety Bureau concluded that the beeping indicated engine failure and that this was the cause of the crash. The investigators did not explain why the engine failed: they could not, they said, because the fire destroyed any clues. But a hundred pages would not have changed the minds of Yilarama's kin. There *were* clues, one of them said: a cigarette packet in the nearby bush with four cigarettes in it. It was Galka. It would always be as Tom and Mangay had warned – what happens when you break the rules and give offence to the country.

The loss to Donydji was great, and probably decisive. Yilarama had been away for a long while, but so long as he lived, he was a presence in the place, and the community never lost hope that he would come back and lead them. And this he might have done. It is likely he would have strayed further from the old protocols than Tom was prepared to, but Yilarama had charismatic qualities that might have yielded more authority both within the community and outside it. Donydji might have been harder to neglect and ignore. His more adventurous mind might have found room for some of the younger residents to prosper. Instead, his death hardened Tom's already hard conservative views.

Neville had not long returned from Donydji when Yilarama was killed. He was in Cairns on his way back there when the funeral was held. He knew his absence would disappoint some people, and very likely set a few others wondering. When he next went to Donydji, not everyone was warm towards him.

It is customary at funerals to hold a 'dhapi'. A dhapi is a circumcision ceremony, an elaborate, long, frightening and painful initiation for three boys about twelve years old. As the old pass on, the young rise to adulthood. The Great Serpent Yurrlunggur having ordained the procedure, the Wagilak Sisters' baby boy was the first to undergo it.

A day is spent preparing the dhapi – the boys: daubing them with red ochre and then, as they lie on their backs and men and women sing and dance around them, they are painted in their fathers' clan designs. The boys are given moral instruction and taught the secret 'power names' of 'all the foods that grow in the bush and that are game and that are fish'. They are told names that women must never hear. As they are to be physically separated from the women who have cared for them since birth, they will also be separated by belief and custom. The men crowd around and tell them terrifying tales. They hear of Galka. The fear, Neville says, shows on their faces.*

At a dhapi when the boys are about to taken away, the women gather to ridicule the men. Ritualistically, they try to stop the men taking the children from the company of the women they have known all their lives. The men submit to their humiliation in silence, recover their dignity and bear the boys away.

When Neville took part in such a ceremony the year after Yilarama died, he was mocked by Yilarama's sister, Wanakiya. She mimicked his habit of taking notes, his army hat, his quick-stepping walk. And when he rose to go with the men and the boys, she flung a spear that grazed his temple. Had it hit him in the eye socket, it would have killed him, and he is sure that when she threw it, she intended to. In the days that followed she ignored him, and she has not mentioned it in the twenty years since.

Warner's informant told him women threw spears at the men in Wangurri circumcision ceremonies, so it is possible that Wanakiya's

---

*   Warner compared these ceremonies to Wagner's *Nibelungen Ring*, the difference being that the Yolngu ceremony was not myth but dogma with the same significance to the Yolngu as the Mass is to Catholics.

throw was established practice and she was expert enough to just miss. But Neville thinks the incident could mean real bitterness and rage underlie the ritual, and that Wanakiya saw the balanda as a 'soft' target for a woman's revenge. He thinks it's also possible that she resented a white man's participation in a Yolngu ritual. A third possibility is that she blamed him for the death of her brother. Wanakiya was not the only one at Donydji in whom he sensed a certain coolness, which he suspected was because he had not been at the funeral. There were Yolngu who said white people had tricked Yilarama into boarding the helicopter. They must have got him drunk, poisoned his mind. No one Neville spoke to believed Yilarama's decision to work for the miners was his own.

A year later, in the middle of a genetics lecture he was giving at La Trobe University, Neville dimmed the lights to project some slides, and suddenly saw a room full of people in jungle greens. For several moments he didn't know where he was, or who the students were. He managed to finish the lecture, but afterwards could not remember what he had said. It was as if a trapdoor had opened, and he had fallen into an unfamiliar room. He saw a counsellor, who referred him to the Heidelberg Repatriation Hospital in Melbourne. He was diagnosed with PTSD and put on medication.

It can take much longer, but the symptoms of PTSD typically show within eighteen months of the traumatic experience. 'A mental health condition triggered by a terrifying event' is the Mayo Clinic's definition. Evolution might be the root of it. You've survived one near fatal experience and you have a better chance of surviving others if the episode has equipped you with hyper-alertness, even paranoia, and nightmares and flashbacks to keep you that way; if you sleep lightly or not at all; are by turns angry and ready to fight; depressed and in retreat from danger or places likely to awaken unwanted memories.

Insofar as the past and present coexist in our minds, we all live in a dual reality, but with PTSD, the present, however tranquil and predictable, coexists with a 'ruinous, ever-present past'. The safe, normal enough person lives with an 'other' who feels anything but safe, and far from normal. With PTSD, the traumatic moment is relived constantly. The body reacts accordingly: in perfectly peaceful moments, it might be busy secreting stress hormones and activating the defensive mechanisms prompted by the threat of death and inescapable anguish.

Many men who showed no symptoms upon returning from World War I broke down fifteen or more years later. PTSD is sometimes slow to manifest. There are veterans among the 70 per cent never diagnosed with PTSD who nevertheless report depression and other mental disorders, and some with no reported disorder who say their experiences in Vietnam come to mind every day and that they have nightmares and flashbacks. 'You just have to put it out of your mind,' a former sapper told me. 'You have to fill your mind with something else.' Not everyone can. Neville managed to put it out of his mind for what he says was 'quite a long time'. But he found it hard to cope with people and frequently 'went bush'. He had flashbacks and nightmares.

Over the next few months, the condition steadily enveloped Neville. He was standing in the chancellor's office, the venetian blinds were filtering the light, and it wasn't an office but a plantation. He remembered the endless patrolling. The sleeplessness and nightmares got worse. He worried that he might have killed women and children. He remembered the moments after they overran an enemy position and knew a North Vietnamese soldier was hiding in a hole, and grenades were the only way to deal with him. In treatment, he met a veteran who had been on a coastal patrol boat with South Vietnamese police. The police had pulled an old fisherman aboard and bashed him to death. The veteran could not forgive himself because he didn't – couldn't – stop them.

It is not that only good and decent soldiers get PTSD, but feeling that you have betrayed your good character, and that it cannot be retrieved, is part of the syndrome for a lot of sufferers. 'All is disgust when one leaves his own nature and does things that misfit it,' Sophocles said. Disgust *and rage* if bureaucracies, politicians, officers, old men and a war as unfathomable as your dreams conspired to take it from you before you could become the man you might have been. Not only were they the few among their generation chosen to face death, they were the ones chosen to kill. Dying for one's country is not the worst thing; killing for it is, one American veteran said. Because that's the memory that haunts. The moral injury tightens the bonds between old soldiers. In the comradeship of the group, memories are preserved, but character too. The best of you is with the men who shared the rush of blood and adrenaline, and who did things that others were not asked to do.

Neville taught the rest of that year, but eventually gave up. By the time we renewed our friendship around 2002, he would not sit with his back to a door, would barely sit at all, but instead walked up and down constantly, and leapt at sudden noises.

Could it be said of the clans, as it is of diagnosed sufferers, that traumatic moments are 'engraved' on the memory at the time they occurred, and recalling them in song and ceremony and talk engraves them deeper all the time?

The thought had often crossed Neville's mind. It was his impression that the sleep of the men he camped with was constantly broken by dreams of ambush and ensorcellment, and portents of violence and death, and their sleeping and waking lives washed back and forth, each colouring the other with anxiety. If true, the tendency might be another reason why, as Stanner has it, balance and the avoidance of trouble are central to the cosmology – and, perhaps, why Galka, the avenger, comes stalking when balance is lost, and trouble is abroad.

'Terror is the normal state of any oral society, for in it everything effects everything all the time,' Marshall McLuhan wrote. Maybe not, but given the terrors of Galka and sorcery, the fear instilled in circumcision and other ceremonies, and the horrors in stories passed down from the frontier, it seemed possible that the hunters and foragers at Donydji might suffer some chronic form of PTSD.

William Rivers wondered if it was colonialism. Could the morbid symptoms he observed among Solomon Islanders in 1908, so like those of shell-shocked soldiers, be put down to the ruinous effect of dispossession and the overthrow of their culture? Could even the steep decline in fertility, also noted by observers on the Australian frontier, be traced not only to the physical consequences of invasion, but to a loss of 'psychological equilibrium' brought about by the destruction of their culture?

On the last night I spent at Donydji, an elderly man loomed out of the dark. With his white, neatly clipped beard shaped to fit his striking angular face beneath a broad-brimmed hat, he had a startlingly ecclesiastical aspect. He wore a clean checked shirt, beige shorts to his knees and, when he removed his hat, his hair was combed back from a receding hairline. His name was Tony.

Neville, who had never seen or met him before, made him welcome and offered him a banana, which he took and ate. We had nothing else. He had a story to tell, he said.

He sat down and in a tired, softly modulated voice, he told us what he called a short version of his long story. Some he told in English, some in Kriol. He was born on Mainoru cattle station, where it seems his father was a stockman, and his mother a servant of some kind. How they came to be there he did not say. The station owners were 'terrible people'. They were 'Yankees'. Here he choked with emotion and waited a minute for it to subside. 'We were not allowed to touch anything ... And there was a schoolteacher ...' He choked again, struggled and at last managed to say, 'It was very bad.' And we sat there in the dark and silence as he cried.

When he had recovered sufficiently, he told us that his sisters had been taken away by the welfare department to Darwin. He had wandered all his life, trying to find his home among the Rembarrnga and the Yolngu. He named many places he had been but had never found people he could call his own or who would welcome him as kin. But he had known Dhulutarama, and Dhulutarama had told him long ago that he was welcome in this country, because his mother was Djambarrpuyngu, and one of Dhulutarama's wives was Rembarrnga. On this basis he was allowed to stay. He told the story in the Yolngu way, Neville said – 'and then'; 'and then'; 'and then'. 'Where is your home now?' Neville asked.

'Here,' he said.

He asked Neville to come and see him in the morning. We did. He told us that at Mainoru the white schoolteacher made them shower every morning and 'he was always raping us'.

There was much more to tell, he said. And he wanted to tell us with his adult son present, because he needed to know. But we were leaving.

One day Neville's counsellor suggested he think about what he wanted to do with his life. He thought about it and reported back: he wanted to go all out to develop Donydji. It made sense. He believed, with sound enough medical reasoning, that his resistance to the neurosis had declined with age. No more sport to let the anger out. The fieldwork and the writing kept him occupied, but not enough to stop the bad stuff creeping in. He needed to do something intense.

The grand idea rapidly took shape. Could he bring together the Donydji clans and the men of his old platoon in a mutually beneficial relationship? The clans would enjoy the better education, health and housing they had been promised but rarely received. The vets would renew their bonds in a less hazardous and more creative cause. The experience might draw them away from the serial replays of the past, which, the psychologists say, stifle imagination and initiative. Their presence and their unsolicited good works might stir up something similar in the Yolngu. The path to a successful homeland would lead through a therapeutic community.

While the plan arose from his own need for therapy and his pact with the old men of the clan, perhaps it was Father Tressider who cast the ghost of the idea in his mind: not the Kingdom of God, but the prospect of redemption and grace. He would recoil at the thought, or at least at the language, but no one surrendered more readily to the claims of the downtrodden and demoralised. Add the seductions of Donydji's soft evening breezes, the arc of the sun over the airstrip, the warmth of companionship or exquisite solitude amid people you care for. 'To love and live beloved is the soul's paradise', John Winthrop said, and science now makes the case, or something like it. From empathetic connections to each other, it tells us, our brains get a hit of dopamine. That might help explain why for some people altruism is addictive. And why, indeed, like Camus, we might decide that Sisyphus is happy to push the rock up the hill. His rock is his thing.

PART III

I cannot bear to think of their passing.

Donald Thomson, 1937

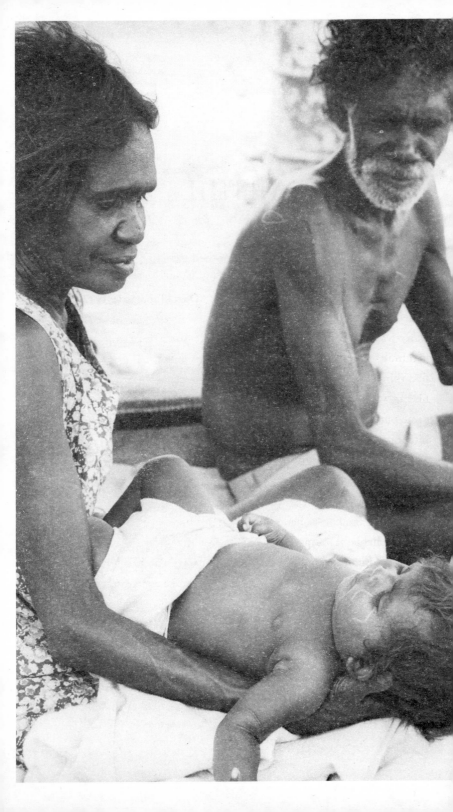

NINE

In the earliest days of the homeland, the Gapuwiyak council agreed to install a windmill. When the drillers struck granite, the senior men feared the bones of the ancestors had been disturbed, but enough water was found for everyone to agree it was worth putting up the windmill. At the base of the mill the contractor installed a tap, and first thing every morning Bayman, the senior man in those days, left his hut, walked to the windmill and turned on the tap. No water ever came out of it. The windmill became a creaking monument to good intentions gone astray.

The windmill was still there when Neville, in remission from his melanoma, set about his plans. There were half a dozen overcrowded houses scattered over the site, but no lavatories, bathrooms or laundries. A couple of the houses had solar panels but they were rarely serviced and unreliable. A pump at the creek brought water to a tank that leaked. Fixing the plumbing and the power supply and building more houses was part of the plan. But Neville knew the centrepiece had to be the school. If he hadn't known it, Tom would have told him. Tom was conservative, and he wanted the children taught in the language of their clans, but he was not so conservative that he couldn't see their life chances depended on a balanda education taught in English.

The other element, as crucial as the school, was a workshop. The workshop addressed the problem that the homeland movement shared with the hub-towns and major centres everywhere – the problem of bored and frustrated young men. In the workshop they could train as mechanics and in other trades. They could make things for the community, and things to sell outside it. With basic carpentry skills they could get paying jobs. With basic mechanical skills they could earn money fixing other people's cars, and *save* money by fixing their own.

Shepherdson College, named after the much-loved reverend and his wife who knew the problems well, set up a school at Donydji in 2001. It was basic: a young woman taught the children sitting in the dust under a shade of boughs and bark. Adults and children were equally keen. Neville asked the Northern Territory government if they would provide a proper building for the school. The government said, perhaps – if the community showed 'commitment'. A year's attendance in heat and dust and rain and mud was not commitment enough.

Neville looked elsewhere. A PhD student helping at the school introduced him to an outer suburban Rotary club in Melbourne. He put his case and they gave him $15,000. He went to the Potter Foundation, venerable Melbourne philanthropists, and they gave him $25,000. He wrote to Nabalco, saying that the community had lost a leader when Yilarama died while helping the company, and the company might now consider helping the community. Nabalco sent two builders. When the little school was finished, the president and some members of the suburban Rotary club turned up on what they called an 'expedition'. They painted the building and erected a plaque saying it had been built with their funds and officially opened by the president. Neville was livid because he and everyone else wanted Tom to open it.

He went after bigger fish. He spoke to the Rotary club of Melbourne. The members were impressed. The Yolngu were surely deserving beneficiaries, and the idea of combining with the hardly less worthy vets in a practical and therapeutic enterprise was irresistibly attractive. Neville made a good advocate: he was articulate, passionate at times, and he had impressive scholarly credentials – the suit and tie only accentuated the evidence of his many years in the field, and lent him the mystique of the hero anthropologist. He was also lucky to find two senior members of the club who had what every homeland needed, white supporters with belief and sticking power. Peter Duncan and John Mitchell became Neville's firm friends, and Melbourne Rotary became Donydji's stalwart benefactor.

The little school built with suburban Rotary and Potter Foundation funds was enough to satisfy the Northern Territory government that the community was committed. They agreed to build a new, better school with a house for a teacher. That was the school being built next to Cowboy's quarters when I first went to Donydji in 2005.

The first vets to go were Charlie Howe and Peter Chapman, a vet he had met in rehab in Melbourne. They went in 2003, soon after Yilarama's death. By then Neville had raised money from Melbourne Rotary to cover airfares and subsistence living. The following year more vets arrived at Donydji, Dave Glyde and Dave Bryan among them. Neville had met Bryan at a counselling session. Another, Wally Magalas, he met at a vets' gym.

To watch them at work was revelatory and inspiriting. They went about it with relentless energy, as if to show every bureaucrat and politician, every rip-off contractor and parasite, what work was, and every Yolngu what was possible. It was work with purpose. As Dave Glyde said, it was work that made you feel good. It was also work that made you wonder how, if a Rotary club and a handful of late-middle-aged men could get so much done, and teach as they went, the nation could be so chronically ineffectual.

Charlie Howe rebirthed the garden, which had only ever existed as 'proof' that the clans occupied the land. Charlie slaved away every day from dawn, clearing the scrub, digging it, fencing it, planting it, irrigating it, until it was a model of agricultural enterprise. The new school's lining boards had already been eaten out by termites, so Dave Glyde and Wally re-lined the rooms with termite resistant sheeting. Existing buildings were transformed, new ones went up, machinery was made to work, plumbing made effective. The young men joined in the enterprise and were mentored as they did.

Neville believes it was because they were vets that they threw themselves so resolutely into the work. They were not put off by the grim conditions in which the Yolngu lived, their desperately dirty houses, the dire plumbing and sanitation. Their army experience had made them resilient. The army had also taught them what it was like to feel let down by your country. They knew a bit about what it was like to not fit. They knew what it was like to be dropped into a life you never would have chosen. If the Yolngu seemed dysfunctional, they knew what that was like as well. Dave Glyde said it was their awful condition that moved him, and the callous neglect – and the waste – that made him angry.

Neville buzzed around like a football coach, and the more he buzzed, the more stoical was the vets' mien. They crawled from their swags as the sun appeared at the end of the runway, by which time Neville had the fire going and the water boiling. They ate their Weet-Bix, drank their coffee, took their pills, and (in the years before they erected new toilets), one by one, army trenching tool in hand, trudged up the airstrip and deep into the bush. Then they got to work.

Neville's plans began to take impressive shape. The workshop was ready and fully equipped to teach young men trade skills which at least would enable them to service their own vehicles and machinery. After the vets left that year, the young men pleaded for more training. Youths from other homelands and Gapuwiyak wanted to come to Donydji and learn. The principal at Shepherdson College sent a primary school teacher with trade skills, who ran a workshop program for twelve months. The results were gratifying. The excellent schoolteacher was an equally excellent trade teacher. The teacher said the trainees showed 'real enthusiasm and motivation in working towards improving their own situation'. When the vets returned the following year, they supervised the trainees who, for the first time in their lives, were paid for their work.

Meanwhile, in the new school, Donydji's children were learning to read and write and becoming familiar with some of the ways of the balanda world; and they were doing it as Tom required – on their own land, without losing their own language, law and culture.

But after twelve months a new principal at the College cancelled the scheme: Donydji was not a 'real school', he said, but a 'homeland learning centre'. The trade teacher was moved on to be a primary teacher at another school. His replacement at the workshop had begun enthusiastically, but then he took a job with the contractor who built the new school and left. The Northern Territory government having pulled out of the field, the principal said he was not in a position to provide technical training to anyone.

Without a trade teacher, the young men began to leave the homeland. Even though, as they said, there was 'too much humbug in Gapuwiyak', they went there because life was so often boring at Donydji, and they didn't want to sit around or just cut grass and clean up rubbish.

To say there was a pattern to these disappointments is to understate the effect on the inhabitants. It was a mill, a grindstone.

Two years before my first visit, a water tank was delivered to the school – by helicopter. The new tank was as big as the tank that served the whole community. The contractors set up the pump to override the pump on the community tank when the level of water in the school tank fell below a certain point, which left the school with water but the community sometimes without it. The contractors installed flush toilets and a septic tank at the school, but in the wet season some of the septic tank's contents washed back into the toilet bowls and a good deal more flooded onto the ground and into the creek from which the community's water is drawn.

Two years earlier, when a toilet was brimming over, Neville rang the Health Department and asked if the contractor who was then building Tom's house could be authorised to fill in the overflowing hole and dig a new one with his big tractor and its earth-moving implements. A contractor had installed a septic tank three years earlier, but the 'tank' turned out to be a 44-gallon drum cut in half. The same contractor laid some pipes but never came back to fill in the trench. He quoted $14,000 to lay a pipe to the workshop. Three veterans bought the pipe in Nhulunbuy for a few hundred dollars and laid it in half a day.

The Health Department said the hole was the responsibility of the homeland's service provider, Marthakal. Neville phoned Marthakal on Elcho Island, but they said the hole was not their job – the Education Department should dig it. It was no surprise when the Education Department denied responsibility. The visiting Health Solutions Broker from the Indigenous Coordination Council, who had advised Neville to ring the Health Department, said on second thoughts he should contact a person whose name and address he wrote on a piece of paper before driving away in his new Land Cruiser. Neville at last rang the Regional Council at Gapuwiyak and their person said go ahead and tell the man to bury the overflow and fill in the existing hole and dig a new one. It took the contractor half an hour. It had taken Neville many months.

The follies came one upon another. When the workshop was finished and the new school almost complete, the Education Department paid a consultant $13,000 to find out if sacred sites at

Donydji had been damaged in the process. It seemed an odd thing to do, given the building was already up, the community had chosen the location, and the protection of sacred sites was the reason for the homeland's being. But the consultant flew in, asked if any sites were likely to be damaged in the construction of the buildings, and then he flew out.

Soon after, another consultant flew in from Darwin to see to the health and safety provisions in the new workshop. The building had been designed with doors at each end wide enough to allow two large vehicles to easily traverse the 10 metres between them. The consultant, however, noting that no illuminated EXIT signs had been erected above the doors, declared the workshop unfit for occupation or use, and flew away. Illuminated EXIT signs were ordered, reached Donydji within a month, and the vets installed them above the doors. The health and safety officer flew back to Donydji, examined the signs, found them satisfactorily installed and declared the building fit for use. Then he flew away again. The signs cost a little over $100; the flights of the consultant were probably about twenty times that.

Planes would come in from the 'service provider' on Elcho Island with one person on board – the teacher, for instance – and fly away, and no one at the 'service provider' ever thought to phone ahead and ask if there was something the homeland people needed. Food, bullets, bandages, a spare part, fuel, a mechanic. A man flew in one day and erected a letterbox on the fringe of the airstrip. Years later another man came with a front-end loader and pushed thirty-six car bodies scattered around the place, not to the tip but to Joanne's front door. In two neat rows.

People were always flying away or driving off in their shiny new Land Cruisers. The residents lived at the convenience of bureaucrats and contractors who came without warning and left after making promises which they forgot before they were airborne or reached the main road. Health workers, volunteers, mechanics, electricians, miners, tourists, school children – even politicians occasionally – they all blew in and blew out. It is a condition of homeland existence to be serviced, studied, befriended and left. Attention is always fleeting. The people who come in person represent the Australian population, including those who count sympathy for First Nations people among their progressive credentials. As guns and missionaries were to early settler colonialism, no less cynical bureaucracy, fine sentiments and hollow promises have been to the later stages.

I was at Donydji late in the Dry season of 2007. Neville had been there with the vets from May to July. They had performed their usual wonders, renovating and painting houses built by the council ten or fifteen years earlier, putting up two shower blocks and washhouses.

But things had begun badly. Dave Glyde found the locks on the new workshop had been broken, tools were missing, and diesel was seeping onto the floor. Men from other communities, calling on the obligations of kinship, had been responsible for the break-in and the thefts.

The people were hungry. There was no vehicle to drive to Gapuwiyak for food and no one knew where the gun was. There was no ammunition anyway. Kevin Gunyanbirrirr borrowed Neville's gun and a couple of bullets and came back with two ibis, which he divided among the hearths. He sent Neville a leg, but Neville sent it back, saying the women and children needed it more. It didn't help his mood that Tom and Christopher had gone to Numbulwar for a funeral and stayed there. Cowboy was back at Donydji and Neville was sure they were intimidated by his presence.

Neville wrote in his diary of his 'disappointment, depression, anger'. The torment was made worse by Tom phoning to tell him he had heard the kids at Donydji were 'starving'; they were eating grass; the women weren't caring for them. They were not showing him respect. The young men should be hunting. Tom was leading vigorously from a safe distance.

Neville couldn't sleep for hunger and frustration, and when he did, he had dreams he could have done without. Then, before dawn one morning, he decided he would not surrender. Dave Bryan and his brother Ken were coming, and Andrew Sharp from the organic vegetable stall in Melbourne. Things would be done. Marthakal, the service provider, had agreed to pay the Yolngu workers a trainee wage. He took comfort from the example of Kevin, a great believer in the homeland, who had heroically mowed the whole place with a mower designed for a suburban backyard.

The first trade teacher had begun to teach him English, and now Kevin was spending hours each day trying to teach himself. He slept in a room in Tom's house and ate at night with Neville and Dave. There was no more sincere, warm-hearted, generous person in the camp. But when Neville asked Kevin to be manager of the workshop, he said no. Too many arguments. To much humbugging.

At the end of Tom's verandah, as if guarding it in his absence, David, Kevin, Djaypi, Bunbuma and Ricky, all lean and hungry, sat looking across the camp. A hundred metres away on the verandah of the house that had served as a medical clinic until he commandeered it, Cowboy sat in his blue director's chair with his favourite wife, Sandy, sitting cross-legged on the boards beside him, and the less favoured May Wilfred bringing him damper. No one went near the big man with the big stomach and the big appetite, in his blue flannel shirt, jeans, stockmen's boots and big black cowboy hat.

A few days earlier, Sandy had come in on a plane with her son and sister on board, and the camp saw them load big bags of food and supplies into a wheelbarrow that Cowboy had pushed up to the airstrip, and they watched as he wheeled it down to his verandah. Tom was still at Numbulwar, worried off his own country by Cowboy, or at least by the trouble he brought with him. Tom was not generally a model of strong leadership, but the community respected him and cohered around his presence, and if by driving him away Cowboy had not yet pulled off his coup, he had taken the first step by creating a power vacuum. And he knew he was winning the psychological war: one day he sent Sandy to Neville's camp to say Tom and Christopher should go and live at Ngilipitji and leave Donydji to him.

Ricky Guyula, who had emerged as a smart and likeable figure in the community, said Cowboy had been going to ceremonies and demanding money from the community account for food and travel expenses. He demanded diesel. He demanded wood for his fire. He monopolised the school phone.

Ricky was knowing and droll, tough and vulnerable. Through his Ritharrngu mother, along with Bunbuma and Damien Guyula and Djikambur, he had the status of a manager at the homeland. Growing up at Donydji, he was Birin Birin, but his name was Ngambirt and he was the brother of Joanne and Sonya Guyula, and Bunbuma (Eric) Guyula. The mother of the sisters was also Ricky's mother, but he had a different father, Burrukala's brother. As a Djambarrpuyngu (Dhuwa) man he had outraged the law by taking a Wagilak (Dhuwa) woman as his wife and having a child with her. He left Donydji for some time, and apparently lived hard, but he came back with a rare feel for the homeland's potential. No one was more desperate to make it a place he could happily live in.

The longer Tom stayed away, the bolder Cowboy grew. A few years back his children had been at Donydji for a while, but they wouldn't stay: 'Maybe they saw something miserable here,' he said to Neville. He was applying for a business loan to establish a cattle station and immediate funding for fencing and stockyards. When Marthakal called a meeting on Elcho Island and invited representatives from all the homelands they serviced, Cowboy made himself Donydji's representative. A plane came to pick him up and as he walked past Neville at his fire, he said he was off to meet an important person. Neville said he should not be representing Donydji, Tom should be. Cowboy said, 'Maybe he's too frightened.'

As the plane taxied away, Neville sat with his back turned, Yolngu fashion, hoping Cowboy noticed. He wrote in his notebook that Tom had to 'grow some balls'. He had to stand up to Cowboy and stop expecting him – Neville – to do it. He thought it might already be too late. The men, Cowboy excepted, went hunting. Neville stayed alone in his camp while six hungry dogs and a dingo stood in a row staring at him.

One day soon after, to calm himself, he left the camp and spent a day among the paintings in two massive rock formations separated by gentle field-like savannah that he had taken me to see a year earlier. He had first seen the paintings one evening years before, when the sun, low in the sky, flashed on the ochre and walking towards it he was amazed to see the panels: finely painted yam figures, with leg tassels, in the style of Western Arnhem Land. But crude symbols had been painted over them. Looking around, he saw more of the same. It was an illuminated landscape. 'A cultural landscape in the literal sense', he wrote later. Tom knew the site of course, but even standing before them he refused to acknowledge the paintings in the Western Arnhem Land style. They were in the rock, he said. On his way back he saw Cowboy and Sandy leaving the camp, each carrying an axe. Eight dogs trotted along with them, while May Wilfred, some distance behind, pushed the wheelbarrow. No one had brought them wood, it seemed.

Neville had a duty to protect the unity of the clans, which meant he had a duty to protect the Bidingal clan and the integrity of their lands against interlopers wanting to create cattle stations. By phone, he suggested to Tom that they elect a council, with Tom as general manager. The council would administer the workshop and everything else that needed administering. And Cowboy would be put in his proper place.

To support the case for Tom's election, Neville found a 1974 diary with entries recording the visit of Cowboy's father, Munuma, and others from the Madarrpa clan to 'discuss compensation' for the miners' damage to the rocks. It had been agreed that the Bidingal-Gulungurr clans of the Ritharrngu would look after the site. Munuma and his party returned to the Roper and never came back to Donydji. As well as the notebook he had maps, showing the Bidingal-Gulungurr lands and the Madarrpa lands to the west and south in the Mitchell Ranges. (He could have shown them the map in Warner's old book – it marks the border between 'Bringel' and 'Maderppa' clearly.) There were also tapes and the five-generation genealogies he had compiled. It all went to show that the clans presently occupying the Donydji lands had proprietary and managerial rights, and Cowboy's rights were only ceremonial.

In Tom's absence, Neville put the plan to the younger men, Kevin, Djaypi, Djikambur, Ricky and Terrence Ritharrmiwuy, a wise and reliable Djambarrpuyngu associate who lived in Nhulunbuy. They all supported the idea. They agreed that, with all the documentary material to back them up, their case was strong. Neville asked if they should use the notebooks or the tapes. They were unanimous: the notebooks, they said – 'for proof'.

He told Tom about it over the phone. Tom also liked it, though he rang a few days later and asked Neville to explain it to him again. Neville told him that to elect the council and appoint him leader there had to be a meeting of the whole community. He told Tom he had to come back.

Things began to look up. Ken Bryan, Dave's brother, was a mechanic and soon had the generator working. The men were working well on the houses and in the workshop with the vets. Ricky told Neville that the work made him feel good. Not working made him sick. Neville saw women sitting on the verandah of their freshly painted house, arms wrapped around their knees, content. The blind old woman sat among them with her cloth hat pulled down over her eyes.

But on the phone Tom complained that the young people were running around too much: back and forth to Gapuwiyak for kava and gunydja. They should stay at Donydji and be (Neville's translation) 'quiet, humble'. The young men should be hunting. He was sick. He needed red meat for his blood. The community needed a reliable working vehicle. When they had one, Djikambur should drive him regularly to Nhulunbuy for injections. At Numbulwar the nurse had given him lots of them. Sometimes Tom's idea of a good community sounded a little self-interested.

He at last returned, with Christopher, by charter plane that Neville paid for. The days had been colder than any Neville had known at Donydji. Tom blamed the cold on ill-disposed people at Numbulwar. He said Gapuwiyak had been cursed by people at Numbulwar too. He had no sooner got back to Donydji than he heard strange sounds in the night and saw a shadowy figure. Ricky reported that his brother Bunbuma had heard it too. Neville told Ricky that he also had heard something. Cowboy had the spotlight on at night.

Tom had returned agitated. It didn't help when Andrew Sharp came back from a hunting trip with his leg grazed by the horns of a wounded buffalo. Andrew lacked his companions' ability to shin up trees. He was lucky to have survived and everyone knew it. Tom fumed that the young men had taken the balanda with them. The leg became infected. Neville feared the worst. Andrew ended up in Darwin hospital, where it took him many weeks to recover.

*

The day came and Tom was on his way to the meeting when he saw Cowboy, carrying his director's chair, heading for the same entrance. Tom doubled back and marked time out of sight before making for a back door. Twenty-one adults sat down in the school classroom, waiting for the showdown to begin. Cowboy sat outside in the breeze-way, listening through the louvre window. Sandy sat in the doorway.

Djaypi, who always seemed a calming presence, chaired proceedings. He read out Neville's notes from 1974, then held up the genealogies and laid them on the floor, where everyone inspected them. Then he put it to the meeting that Tom be elected general manager of Donydji. There was never any doubt: Tom was elected 'on the voices'. But later everyone marked off their name on a voting sheet to put it on the record and beyond question. Only Cowboy, Sandy and May Wilfred did not vote for Tom.

It was decided that a council of four men would help Tom to run the community. Christopher, Ricky, Djaypi and Kevin were elected, but they were not to take decisions without Tom's approval. No one wanted cattle. Cattle would make Donydji 'dirty country'. They would wreck sites, ruin waterholes and streams, and bring uninvited visitors, booze and drugs. So it was recorded that Donydji was not to be a cattle station.

Joanne Guyula, the young, dedicated trainee teacher, would have been a valuable member of the council, but that could not be. She had already spent a year trying to get the training she needed to become a qualified teacher and she would spend more years trying, without success. (Her sister Sonya could run so fast people thought she might one day be as good as the world champion Cathy Freeman, but with no one to coach her, that too could not be.) As she struggled valiantly with her studies and taught at the school, ever more burdens of caring and management fell on Joanne's shoulders. What she told the meeting typified her daily struggle: the school bank account, she said, should be used only for the needs of the school children.

Someone in the room must have been using it for something else.

Tom went further. In a long speech he said people should not be spending their time driving around looking for gunydja. They should stay at Donydji and care properly for their children, instead of leaving them to run around in the long grass, risking snake bite and attacks from buffalo.

Neville suggested that Cowboy might be reconciled to the new arrangements as council chairman. But Cowboy rose to his feet in the breezeway and said he would not accept the position. Too many people had been criticising him. He didn't like to be criticised. He didn't like to be 'cut out' and 'blocked'. He would search and find the people who were spreading stories about him. If they kept it up, he would leave Donydji but he would stay very upset. He had said the same privately to Neville and left him in no doubt that it was a threat.

Yet there was something sad about Cowboy's spiel. He might have looked as if he had never gone a day without a feed, but no one could say his life had been easy. He'd been born in the cattle and raised in the mission and probably suffered as many humiliations as most of the people on the homeland. The young people at Donydji did not know about his rights, he said. They didn't know about the Madarrpa relationship to the Donydji lands. At this point, Djaypi leaned over and told Neville he should leave, because now it was 'private talk'. Later he heard that Sandy had spoken to the meeting 'with moist eyes'. She said Cowboy had been hurt by the words spoken that morning.

The meeting was judged a great success. Relief spread through the community. There could be a new start. Work on the houses continued. Djaypi said to Neville, 'Look, they [white people] think we can't work but this will show them.' The pay packets were handed out, and it seemed just then that this could be the homeland of the future.

*

I went back with Neville a couple of months later. The grass and weeds were halfway up the red, yellow, and blue plastic slide in front of the new school, the plastic play tunnel in the same bright colours and the torn and rusted 44-gallon drums that do for rubbish bins. The crows were talking in their sardonic tones, a bull calf found in the bush and called Ringo was asleep in the shade of the house where the unmarried men slept and played their music, and lean and bony Betty was getting water from a tap. Looking from the old school towards Neville's shed and the caravan he parked there thirty years ago, three small girls were giggling in a mango tree. When they came over this morning Neville gave each of them a muesli bar and they ran away laughing. Donydji, slipping between Chaos and Eden.

That morning, Christopher wept. He was saying how difficult it was to keep the young people out of trouble, when the tears rolled from his eyes. Tom said (Neville was translating) that on the outside the young men seem happy but inside their eyes they are 'dry'. David and Damien, two of half a dozen men on whom the homeland's future rests, had gone with some youngsters to get marijuana from Gapuwiyak. That was bad enough, but Christopher and Tom had also heard Yolngu bureaucrats were supplying gunydja, and that youths sent to Batchelor College, south of Darwin, were picking up drug habits there and bringing dope back to the homelands.

Yet when one of the alleged offenders turned up that morning, Tom smiled and politely accepted him into the circle of conversation. The man is connected to Donydji through his mother's family and therefore has a right.

We were joined by a veteran called John, a big man with a broad open face and a disarmingly gentle manner. Neville had met him at a PTSD therapy session five years earlier. John gave the impression of having lost something of himself.

After we arrived, half an hour went by before Tom sauntered up, smiling, unable to hide his happiness at seeing Neville. He sat cross-legged on top of a 44-gallon drum. Kevin Gunyanbirrirr strolled over soon after. They talked for an hour or so, then Neville asked for the key to the workshop. We found there was no need for it: the door was unlocked. Inside, the truth was plain to see. The place had been ransacked. Louvres had been pulled out. Many of the tools were gone and those that remained were strewn around. Later we found several lying in the grass around the camp, but many more were missing. The trailer was gone.

Neville was devastated. For a long while, he didn't speak. Tom told him that people had come from Gapuwiyak and other homelands to fix their Toyotas and took a lot of the tools. The kids had got into the place and taken them to fix their bikes. Cowboy had taken the trailer. Tom didn't explain the tools found strewn around. Maybe it had something to do with their nomadic heritage, the millennia when mobility and property were in contradiction. Warner noted the Yolngu were 'not particularly interested in ... material culture and would rather not be disturbed by its burden and responsibilities'.

It was easy enough to understand the men who brought their clapped-out cars for repairs. When the repair shop in Nhulunbuy did the work, they confiscated the vehicles until the owners paid bills that often ran into thousands of dollars. So the owners brought them to the workshop, where David and Ricky, both good bush mechanics, repaired them. But they didn't pay. Kinship obligations rule.

It occupied the same confounding realm in balanda minds as the question of why some of the houses they had renovated were later vandalised. One unpalatable answer was that while the houses, like the tools, had been given generously, those who gave them could not set the terms of their use – not unless the gifts were, like beads and tomahawks, a blind for expropriating not their land this time, but their customs and manners. This reasoning of course did not help the likes of Ricky and Kevin, who wanted to learn a trade and make an independent living.

Neville spoke of getting the trade teacher back for at least a day a week to train young men in the basics, and of the young men, once trained, being paid for their services, and of Donydji charging a modest amount for use of the workshop. The young men, as always, lit up at the prospect of something to do. But the trade teacher never came, and the workshop remained a cruel reminder of what might have been.

If teaching had continued in the workshop, there might have been less incentive for the pillage. Perhaps someone would have defended the community's asset. The school was never looted, presumably because the community valued the work that was done there. Though it was known to contain many items of value, including food and tobacco, Neville's hut had never been burgled, because Neville's work was prized. But neither his hut nor the school contained the means of satisfying every young man's greatest desire – a functioning vehicle.

Cowboy at last departed Donydji and the verandah from which he had surveyed the world for so long. By way of leaving a foothold in the community, before he departed with the trailer, he stowed his gear in the house, and put both a lock on the door and a spell on the building. Defying his sorcery but unable to break the lock, Djikambur and his family, who had recently returned from another homeland, now slept on the verandah.

Tom was hungry. 'Look at me, I'm starving,' he called pathetically to Neville. He was on all fours outside the door of the single men's house, putting on a comic act: 'Sugar and Winfield,' he called feebly.

But Kevin never complained. His teeth were broken and rotten and his big toe was so badly infected it was soon to be amputated, but he said all he wanted was something to do.

John was wonderfully adept with ropes and machinery. In no time he built a strong room in the workshop for all the surviving tools, some of which were found and returned by the children within a day of our arriving. A signalman in Vietnam, John had been in a bunker one day when he realised an Australian outfit was about to run into a New Zealand one. The signals unit did not get the message through, and Australian soldiers died in 'friendly fire'. The fatal stuff-up left John oppressed by both guilt and anger: anger because it was his American commander who failed to send the message and, what was worse in John's mind, told him to forget the episode and never tell a soul about it. John hated the Yanks, the white ones at least; he liked the Black servicemen and used to hang out with them.

He told me he had been spat on when he got back to Australia. He dropped the bloke, he said, but that didn't help much. His father, he reckoned, got a ticker-tape parade in 1945, but in 1970 his son got a gob of spit.*

Back in civilian life, though he found work easily enough, John could not settle. A marriage lasted just eight months. He got into a fight with some cops, but a sympathetic magistrate let him off with a $1000 fine. If John was still angry in 2007 it did not show, but sadness and loneliness hung about him. Signals did not have the comradeship of the infantry, he said. No one knew what a signalman did. Some infantrymen thought he was the commanding officer's valet. John had fought the same war as Neville and the other vets

---

*   In fact, while some World War I and II soldiers returned to big public welcomes, plenty drifted back into civilian life as unnoticed as the Vietnam vets. No doubt some soldiers were spat on and abused, but, researching his book *The Nashos' War*, Mark Dapin could not find a single case.

who came to Donydji, but he had been denied the one saving grace of their experience. They had their bonds of friendship. John had only his torments.

John, Neville and I spent an afternoon exploring jungle by the creek. We were joined by another Damien, a lively young Rembarrnga man with a trimmed beard and ponytail. He came from the Beswick community, west of Donydji, and spoke Kriol which Neville could only just understand.* John broke his sandal, and Damien repaired it in no time with a vine. Neville talked about the jungle fowl that used to live along the stream. Twenty years ago, they had disappeared from all the Donydji lands. Feral cats and the use of guns instead of spears were two likely reasons. Neville had suggested importing a breeding population, but Tom said no: they had just gone away, it was their business, they'd come back if they wanted to. Damien listened to Neville, cocked his head, walked a little way, and pointed up in the branches of a tree. It was a jungle fowl. I dropped my sunglasses somewhere in the dense undergrowth, and Damien found them as well. It would be easier to find them next time, because as we left, he set fire to the place. It was not a 'cool' burn. Back at Donydji, we could see the great cloud of smoke billowing in the distance and wondered if the antilopine kangaroo we had seen there had managed to escape.

Well upstream from the old waterhole which the buffalo had fouled, we washed in the creek while the bee-eaters did aerial acrobatics. We spent the twilight listening to stories of negligence, greed and rank stupidity from Neville's limitless array. A mechanic came from Marthakal to fix the generator, but soon after he left the

---

* Northern Territory Kriol grew out of a kind of pidgin which evolved among the children of different language groups that came together in the early days of white settlement at Roper River. As more groups were brought together in the missions, Kriol, with several regional variants, became more common and is spoken by more Indigenous people in the Territory than any other dialect.

battery was flat. They recharged it but it soon went flat again. The pattern repeated until the vets arrived and found the mechanic had put the bushes in the alternator back to front.

The vets could not fix everything. The flooded ground around the 'septic tank' stank and teemed with parasites. They did their best to drain it, but a year later it was still flooded. Contractors installed solar panels on several houses, but some failed within a few weeks. No one had come back to fix them. A year later, not one of them was working.

'I won't give up,' Neville said. 'Look how healthy everyone is.' Maybe not as abundantly as they had been when he arrived all those years ago, but so much healthier than people in the hub-towns. Hungry sometimes, but healthier.

Where did his sense of obligation come from? Was he Gwen White's son, Leo White's, the boxing gym's, Dhulutarama's, or was he a son of Vietnam? Were his motives benevolent and empathetic, or more those of a control freak, a missionary, a masochist, a fanatic? Was he a marvellous hybrid of empathy and pragmatism – like Christ; or a man trapped in a delusion and drawn to mortification of the flesh – like Christ? Was it all to redeem himself, the fallen self of Vietnam (if somewhere in the darker corners that is how he saw it), or to redeem the whole world? Was it always war with him, always duty-bound? Always under fire and returning it? To reproach the world, or himself?

He did know doubt. His doubts were monsters. It was no accident when Galka turned up in his nightmares. Doubt was more than asking himself what the point was. It was not ennui, but more like terror. He had to stop himself from thinking that he had given birth to a thing with dimensions he could not control. He could run from it, of course. Most people would. He could become a recreational humanitarian, like the rest of us. But he wasn't like the rest of us. Whatever it was that drove him – empathy, ego unrestrained, a crease in his psychology – all that mattered to him was what could be fixed, the concrete expression of a man's duty to others.

The buffalo crossed the airstrip every night we were there, and every night in protest the dogs – gaunt, indomitable creatures with bits out of their ears and hides, some with limps, and most with ungovernable libidos – set up their hilarious chorus. Each morning on the airstrip, in the shimmering gold of the sunrise, the camp packs, joined for a while by sleek red dingoes appearing like phantoms from the bush, staged the canine equivalent of *The Sopranos*: strutting, snarling, warring, copulating, cuckolding, bullying, lying on their backs begging for mercy.

In the days when the clans moved in bands, they always had dogs to protect the camp and warn them of approaching danger. The women still take dogs with them to warn them of buffalo and to flush out lizards, echidnas and feral cats. Men take them hunting for much the same purpose. Good dogs will stand a buffalo or bullock long enough for men to spear or shoot it. There are favourite dogs, with names, even subsection names, as if they are at least informal kin. Some are given burials and their graves are marked with crosses and other symbolic objects. Traditionally, dogs enlarged the group. Their usefulness still extends beyond services to security and food gathering, to the company they provide. They are a social element, if at one remove from the human. This is to speak of favourite dogs. Dogs that are not favourites lead a thoroughly miserable existence on the fringes.

The women came back one afternoon with half a dozen turtles: they always come back with something. But men and women both say hunting is not what it used to be. Cane toads have killed off the goannas and pythons, water monitors, lizards and file snakes.

The quolls have gone too, and though no one knows why, they rarely see a kangaroo or wallaby. Buffalo and wild cattle (bullocky) are the most reliable source, at least when there is ammunition for the gun. One of the young men had a rigid little finger and a deep scar stretching across his palm and down the side of his hand. He was clinging to the back of a wounded buffalo and stabbing it, when in all the blood his knife slipped, and he stabbed himself.

One night, after his evening walk up the airstrip taking potshots at mudlarks with his slingshot and stopping occasionally to examine signs of animal life in the dust, Tom joined us for our usual dinner of rice and tinned tuna. Kevin had also walked on the airstrip, a couple of hundred metres in front of Tom, deep in thought, it seemed. He came to dinner as well, along with Damien. They all left around eight o'clock and John took to his tent soon after. Around nine o'clock Kevin came back and asked Neville for some wood. A short time later there was a fire outside the single men's house, and soon after Kevin came out with a blanket, threw it on the fire and went back inside. A few minutes later he reappeared with more bedding and threw it in the blaze.

We could feel general consternation around the camp. A couple of young boys went to the house and went away again. Campfires blazed higher; lights flashed in the dark. The lights went out and the fires dimmed. It was as if the community's blood pressure rose and fell. In the morning Kevin said nonchalantly that he was fine.

The fire, a signal of Kevin's angst, had its roots in an act of the Australian parliament. In August 2007 the federal government suspended the *Racial Discrimination Act* and provisions of the *Native Title Act* and passed the *Northern Territory National Emergency Response Act 2007* – widely known as the Intervention. The act was the Commonwealth government's response to *Ampe Akelyernemane Meke Mekarle*, the 'Little Children Are Sacred' report from the Board of Inquiry into the Protection of Aboriginal Children from Sexual Abuse. The principal justification for the Intervention was evidence of sexual abuse of children in Aboriginal communities, though only two out of ninety-odd recommendations in that report were taken up, no 'paedophile ring' of which the minister spoke was ever discovered, and no charges were ever laid against an abuser. Yet anyone who had seen the violence, self-abuse, suicide and squalor of some Aboriginal communities knew there were solid grounds for radical action, and the Intervention was applauded by several Indigenous leaders, including Marcia Langton, Noel Pearson and Galarrwuy Yunupingu.

Large amounts of money were invested in child protection and housing. Numbers of police – and soldiers – were sent to hub-towns with instructions to crack down on violence, drugs and alcohol – and pornography. In deciding bail applications or sentencing, Northern Territory courts would no longer take into consideration Indigenous custom or law. The Community Development Employment Projects (CDEP) scheme was scrapped. A proportion of all benefits paid to Indigenous people through the government welfare agency Centrelink was withheld, and payments to any recipients found to have neglected their children were cancelled. Neglected children were to be taken into care. Income support became conditional on the recipients' children attending school.

Some human rights groups and Indigenous leaders, the Greens and the Northern Territory government all opposed the Intervention on the grounds that it was discriminatory, draconian and regressive. Three years after it was introduced, the Intervention had as many critics as it had supporters. Galarrwuy Yunupingu became one of the critics. But even those who distrusted the government's motives, or saw self-interest and hypocrisy in the rhetoric, conceded the need to do something. It had to be, Marcia Langton wrote, after 'the failure of Northern Territory governments for a quarter of a century to adequately invest the funds they received to eliminate the disadvantages of their citizens in education, health and basic services. It was made worse by general incompetence in Darwin: the public service, the non-government sector (including some Aboriginal organisations) and the dead hand of the Aboriginal and Torres Strait Islander Commission (ATSIC) all presided over increasingly horrible conditions in Aboriginal communities.'

In Gapuwiyak, the Intervention was getting into gear. Two Yolngu men in khaki uniforms were training a hose on some large rocks piled in a row along the verge of the road in front of the Community Centre. A third man was picking up rocks and throwing them in the back of a Toyota. Another row of rocks had been painted white.

Helen Westbury had just retired from the Commonwealth Public Service, and was on holiday with her husband, when the call came asking her to manage the Intervention on Yolngu lands. This she was attempting to do from a Toyota and a converted shipping container in Gapuwiyak.

Untangling the various bits of government-issued hardware – telephone, pager, iPad and their various aerials and connections – was management challenge enough. Helen came with lashings of management speak which required more untangling. But she was fervent, she had heart, she listened, she quickly came to understand and she turned up when she said she would. She went out to the homelands. At Donydji, she did the unthinkable and stayed overnight. We grew rapidly to like her, and often said that half a dozen Helen Westburys could have made a world of difference.

No doubt the Intervention helped in some Territory communities, but at Donydji it caused mainly harm. With more police (and soldiers) in the hub-towns, people with drug habits and little respect for the local rules turned up in the homeland and brought trouble. A rumour spread in Gapuwiyak that children were being abused in Donydji. Police and nurses went out to the homeland and conducted examinations. The adults could not understand why they were there, and when it was explained to them, they were bewildered. When Neville spoke to Djaypi and Sammy, he said, they told him such things could never happen at Donydji, and they cried for shame.

That was also the medical officer's view. She said until the Intervention no one had ever seen a sign of sexual abuse among Yolngu children; yet, she said, the entire Australian population thought sexual abuse was the reason for the Intervention. She had been visiting Donydji for years and had never seen a sign of abuse. It was Cowboy, she said, who told police Kevin was abusing an underage girl, and that was why they went to Donydji. Cowboy of course had an axe to grind. Hearing the rumours, the medical officer checked again and found they were false. She hated the Intervention and intended to leave her job.

Kevin was not abusing anyone, but he was having a relationship with a twenty-three-year-old woman who had been promised to another clan. Taken as an object of exchange, she was the 'wrong' woman. Kevin burned his bedding that night because, inadvertently, the Intervention had flushed out the affair. The young woman had confessed to the relationship and to being pregnant to Kevin. Only later, when Kevin had been expelled from the community did Neville find out. But that night the whole community likely knew that Kevin's fire was a plea for sympathy.

Wrong relationships were far from uncommon. If her son could not stay at Donydji, Kevin's mother said, others who were guilty of the same or similar offences should go as well. Not for the first time, Wanakiya declared the Guyulas – Ricky, Joanne and Sonya – did not belong at Donydji. From time to time she would say the same of

Ronnie, the adoptive brother of Tom: 'You're Gulungurr, Ritharrngu, not Bidingal, your country is Dhunganda, not Donydji – you don't belong here!' Ronnie seems to have thought it better to clear out with his family, though he left his dogs behind, and they went hungry. Then, feeling the camp's disapproval, Wanakiya left with her adult daughter and her daughter's children.

When the Wet set in, the people followed tracks through grass so high the houses and the school could not be seen. Christopher was at Walker River with his new wife, and Tom was forever in Nhulunbuy getting his chest X-rayed, a procedure which he felt was keeping him alive. The medical officer who made fortnightly visits to Donydji later told me she thought the homeland might be finished.

Yet it was a pattern repeated over all the years that Neville had been at Donydji: every major dispute saw families and individuals leave. He had mapped it in his thesis: in 1974, after a sacred site was damaged and there was an argument about permitting alcohol on the homeland, fifteen of sixty in the community left. Another fifteen left the following year after a dispute about the ownership of a community vehicle. Arguments led the Wagilak households to move to the other end of the airstrip. The pattern was as old as the clans themselves. The anthropologists called it 'fission and fusion'.

It was the police, acting in accordance with the stated aims of the Intervention, who had blundered in and left the community riven and reduced, yet the core of the matter was customary law running up against the reality of life on the homeland. The homelands cemented or re-established the authority of the old people which the missions had substantially broken down. The missions permitted, even encouraged, young women and men to meet and court and marry each other. But homelands reimposed traditional sanctions. Kevin's liaison not only breached the 'letter' of customary law, it cost the community the dues paid by the man to whom she was promised, and risked retribution for the offence. It was to put purpose and meaning in the lives of young men that Neville set up the workshop, but that would not have relieved their frustrations under the marriage laws.

Kevin's banishment broke him after months of torment, and not only over the affair. In the spirit of the Intervention, police alleged he had been apprehended in Numbulwar driving an unregistered vehicle, without a licence and without wearing a seatbelt. In fact, on the day the offences were committed Kevin was in the hospital in Nhulunbuy having his big toe amputated. Neville provided the police with documentary evidence from the hospital, but for months the police and the court would not relent, sending letters to Kevin (that he could not read) demanding that he appear in court to answer the charges or be taken into custody. Nor would the Donydji resident who had borrowed the car registered in Kevin's name – and driven it without a licence or a seatbelt – relent in his refusal to own up to the authorities.

Neville did his best to save him, but Kevin fell apart. He went out to Donydji determined to see his child. He caused so much trouble there that the police came and took him away in a divvy van. In what must have been general confusion, they also took Christopher, who, furious and humiliated, blamed the schoolteacher and everyone else at the school, including Joanne. He said he wanted the school closed.

In Gapuwiyak, Kevin vandalised buildings. He spoke of suicide. He shut himself in a room and rarely came out. Some at Donydji wanted him to come back, but the medical officer told me that Tom had said he would kill him if he did. The young woman could not go back to her people: she tried once, and they threw stones at her. Neville told the police it was pointless to press charges against Kevin: he was in crisis and needed counselling. In the end the court issued a restraining order, thus confirming in European law Kevin's exile under customary law.

TEN

Donydji in late November, the hottest time of the year. The tattered windsock hung lifeless, the crows stood staring with their beaks open. To escape the blistering sun, we edged around the half-metre strip of shade thrown by Neville's little shed. It was a contest, and enjoyable in a way.

Neville wanted to revisit some sites he had seen long ago, and Tom had agreed go with him and explain them. He also wanted to do some mapping with his GPS. He planned an expedition with Tom, Christopher and Djikambur, and they had cautiously consented to my joining them. I would venture nowhere without permission, do as I was instructed and be careful not to utter any place names I overheard. As proof of my willingness to comply, I left my camera at Donydji.

Djikambur came because we were going to his mother's country. He was about fifty, and like Tom and Christopher he had grown up as one of a nomadic band moving up and down the waterways. As a young man he'd had leprosy, which left him with no feeling in his feet and unable to hunt with the other men. Possibly this was the reason for his sad and weary face.

An old Toyota troop carrier had come into Christopher's life, and he led the way with Neville and me following in a HiLux hired in Nhulunbuy. We were heading north in the general direction of the

Arafura Swamp. After two hours we stopped at a creek whereupon Christopher took the rifle and disappeared into the scrub. A few minutes later we heard four shots and soon after he reappeared to say he had shot two buffalo – one big and one small – and did anyone have a knife? We had only one between us, my little pocket-knife with a blade an inch long. Christopher took it away with a look of contempt and returned with a piece of the smaller buffalo about 50 centimetres long and 5 centimetres wide. He placed it on the dashboard in front of me and there it stayed for the next three days, drying and shrivelling in the sun. I gave everyone a muesli bar, which they ate with sugar bag (wild honey) Djikambur found in a tree that Christopher had tangled his truck in. Then we set off, revitalised.

Christopher zigzagged through the bush, guided it seemed by Tom who, with his arm out the window made looping hand signals that also guided us. A couple of times the convoy stopped and examined Neville's maps and GPS, while I stayed in the truck with gaze averted and ears tuned out. Then we resumed the journey, and Tom resumed his hand signals until, after four and a half hours, we came to a place that our companions reckoned was near enough to where we wanted to be. We followed them across a shallow stretch of water in a deeply eroded creek bed and pitched camp next to a tannin-stained waterhole in which catfish swam indolently in the shadow of pandanus and paperbarks 20 metres high.

Christopher immediately sat down under a tree on the bank and remained there, very still, for five hours. Unlike all the other men, Christopher rarely wore a shirt. The cicatrices on his chest defined him. Tom and Djikambur went downstream to fish and returned with bream. Then Tom retreated to the new transparent tent, big enough for a dozen adults, that Neville had bought for him. He sat cross-legged in the middle of it for a while, then laid his little body down and slept.

That night they talked softly: about the place we were in and the paintings they would see the next day, Neville told me when the conversation ended. He said how mistaken it was to call this country wilderness. For these men nothing could be less like wilderness: that 'veneer of religion' means that they live in a constant state of religious awareness and observance. It is more than a veneer: it runs underground with the spirits that move there, and live in rocks and rivers, and in the air.

Dawn came with the languid two-notes of a koel. Another one answered and they went on communicating in this melancholy, strangely dispiriting fashion for some time. Neville and I set off at 7 am to find paintings which, for reasons I did not understand, I was permitted to see. He took two cameras, still and video, and lights. We crawled and slid on our backs into caves and overhangs, Neville filming paintings done no one knows how long ago, while I held a light. We could see the wasps, bats and green ants; the pythons and brown snakes we could not: but on one big rock pitted with smooth, deep, saucer-shaped indentations in which the paints had been ground and mixed, Neville identified python urine.

Such a creature – a serpent about 4 metres long – was the subject of one of the paintings. Another portrayed an ancestral figure with a head in the shape of a swastika, and a phallus of unlikely size, a symbol, Neville said, of social as well as sexual reproduction.* Among many other images were several beautiful freshwater crocodiles, a Makassan prau, jabirus, turtles, a saltwater crocodile and stingrays. These were inland, freshwater clans, but plainly they knew the sea. There were stencilled hands and feet, hatchings, clan symbols

---

*   'The Aboriginal aesthetic . . . is intensely social', Peter Sutton wrote. As sexual affairs have the capacity to create disorder, sexual imagery is 'usually concerned as much with social and political reproduction.'

and – the most important, Neville said – a bathi, like the one given him, the 'power bag' that contains great secrets.

When we got back, two big fish perfectly cooked and wrapped in pandanus leaves were lying by the fire for us. Next morning Neville and the three men went to the cave and, while he filmed and recorded, they explained the meaning and significance of the paintings and the place. I had asked Neville to be sure to tell them that I understood the importance of the material and would stay at the camp. He did and I rose a little in their estimation, he reported.

It had been too hot for much sleep. I sat drowsily in the shade of a tree by the steep sandy bank of the waterhole and watched the fish idling the day away. A kookaburra occasionally gurgled before deciding it was too hot to really laugh. The insects' whirring din pulsated in the hot air, melding sound and space. A koel flew low across some nearby rocks and left me with the impression that it had been watching me from the time I sat down. A kingfisher with a red breast and brilliant blue wings sat on a low branch and looked with one eye into the pool. Every so often the lightest of breezes rippled through the pandanus leaves, and they rustled with relief. The orb spiders' webs stretching across the water swung in the breeze, and the spiders swung with them gently and, it seemed reasonable to think, pleasurably. I thought – anyone would have – 'Fifty thousand years. Sixty thousand. Sixty-five thousand.'

In the pool a big saratoga made a slow territorial sweep. A skink chased a spider through the long, dry pandanus leaves. The spider hid and ten minutes later the skink gave up looking and darted off, but I could see the spider's leg sticking out from under a leaf. The fish, Neville had relayed to me, were waiting for the Wet to flush these waterholes down to the swamp. But who can say if fish wait?

The men returned mid-afternoon. Neville looked contented. They all did. Around five in the afternoon, two thunderheads appeared in the northern sky. Christopher said we should pack up and move or we would not get across the creek. Neville thought the clouds would move away, and indeed when we looked back after the half-hour spent trying to push Christopher's vehicle up the other side of the crossing, there was no sign of them. Once on the other side Christopher confessed his four-wheel drive mechanism did not work, and the briefest of showers would have made the gully impassable. Very soon it was dark.

Somehow Christopher and Tom could see the tracks we had made two days before and we bounced along behind them under an immense blanket of stars. Then they lost the tracks and we meandered for a while, bounding over tussocks and weaving through scrub, and suddenly we were back on them, and we drove resolutely on for half an hour or so, until on a tussocky plain Tom signalled a halt.

This was a good place to camp, he said. Why it was a good place was not clear. For one thing, we had only about half a litre of water. But Tom said there was water in the part of the starlit dark to which he pointed and so we camped on the bristling tussocks. The sky was magical and near. The smothering heat on that silent, airless, sleepless plain was also something to marvel at.

Djikambur had hardly spoken since we left Donydji, but I heard him talking quietly to Christopher well into the night. Only occasionally did Christopher softly reply. Like Bayman, Djikambur's father had suffered with yaws. He was taken to Darwin hospital, where he became a curiosity for medical students. He did not enjoy the attention and cleared out. There was no road then. It took him six months to walk back to Donydji, a feat remarkable not just for the stamina it required but for the fear to be overcome and the guile needed to cross country unknown to him.

Tom coughed terribly. Neville's snores were interspersed with panicky gasps for air, which seemed natural in that stifling atmosphere, but might have been sleep apnoea caused by sedatives which can relax the muscles in the throat and stop them functioning.

Next morning, sure enough, 200 metres away in the direction Tom had pointed, a stream was running. When the Wet descended in a month or two, the plain would become a swamp.

Twice that morning we stopped, and my companions visited sites of significance. From the vehicle in which I dutifully remained I saw them sitting on the ground while Tom waved his arms in various directions and Neville took readings on his GPS, made notes and revised his maps. Jeremiah and Baruch, his scribe. Neville cannot stop what began in Vietnam: doing everything as it should be done, making light of any discomfort, abjuring self-interest. The record must be kept, the story told, all that can be understood he must understand. And Tom, keeper of the faith, prophet of doom, voice of lamentations, tells him what that story is, how the world works and what will befall those who don't understand or who break the laws that govern the land.

It is poor form to return to camp without bounty from the hunt, and it was probably for this reason that we stopped at the old outstation, Dhunganda, about half an hour from Doyndji. It was here by the stream that the worshippers had gathered to sing in the days of the Fellowship. Neville had brought the vets to the site a few months earlier, for a spot of R&R, including fishing. But Ronnie, whose home country it is, had been there before them and set fire to the place. When the vets arrived, they found only smoke and ashes, and a few women and children in meagre shelters by a creek barely a metre wide. They called it Napalm Village.

Now it was a glade bursting with new plant life, a garden of cycads, pandanus, paperbarks and eucalypts. Red-tailed black cockatoos squawked from the trees; a catbird wailed like a half-throttled cat; their long tails trailing, a pair of koels – he black, she grey – glided intermittently through the suffocating air and took up vantage points in various trees. The place is associated with the koel, Neville said, and it seemed likely that this was a fact the birds were determined to establish.

Tom pursued a water monitor into the creek but failed to catch it, and Chris went off with the gun and came back without firing a shot. He climbed into the back of his truck and though it must have been 50 degrees or more in there did not come out for several hours. Tom and Djikambur went off with the gun but saw nothing to shoot. The constant burning that recharges the vegetation also leaves the soils deficient in nutrients, which limits the land's ability to feed large numbers of animals. One does not see mobs of kangaroos, only occasionally a turkey, rarely an emu.

We returned empty-handed. Tom reported soon after that with Ronnie, his wife Nellie and their seven children in his house, he thought he might move into the spacious new tent Neville had given him.

Dave Glyde cared deeply for the people and the place, and they were manifestly fond of him, but culturally speaking, he found Neville at least as interesting. Neville was a 'mad bastard' who did mad things like thinking he could change the world, or even change those other mad bastards at Donydji. Neville's likely to take you on a day's walk, in blistering heat, to see hand stencils on rocks and paintings. But that's Neville. It's important to him. And the lunch he told you he'd brought turns out to be a couple of carrots Christ knows how old, and black. That's Neville. Then there's the story about how he went up to Donydji with baby food in little glass jars. He was planning to live on the baby food and use the empty jars to put native vinegar flies in – Christ knows why.* But in the heat inside his tent the jars popped their lids

---

*   *Drosophila* – fruit or vinegar flies – are popular with geneticists because they carry 75 per cent of the genes that cause disease in humans.

and the baby food oozed out as orange foam. The stink of the stuff attracted the dogs. A drooling pack of them circled his tent, and he's inside breathing the fumes and bloody terrified the rest of the camp will see what's happening and think he's hoarding food. That's the sort of thing the mad bastard did. He took one of the vets on a long walk and got so far ahead he lost him, and the vet couldn't find his way back before it got dark. The vet had to spend the night in the bush. That was bad. He shouldn't have done that.

But Dave Glyde loved the bloke, and he wasn't afraid to admit it. He was the best mate a man ever had. When Dave was dropping him off at Brisbane airport and Neville told him about the melanoma and the doctors' grim prognosis, he held himself together as he drove away and then he pulled over and 'bawled'. Dave would like to change the world too.

In May 2008, Neville and I drove from Melbourne to Brisbane to pick up Dave and go on to Donydji. On the shady balcony where he spends a fair part of his days, he feeds the tame, melodious butcher birds. He had already baited, ribbed and cursed the left-leaning 'bullshit academic' within ten minutes of our arrival, and he kept it up sporadically for the four nights and five days it took to reach Donydji. But when Dave was not baiting and ribbing and cursing, he was all affection.

Dave is prone to anger, easily outraged. He told me he was standing at a bus stop in Brisbane a few years ago when a young man rushed past pursued by four others plainly intent on violence. Dave's palms are the size of mud crabs, and with one of them he grabbed the lead pursuer by the scrotum and told the others that he would tear the whole thing off if they did not abandon their chase and bugger off. They buggered off.

And then there is the Dave who, on the way to work one day, dragged a man from a burning vehicle and with bare hands pulled the red-hot leads from the car's battery terminals. He took himself to hospital and had his burns treated and continued to his workplace. Dave doesn't believe in heroes, and never did. His father, who saved the Italian prisoners, might be the exception. Honour the father – for the Yolngu, of course, it was a first principle.

Neville, too, concedes his anger frequently gets the better of him. It tips him into another reality, he says, imprisons him there. It does not need the frustrations of Donydji or the outrageous acts of others to overflow. He can be engaged in a mundane task, such as washing dishes, and feel it surging in him. Running in the streets of Eltham, as he does every day when he's home, he hears a remark – or half-hears it – and thinks it might have been offensive, and even though he doesn't know for sure that it *was* offensive and he's telling himself to keep running and ignore it, he turns, runs back and dares the villain to repeat what he said (if indeed he said anything) or have it out with his fists.

If the army offered Dave Glyde a way to live up to his father's example, possibly Neville went to Vietnam in the spirit of Kid Young, getting into the ring and facing the enemy like the man who literally fought for a living and by acts of bravery raised his family from poverty. Leo White taught Neville anger management by his example in the ring. Good boxers never give in to pain, fear, or frustration. They blink it away, stay resolute, cool and upright. They keep their form, or they lose the fight. Neville saw enough of Leo and heard enough to learn the lesson. Among the bouts Leo won by knockout were seven in which he had been the first to hit the canvas but got up and fought on. He had not given in to the pain or the shock or the indignity. That was courage. Neville knows better than most how rage can bring you undone. But he rages. Like Flaubert, without indignation he would fall flat on his face.

In the mining town Mount Isa, we stopped for a night with Tom Donovan, another old member of their platoon. Tom was tough as leather and lean as a whippet, weather-beaten, hipless, and bandy-legged from years on horseback. He was then a mineral surveyor and, Robyn his wife said, still tormented by Vietnam. Both are descended from Kalkadoon survivors of the frontier wars. When I saw them ten years later, they had moved to a cattle station 2400 kilometres away, and Vietnam had come with him. But that afternoon in Mount Isa, when the three vets met at Tom's big shed the delight was palpable, irresistible. Maybe it's the same in the aftermath of all wars: only in reunion with comrades can the returning soldier find his old self. Only other veterans can attend to his need. And when they do, the hard man, the loner and the depressive give way to something which to an outsider looks young and vulnerable, and very much like love.

The Toyota sounded unhealthy and was burning fuel at an alarming rate. Tom sent us to the only mechanic he trusted. The mechanic diagnosed a major problem. He reckoned he would have to take the head off and we wouldn't have a car for at least a week. As a last resort we tried the Toyota dealership. The manager saw Neville's old army jacket stuffed among the camping gear in the back. 'You blokes vets?' he said, and in no time he was saying he could fix the problem in an hour. He had been in the navy and spent time off the coast of Vietnam without ever seeing the sort of danger the infantry had seen. He'd had it easy, he said. He did fix the car, while Neville and I went for a walk and Dave stayed and talked to the man as vets do.

The day before, while we were filling up at an outback service station, a little truck ingeniously equipped for camping pulled in. The number plate said 'NAM'. The driver, stocky, groomed grey hair and moustache, had an unsmiling stoicism about him. His partner, in a bright pink sweater, was taller and smiled more. When I came out after paying for the fuel, the three vets were talking about platoons and battalions and years and tours. 'Take care', 'You look after yourself', they all said to each other. A common vein of sentiment runs through the tribe.

We camped in the scrub that night and the next one as well, when we were a day's drive from Donydji. In the middle of the night, I heard the crackle of fire and, peering out, saw dimly Neville rolling up his tent. I asked him in a semi-whisper what the hell he was doing. He said he was getting ready to go, as if I were a fool for asking. But it's 3 am, I said. He'd been watching the stars and thought dawn was approaching. Once woken, Dave, despite the Temazepam and Stelazine, could not get back to sleep and spent the rest of the night smoking, and Neville, despite a similar ration of sedatives, doubtless lay awake till sunrise.

Inevitably this evidence of his friend's agitated mind provoked an extended bout of grumbly mockery from Dave, which in time gave way to silent forbearance as Neville drove a double stretch at a fiendish pace over the corrugated road. Our teeth rattled and the mood grew sombre. We could sense the dread prowling in Neville's head. At the Goyder River we stopped for water. Feeling much as I did, that he'd rather walk the last 80 kilometres than get back in the car, Dave told me out of Neville's earshot that he'd decided this would be his last trip to Donydji. What's more, he said, he doubted if his old mate would be able to persuade the other vets to make the trip again.

The track into the homeland had been bulldozed as wide as a freeway but was still barely passable. We wondered how many hundreds of thousands of dollars had been spent. But at least it meant someone knew the place existed.

The monsoon had been weak, and the land was parched. Most of the grass at the settlement had been cut short, heroically, with a whipper-snipper, and other parts burned, so the settlement looked both desolate and cared for. There were not many people there. Tom and Christopher were in Nhulunbuy, where Tom was having his chest X-rayed. The doctors would, as usual, find the scars of TB and Tom would come away feeling some good had been done him. The families that left in the wake of Kevin's scandal had not come back, but there were plenty of children, some from Donydji, some from Gapuwiyak sent there by their parents to attend the school. The pity was they did not send money or food with them, and it was left to three or four women to provide both the care and the sustenance. This they seemed to do as they did everything else, with unhurried calm.

The people were hungry. The dogs were starving. They came to our camp and dragged burning vegetable peelings from the flames of the campfire. Tom had given Neville a gracile angel-like dog called Barkooma (the word for a quoll). She came over and stayed, as if with his arrival her home had been restored. By then we had discovered that once again the workshop had been pillaged. Tools worth thousands of dollars were gone. Neville fell silent. No one came near us. Ricky, for whom the workshop and the tools meant a life worth living, continued to occupy himself in the vicinity of the women's hearth making spears.

As a young man, Tom once told Neville, he went with a group of Donydji men on a 200-kilometre walk to the Mainoru store to get tobacco. On the way they met a band of men from neighbouring lands. Each sat down and watched the other. The neighbouring group at last decided to teach the Donydji men a lesson and let fly with a volley of spears. The Donydji men retreated, until one of them picked up an enemy spear and hurled it back. The spear entered the side of one man's head and came out above the eye. The Donydji men walked on to get their tobacco. Tom told Neville the speared man survived his injury and died 'in his own time'.

The day after we got to Donydji, Tom arrived in a new Land Cruiser driven by a Northern Land Council officer who was on his way to a big NLC meeting in Mataranka. Tom had hitched a ride from Nhulunbuy. Gaunt Ricky and even gaunter David watched impassively as representatives of the common Indigenous interest drove away. A second-hand vehicle like mine would have left enough to pay most of a trade teacher's salary.

At Neville's call I went down to Tom's house, where he was sitting with Tom and Christopher. They were friendly enough but I felt as usual that something put them off, and I presumed it was my whiteness. That, and the fact that, not being a builder, I was useless to them; and not having been a soldier, lacked a warrior's prestige. Without language or knowledge or anything of value to say, I felt much as I remember feeling in adult company as an early teenager. I wondered if to feel stripped of character and substance is what the losing end of colonialism feels like. To never be in the conversation, except for some skerrick of knowledge or usefulness. I was more comfortable around Neville's camp, serving tea and coffee, dispensing the sugar and biscuits with a grin, disappearing into servitude to spare myself Christopher's disdain.

Perhaps because he spoke English and was a virtual fixture at the phone-booth pursuing a hazardous and doomed affair with a 'wrong' woman in Maningrida, Djaypi always seemed to know what was going on in the wider world. That telephone box, on the days the phone was working, was a listening post: the tall antenna and the little solar panel that drove it picked up information from across the known universe and relayed it silently to every hearth at Donydji, including, eventually, Neville's.

Djaypi had taught Ringo the pet bull to kneel and lie down on command. He also told him not to hang around our camp, but that instruction Ringo ignored. He was now a yearling and feeling his oats. He came with the dogs, looking for a feed, sniffing and rubbing his head on the females, which had learned to sit down at his approach, as had the cats.

The tall, athletic, formidable Dick, whose two beautiful, smiling daughters draped themselves around him and rode on his shoulders, led the young men off on a hunt one day. I had not met Dick before. He had a look of broad experience, as if he could operate on both sides of the frontier. Ringo the bull joined the hunting party. Dick, the young men, the dogs and Ringo. On a recent excursion Ringo had brought a rampaging wounded buffalo to its knees when he stepped from behind a termite mound and met it head-on. The buffalo was dispatched, Ringo got over the symptoms of concussion within a few days, and his fame as a hunting bull spread throughout the lands.

The second pillaging of the workshop had produced a tense stand-off. The whole settlement seemed to know about it. We heard that people in a homeland a hundred kilometres away knew about it. There would have to be showdown. A meeting of all the adults, men and women, was called. They met with Neville at the school. Tom opened the meeting and Neville followed, telling them that Dave and the other vets would not come back if tools continued to be stolen and the workshop was broken into again.

Meanwhile, Slater and Gordon, a Melbourne law firm well known for pro bono work, offered their services to the community. The company not only took on the legal work but agreed to pay for a community tractor. In the Wet the grass grew roof-high and the houses were connected by tracks through it that swarmed with mosquitoes, march flies and ground-dwelling, bird-eating spiders whose bites, the people say, hurt like hell and won't stop bleeding. With a tractor they could slash the grass, they could grade the airstrip, take rubbish to the tip, bring in wood for fires, bring in shot beasts for food. A tractor was just about an essential item for a sedentary community.

On the northern fringes of Melbourne, Neville and I had bought a remanufactured Kubota L2402DT 28-horsepower four-wheel drive tractor, with a front-end loader, roll bar and grader blade, for $27,000, and arranged for it to be shipped via Darwin to Donydji. But Neville told the meeting there could be no tractor if it was going to be treated as the workshop had been. Christopher drew the line that had to be drawn: Yolngu law of sharing and reciprocity did not apply to the workshop anymore, only white law. Ricky was put in charge. This was what he wanted and deserved, but he knew he didn't stand a chance. He came to us later, and with tears in his eyes said there were too many untrustworthy people at Donydji. As soon as he turned his back things disappeared. What he didn't say, but knew well enough, was that not everyone would recognise white law or his right to administer it.

Yet it had been a good day at Donydji. The meeting had released the tension. The place got its spirit back for a while. If Tom shared Ricky's misgivings, it didn't show. That evening as usual he sat on the airstrip watching the sun set, his head haloed in grey hair and beard.

There were twenty children at the school, but the current teacher came only five days a fortnight. In truth, four days was an exaggeration. We watched as the plane landed at 12:45 pm. As she would leave mid-afternoon the next day, the children would have one and a bit days, to go with the three days the following week, the first of which would almost certainly begin, like this one did, after lunch. I watched one morning: an hour of instruction followed by an hour of soccer. Then the plane came in and the teacher flew away.

The people who ran Shepherdson College, which supplied the teacher, told Neville that anything more than five days a fortnight would 'set a precedent'. But they were intending to add another two days by supplying the school with computers through which the teacher could conduct virtual lessons. The teaching assistant, Joanne, would oversee this procedure and keep twenty kids aged five to fifteen in order and with their minds on their tasks.

Joanne lived in a household of women and children and caring for the oldest of them was one of her many responsibilities. Neville was determined to get her the training she needed to become a qualified teacher. She was as conservative as Tom and determined to teach not only the general curriculum in English but Yolngu culture in their own languages – Ritharrngu-Wagilak and Djambarrpuyngu, so they would 'know how the old people lived'. It seemed a reasonable ambition, if only because it was a given in the education of all other Australians. She spent years trying to qualify, including a month in a Melbourne suburban school as an assistant, and a year alone in a dormitory at Batchelor College outside Darwin. In one exam, Neville saw she was asked to 'estimate the number of elevators in the town in which you are living'. She failed one assignment because she entered the wrong course code.

Neville complained to the college and the department that they seemed determined to crush her spirit and self-esteem. An Education Department official came to the homeland one day. The adults told him they wanted their kids to go to Donydji school, not Gapuwiyak. One woman said, tapping her chest: 'It hurts me inside. I want the young people to come back here.'

Capable and willing as she was, for now Joanne had neither the training nor the confidence to carry the burden the Shepherdson arrangements placed on her. Part of the burden, surely, was denying the reality of life at Donydji: the school was to pursue abstract and nonsensical 'national benchmarks' and pursue them through a curriculum and language that defied understanding among English speakers, much less people for whom English was a third or fourth language. The Northern Territory Indigenous Education Strategic

Plan 'Action Wheel' would allow schools to 'prioritise the actions and outcomes according to the needs of its clients or the specifics of its context'. Furthermore: '[D]epending on what the issue is (which outcome is most important) it is possible to align the outcome against any of six Action Areas to develop specialised and localised activities that will address that outcome.' At the end of one day, we found Joanne on the school steps with tears in her eyes.

Donydji had a new school, a new schoolhouse and a new workshop, but less than half a teacher. It was hard to see any justice in it. The kids in most need, whose lives without an education were most likely to be perilous, got the least. It was as if to say that people who wanted to live in remote homelands could not expect to get the education available in major centres. If that was the official view, it went unspoken, perhaps because such discrimination never informed education policy for remote white settlers. In my childhood, hundreds of schoolteachers taught from 9 am till 4 pm five days a week in schools accommodating at most a dozen sons and daughters of farmers who, averse to the suburbs and wage slavery, had chosen to eke out a (heavily subsidised) living from the land. People chose to live at Donydji because it was a safe place for their children and because, even more than the poor white farmers, they had an affinity with the land and believed the lives of men and women were meant to be connected to it. Two good, dedicated teachers at the school, and a trade teacher at the workshop, all full-time, would have been reasonable – and an investment consistent with the stated aims of the Intervention.

A plane landed unannounced and from it stepped a white woman and two Yolngu assistants. They were from Marthakal, the Elcho Island body responsible for providing services to Donydji. Without a word or a sideways glance at anybody or anything, they marched past our camp and down to the school – which had finished at 11:45 am – and set up their computer in the classroom, there to process the personal details of people on the government employment scheme and any wishing to enrol. Sadly, the computer could not process those in the first category who did not know their birthdays and could not remember what date they had given last time they were asked, and some of those in the second category had not been told she was coming and were in Gapuwiyak or more distant places.

There were forms to fill in. As the people could not write, a teacher who was interested in the general welfare of the community, or indeed in the relationships and culture of the people living there, might have helped them with this task. There could be no effective teaching unless the teacher was prepared to join in the community, know the people, their relationships and their language. Some of the missionaries, Harold Shepherdson, for instance, knew this. But Donydji did not have that kind of teacher and, because it didn't, a central element in the project was missing.

Helen Westbury from the Intervention joined the meeting next to Neville's shed. There was a belligerence to the Marthakal contingent, part missionary, part managerial. The manager said 'removing rubbish' was not a proper job and she would not grant funds to anyone who used it as a job description. She did not say what jobs she thought proper. That very day, Ricky, who would have called himself 'mechanic' if by now he had been trained, had removed rubbish in a trailer he had tied with rope to the back of a ruin of a Toyota. He sat bravely on the fringe of the meeting but said nothing and at first showed no emotion. Neville, by contrast, sat rigid, his hands clenched tight, his face reddening, his mouth open.

Reading from a sheet of paper, tolerating no interruptions, and speaking, she said, with the authority of one who had spent a year and a half among the people of Elcho Island, the manager presented a damning account of Donydji's affairs and a documented record of her organisation's diligence. Their mechanic had gone beyond the call to clear blocked toilets. He had tried to keep the generator and the slasher going but had met with nothing but incompetence and negligence. At this point Ricky showed signs of agitation. He, Ricky, had rebuilt the slasher, but Marthakal had never delivered a missing part. It was Marthakal's mechanic who replaced the bushes in the alternator incorrectly.

The manager's offsider entered the conversation in fine management style: 'What we must do,' she said, 'is identify the problems, then find the solutions so we can move forward. Write that down,' she said to the other Yolngu woman, who had a notebook. There was no stopping her until her superior referred to her as a 'receptionist'. 'Executive!' she snapped. This moment of crossed wires gave Neville his chance. 'I beg to differ with your account,' he said. He declared his thirty-six years of experience and fluency in the languages gave him some authority on the subjects under discussion. The manager protested, but Neville was underway by then and did not intend to stop. The mechanic's account was false. It was Marthakal that lacked diligence, he said. On the rare occasions their mechanic had been seen, he had either failed to attend to the community's needs or attended to them badly. 'Write that down, write that down. Yo!' said the Yolngu executive.

The plane had come back in and the pilot was wandering; a lean, Nordic-looking chap in a pale blue uniform with shorts and knee-high socks. The manager said they had to go. Neville said, 'Not until you have seen the toilet and the septic tank that is meant to serve a household of fifteen.' She said it was not necessary, but Neville said it was very necessary and the Yolngu executive said helpfully, 'The health of the people must come first.' Neville led them to the toilet and went inside, stepped out and beckoned the manager and her colleagues. One by one, in they went, and instantly recoiled. Neville pointed to the rusted iron on the ground that had been installed as a septic tank. Then he took them to the water tank, streaming water as it had since the day it was installed. The manager said they planned to put a 'big filter' on the water supply because probably it was contaminated, with uranium among other things. Neville said there was nothing wrong with the water but a lot wrong with the tank.

As we walked back to the airstrip, I told the manager that Donydji was getting a new tractor. 'Take it from me, it won't last a year,' she said. 'That's what these people do.' Her husband had been until his recent retirement responsible for the 70-acre grounds of a Melbourne private school. 'When he sees the state of lawn mowers on Elcho, he cries,' she said. They all piled into the plane and, her day and a half done, the schoolteacher climbed in beside them.

Next day we drove into Nhulunbuy. While Neville was talking to a woman from one of the health services, Dave Glyde talked about Vietnam. 'When I left Vietnam,' Dave said, 'I was sick of killing people. I hated killing people.' Then, after a pause, 'but I would have killed more of them if it meant less of my mates were killed.' That was the thing: no Vietnam meant no Neville, no Freddie Howell, no Charlie, no Ossie. No Donydji. The platoon is the clan, the band of brothers: all meaning lives there; all must be gathered into the embrace of imperishable memory.

There was a gleaming new building in Nhulunbuy, home to the Indigenous Coordination Centre – the ICC. Inside everything was state of the art: the high-security doors, the airconditioning, the electronic equipment, the furniture, the fittings. The deputy manager of the ICC had come to the job from the office of the Commonwealth Minister for Indigenous Affairs, and the department before that. She was welcoming, admirably so given that we were red in the face and dirty. The boardroom was bigger than some of the houses at Donydji; the table could seat a couple of dozen.

The deputy manager said she didn't know where Donydji was, which explained why she called it Doomadgee, a settlement 1600 kilometres away in Queensland. Neville said he could help to acquaint her with Donydji with a DVD about the place if they could provide a laptop on which to play it. The deputy manager's assistant went to get one. The deputy manager said that SRAs were being replaced by FFPs. It wouldn't be an 'SRA world anymore'. What she meant wasn't clear.

Neville said he was asking the government for $60,000 to match the amount he had raised from private sources. He wanted the money to be paid over two years to fund the training of young people, especially young men. She said she didn't know, but she would do her best. Neville read from a note he had taken at a meeting with the Wellbeing and Behaviour Officer (WBO) of the Department of Education and Training, at which the WBO said such funding was deserved. It was indeed the task of the ICC to see that money got to the 'grass roots', the deputy manager said. But the problem, she said, was that no one had a big bucket of money. All the buckets were small. The trick was to find the right one. That was the role of the Indigenous Coordination Centre – to move the buckets around until they found the right fit. We said that if the TV and sound system in the corner of the boardroom were put in a bucket it would be enough to put in a long drop at Donydji, with some left over for training.

The assistant to the deputy manager came in with a laptop, but she couldn't make it work. She left and came back with another one, but she couldn't make that work either. I brought out my computer, but they couldn't find an external CD driver. We gave up. Meanwhile, Neville's spring had wound tighter. He told the deputy manager, who grew uncomfortable, how much the volunteers and charities had done, and how the government had done nothing. He told how the failure to provide an education for the children made a joke of the Intervention and of the minister for whom she worked, who invented it. Neville got passionate: the failure to provide education and basic services made young Indigenous people bitter, resentful, without hope. It meant their lives were ruined from the start. The deputy manager said it was the responsibility of the service-provider, Marthakal, surely. But you said it was your responsibility to see that the money 'gets to the grass roots', we said. Isn't it therefore your responsibility to oversee Marthakal? What do you 'coordinate' if not the distribution of the money?

At this point Glydey, alone on the far side of the table, cleared his throat and said, 'I'm not like these blokes. I'm a poor dumb bastard. What is the ICC? What do you do? I'm just a fat, dumb, bald bastard but . . .' and he told the deputy manager about the shameful treatment of the people at Donydji. 'I'm bloody near crying.' He was. 'I'm bloody ashamed to be Australian. Bloody ashamed!' And he stood up and walked out.

The deputy manager coloured. She said if she couldn't help through the organisation, she would help privately. Her pledge lent a certain poignancy to the moment, even if no one in the room, including the deputy manager, thought it a very solemn undertaking.

ELEVEN

The tractor was 40 per cent more powerful and a hundred times more refined than the petrol-fuelled grey Ferguson tractor with which farmers conquered the hill country of south-eastern Australia and saved towns from the great floods of 1956. But when Christopher saw it unloaded from the truck, he said it was too small. Sadder even than Christopher's disapproval, the machine arrived in a pool of oil. In the last half-kilometre of its 4500-kilometre journey, on the cratered track from the main road, the truck hit a hole, the tractor plunged through the palette on which it rested and broke something in its back axle. Without parts, the vets could not repair it. It sat forlornly and frustratingly in the workshop.

I went up there a few weeks later. It was late August and the land had not seen rain for months. Green cycad and the orange flowers of silky oaks were the only splashes of colour in the dusty land. The usual fires were burning drowsily by the roadside. Kites and hawks in numbers hovered at the front margin to pounce on fleeing animals. Ibis stalked the rear.

I brought the parts the tractor needed, but the vets had left and taken their know-how with them. Ricky Guyula was not deterred. There was such a longing in Ricky, it made you fear for him. When I went over to the workshop in the morning, the rear of the tractor had been raised with a car jack and a wooden crate, one back wheel was off, and several bits of the inner workings were spread around the concrete floor and swimming in transmission oil. Ricky was sharpening a wooden stake. I gave him the oil filter, secondary filter, transmission seal, and several other necessary items, along with the instructions the tractor salesman had written out for me, together with a diagram he had drawn. As I put each item down, Ricky said, 'Yo.' He ignored the instructions, which he couldn't read anyway, and seemed unimpressed by the diagram. He would put them in, he said calmly, and went back to sharpening the length of wood.

I couldn't help asking what he had in mind with the stake. He said it was a 'bolt' and nodded toward the missing wheel. I knew without looking that there was nothing about a wooden stake in the instructions, and said something to the effect that, surely, he wasn't going to put a piece of wood in the axle of the tractor, and just as I feared, he said, 'Yo.' 'But Ricky,' I said, 'you can't . . .'

Our conversation went poorly after that, and at last he told me to go away and leave him alone. He would get David to help. An hour later he drove the tractor out of the workshop. Very soon after that he was grading the airstrip. I wandered over and cast a furtive eye over the floor to see if any bits he had taken out had not found their way back in. There were none, and I was even more relieved to see the stake. Later he managed to make me understand that the 'bolt' was just a device to steady the assembly and draw it into the wheel.

Alas, next morning there was Tom, guided by Ricky sitting on the mudguard, steering the tractor down the airstrip to his house. Word reached us that Tom had taken the key and decreed the tractor was to be parked at his house, and only he and Christopher would be permitted to drive it.

For Tom, Neville said, the tractor was a 'cultural matter'. With a ceremony soon to begin, and visitors arriving for it, Tom wanted the tractor as evidence of his status. Poor Ricky wanted it to take rubbish to the tip, grade the anthills off the airstrip, bring a shot buffalo back to the camp. Once again, he was in despair.

But Neville, for the moment, had hope. The vets had built a house for Christopher, one for Damien and his family and one for David and his family. They had cleaned out and refurbished the single men's quarters and the old school. The homeland service provider, Marthakal, had at last put in a septic tank, dug a long drop and erected a new water tank. Christopher said they had put his house in the wrong place. No one volunteered to move it.

But the Marthakal people were unhappy. They reckoned that by providing housing and services for which they were responsible, Neville and his vets had jeopardised their funding. They were also dirty on an article in the Fairfax newspapers about the travesty of the Donydji school. I had written it, but they suspected Neville was involved. They were right in this case, but they would have blamed him anyway. They blamed him for everything, a Marthakal employee told him on the phone. Soon after, Neville arranged for Laynhapuy at Yirrkala to take over as Donydji's service provider. Marthakal were even more unhappy.

The teacher being absent, the vets had taken classes at the school. They discovered that reports indicating the students had reached national benchmarks were laughable. Teenagers who had been given 'B' in mathematics could not do the simplest sum. They had done projects about Russia but could not point to that country, or to the Northern Territory, on a map. One fifteen-year-old girl had written her own report in a sentence of thirty words, only five of which she recognised when Neville checked with her. The same girl was said to have a good understanding of 'the birth of the solar system'.

In fairness it must be said that if the school's assessments were exaggerated, claims made by the Northern Territory Education Department on its website and the curriculum itself not only encouraged the tendency but led by example. The minister spoke of 'a strong and relevant education system that gets results for Indigenous Territorians' and 'a road map for implementation of the vision' and so on. It was a fine example of official language concealing what it purported to reveal. All the rhetoric extolling their energy, goodwill, care, attention and meticulous planning collaborated seamlessly with chronic inactivity and dysfunction. The education minister's office continued to insist the school was but a 'community education centre' and entitled to a teacher for only three days a week. Yet it had been called a 'school' when approval was given to build it, and again when it was opened by the minister, which meant it was on the 'road map' and in the 'vision'. The children certainly thought it was a school, and the teacher thought she was a schoolteacher, and she was paid to be one, even if the children rarely got as much as ten hours' teaching a week.

Still, the tractor was proving a great success. Tom parked it outside his house every night, wiped it down and washed it. In the morning he drove it in first gear up the airstrip to the workshop, where the young men took over. The grounds and the airstrip were impeccably slick, and the old garden had been cleared of weeds and scrub and planted with bananas, cassava and sweet potato.

Christopher had taken a stick and drawn in the gravel an explanatory diagram of the community they were trying to establish at Donydji. He drew three circles of different sizes: the innermost one represented the Bidingal clan of the Ritharrngu – Tom and Christopher's people; the one surrounding it represented their mothers' people, the Wagilak and Djambarrpuyngu clans. The third circle, on the outside, represented the vets. He drew another series:

the inner one he called Yolngu culture; the one surrounding it was the workshop and the school; and surrounding that, the vets.

I went back to Donydji nine months after the tractor. The night before driving out from Nhulunbuy I met Neville, Dave Glyde and another vet from the old platoon, Fred Howell, in the cafeteria of Gove House, the workers' hostel where you could eat as much as you liked for $21. The banter started at once: Neville's bullshit cooking, Neville the bullshit intellectual who couldn't drive a nail, Neville's bullshit hat.

The teacher had spent one day at the school in the past six weeks. She arrived at 11:45 am and by midday the kids were playing basketball. She left at 2:30 pm. Neville, Fred and Dave had been teaching the kids in her absence. Shepherdson College touted Donydji as an educational success and used a picture of a smiling Donydji fourteen-year-old who had reached nationally benchmarked Level 8 standards. But the vets found the youth could not read or write. Another student, seventeen years old, could not spell the simplest words in English or his own language and when Neville gave him the sums 3 + 3 and 3 + 4 answered 4 and 5. He was awarded the Northern Territory Year 12 Certificate.

The other news was the familiar tragicomic mix. The vets had arrived to find the hunters had sawn off the terminals on every battery in the place and melted them into shotgun cartridges for shooting buffalo. This house had been declared too small; this one was in the wrong place. This one, renovated by the vets a year ago, had been vandalised. As usual, Christopher was behind much of their annoyance and bafflement. As if to prove that the tractor was indeed too small, he had set out to make a wreck of it by setting it tasks only a much bigger tractor could perform. It was not quite a wreck but getting there.

To think more pride than malice might underlie his behaviour was probably too kind, yet the mean streak in Christopher could be read as his way of asserting not only his status in the community, but the status of Yolngu law and culture against European influence and European condescension, real or imagined. Weren't his complaints just the inverse of the colonial relationship, wherein the colonisers tell the colonised where to put things? And who were Europeans to talk about vandals? For all that Neville and the vets were doing for him and his community, they were still trying to redefine him, confine him to a space between their margins. Every now and then there was a glimmer of the resistance fighter in Christopher. Not that he wasn't also a schemer, and a menace.

It was the school that tormented Neville. The school lay at the heart of the community's hopes. It was at the heart of his promise. But it had failed the children. It was as if nothing could be done properly if the vets did not do it.

Dave had given up smoking and reduced his intake of instant coffee to six cups a day, but he still took a Stelazine and two Temazepam at bedtime – and kept a spare under his pillow if he couldn't get to sleep. He said, 'Oh, another thing,' and he told me how Christopher had taken the diesel that was meant for the generator and put it in his vehicle and cleared out; and some of the young men were following his example and taking what remained of the fuel when the vets told them that if there was no fuel for the generator, no houses would be built – at that point young Bunbuma 'lost it' and threw diesel everywhere.

It was one of the mysteries. The authority of the law (Rhum) is absolute in ceremonial life and in the hunt, and the penalties for breaches are certain and severe. But the social rules are different, and Tom, the voice and embodiment of the law, seemed unwilling to impose any. The relatedness of all people within the kinship system does not bestow any system of hierarchical authority in daily life: no one gives orders, and no one admonishes, much less punishes antisocial behaviour unless it infringes religion and custom. Like the Hebrews in the Book of Judges, every Yolngu does what is right 'in his own eyes'. If someone wants to run the generator all night, the generator will run all night and the community will be left without diesel. If Ronnie doesn't do his job properly, and rubbish builds up outside houses and the school, it's no one's business to tell him to do his job properly. If the kids pick the mangoes green and throw them at each other, or if they take tools from the workshop and lose them in the grass, no one will correct them. If Christopher commandeers the community's one vehicle and goes to Gapuwiyak to buy food for himself but not for anyone else, no one will complain to him. If he wilfully wrecks the tractor, no one will confront him: but Ricky in a rage at him will get hold of a car and go roaring round the camp, frightening everybody and prompting Joanne to email Neville, 'Dear Father, I have to leave Donydji.'

Nothing so grieves a balanda – especially, perhaps, a balanda army veteran – as the casual anarchy and selfishness the philosophy allows. 'A philosophy of life . . . a system of mental attitudes towards the conduct of life, may or may not be consistent with an actual way of life,' Stanner wrote. It is true that the absence of authority in day-to-day life has made the Yolngu's long struggle to maintain their culture and accommodate the European more difficult. When no one commands or admonishes, and wrongs go unpunished, sullen resentment and frustrations periodically tip over into destructive – including self-destructive – rage and violence. So, on another occasion, after a dispute with his family, the same Christopher took the four wheels off a four-wheel-drive he prized and burned the rest of it. No one chided him. Another person had possession of him. He went to Darwin and came back a Pentecostalist.

And yet there were times when 'the system of mental attitudes' governing white functionaries of all kinds was as remote from anything resembling fairness and good management as the Yolngu, and just as certainly served up anarchy. In truth the great majority of the white population, whatever their moral avowals, could not have cared less if twenty kids in north-east Arnhem Land went without an education. *Everyone* did right 'in his own eyes'.

Ricky was the counterpoint. The vets had built a row of one-room houses for single men. Ricky kept his impeccably. He had a patch of lawn out the front, well-watered mango trees, tomatoes and basil. Inside he painted pictures in the clan designs. His importance to the community was growing, and resentment was growing in proportion. His mother told him he should think about leaving because he was being blocked by the older men and there was jealousy afoot. He came to Neville and asked him for Panadol because his back was hurting, and told us with a grin that he had been hit by a car in Katherine last year and cannoned into the windscreen. There was Ricky of Donydji and there was Ricky of Katherine, smashed and staggering, and living in the long grass.

To say that he was caught between two worlds is only half true, for neither world was really open to him. Even if he had wanted to join it, the white world of Katherine, Nhulunbuy or Darwin might as well have been Paris or Rome. The only place truly open to him was the long grass – the camps for the homeless on the urban fringe. 'Long-grassers' are outsiders twice over: alienated from their homelands, hub-towns and the customary laws attaching to them, and from the white population and their white laws. They come, as Ricky did, to escape 'family problems', tension, disputes, fights, frustration, boredom. They come to catch up with relatives and friends, to get booze and other drugs they can't get in the homelands. Old people come to escape abusive youths; young people to escape the oppressions of the old. Many of them come for medical attention and, with nowhere else to stay, camp in the long grass while they're there. Katherine has very little accommodation for homeless people, and camping by the river and sleeping rough in the open or in a tent is the only option for most of them. A lot of the long-grassers are chronically ill, a lot suffer mental illness, a lot more are alcoholics and addicts of other kinds. Long-grass people present to emergency at Katherine Hospital at sixteen times the rate of the rest of the population.

The long grass goes back to the earliest days of European settlement. It goes with post-European mendicancy, alcoholism, debility, illness and early death, which are as old as settler colonialism. The long grass is the frontier continued *ad infinitum*. Long-grassers live not only on the margins of the town, but on the margins of the law. They are always in breach of by-laws and accumulating fines; always poor and getting poorer; always exposed to violence and incessant humbugging. Long-grassers know the white population either holds them in contempt or looks past them as if they are not there. They are the universal 'poor in spirit' outside the temple. They escape from loneliness and alienation among the lonely and alienated.*

Ricky would have been *happy* to live between two worlds. At Donydji that was precisely what he wanted to do. He could be a Yolngu hunter, provider, artist, bearer of ceremonial and environmental knowledge, and a mechanic, teacher, householder, gardener. It was not that one made it impossible to live in the other, but rather that

---

* There is a defiant, solidarity song called 'I'm a Long Grass Man', sung to clapsticks. Among countless others from all over the Northern Territory, for a while David Gulpilil preferred being a 'long-grass man' to being a famous actor. Ricky chose it over his homeland. After decades at Donydji and other homelands, Ronnie took his wife and family into the Katherine long grass and stayed. Ronnie had never drunk alcohol. But in Katherine he did.

he was refused admission to both. It was Aboriginal tradition which left him feeling unwelcome and undervalued at Donydji, and which invested the Ritharrngu men, as owners of the land, with status and authority above his – a custodian of his Ritharrngu mother's land – and stymied his chance to lead.

Tom and Christopher had told Ricky, 'We want you to live here. Your grandmother is buried here.' For a young man that was not much of an inducement. It was a bit like a workshop without a teacher or tools. Ricky lived with the condition Bill Stanner called the 'torment of powerlessness'. For all that, in Katherine he exercised the one agency remaining to him, his right to seek comfort, pleasure or oblivion in booze, gunydja or recklessness. Ricky was not the first talented person with a tendency to self-destruction, or the only man in Australia to enjoy getting drunk.

Neville had been working on a food plan for the community. A proportion of fortnightly government income would be set aside for groceries at the ALPA (Arnhem Land Progress Association) store in Gapuwiyak. Each Donydji household was to provide a list of groceries, and these would be boxed and delivered. Nothing could be easier. But who would box the groceries? Not the store. Helen Westbury took on the task, and Andrew Sharp, recovered from his buffalo wound and working in the Territory, did it the second time. The third time Neville and I drove in to do it. We arrived at the store to find there was no money in the accounts. No one knew where it had gone, but after a phone call to the store management the money appeared.

The orders all included bananas and oranges as well as the usual cordial and sugar, but there were no bananas in the store, and the oranges were bad. We filled the trolleys, checked it out and, amid the usual dismal scenes outside, loaded the car. The rocks painted white at the beginning of the Intervention had yellowed.

The next time I went to Donydji I arrived a couple of days before two lawyers from Slater and Gordon. They intended to stay two nights, which was more than any government official or NLC representative had done in forty years. Neville had arranged their visit to coincide with the arrival from Melbourne of three archaeology postgraduates, half a dozen high school students and the La Trobe deputy vice chancellor, who had come to see what the university could do to help.

Ricky was anxious about the condition of the tractor.* Already the thing had a broken headlight and many other scars and debilities, most of them brought on by Christopher's campaign to prove the gift was not something for which any self-respecting Yolngu should feel gratitude, nor a vehicle for the furthering of Ricky's status in the community. It was not a sight to please the lawyers whose firm had paid for it just a year earlier. For now, Christopher had locked up his house and taken himself off to Mangay's at Mirrngatja. People making do with overcrowded old houses at Donydji were unhappy to see his

---

*   Day after day for weeks, Christopher drove the tractor 40 kilometres to and from Dhunganda, Ronnie's Country, where he planned to use his stepbrother's clan credentials to re-establish an old homeland and get funding for houses, royalties from a gravel pit and status for himself. Put to work pulling trees out of the ground and other tasks for which it was not made, the tractor was all but destroyed. It was trucked to Laynhapuy to be repaired but never came back, despite phone calls from Neville and letters from Slater and Gordon demanding to know where it had gone. One day Neville was at Laynhapuy and saw a familiar bit of tractor on the ground. It was what remained of the Donydji tractor. The rest of it had become spare parts for all the other tractors provided to homelands that had demanded them when they heard that Donydji had one.

new house empty. Neville had raised the matter with him, pointing out that the people in Melbourne who provided the money did not provide it for a house to be unoccupied. But as if he saw through to the dark side of philanthropy and refused to succumb to the 'tyranny of the gift', Christopher replied, 'Their money, but my house.'

In a development probably not unrelated to the imminent arrival of the La Trobe people, the schoolteacher and a person from the Northern Territory Department of Education and Training had arrived to put in a four-day week, albeit one that started on Tuesday afternoon and finished at 10 am on Friday – little more than two days in real time. Neville and I had just arrived when the teacher came and invited us down for a cup of tea. The motive, we knew, was not an entirely hospitable one, but we trooped into her pleasant little school house with indoor bathroom and toilet, airconditioning, a gas stove, ADSL broadband, phone and fax, and soon we were hearing that she had been teaching the sixteen kids that afternoon and working so hard, you just wouldn't believe it, and she had to spend so much time in curriculum preparation, we wouldn't believe that either. Just the same, for all her best efforts, much that Neville thought should be done, sadly, could not be.

The arrival by plane of the deputy vice chancellor and the lawyers and, by Toyota, Helen Westbury, bubbling with energy and good intentions, brought a dramatic change in the community mood. The people gathered in abundance and the children sparkled as children do when guests arrive. Even the recently neutered dogs were amiable. The guests from Melbourne, several Yolngu adults and many children piled into two Toyotas and went out to a waterhole in the jungle creek. At Joanne's request, David went with a gun in case of buffalo. When we picked them up a few hours later, the bush on the other side of the creek was burning gently, the kids were laughing and playing in the water, and everyone seemed energised by the smoke-filled air.

Neville's face was burned by the sun, his eyelids were swollen, his cheeks hollowed out with exhaustion. But this was a moment to be relished. He told them of the possibilities he saw and the plans he had to make them real. The visitors became believers. Joanne would go to Melbourne to study. Slater and Gordon would draw up the articles for a Donydji Association and do whatever else was necessary to establish such a body.

At night Neville sat by the fire regaling his guests with tales comic and tragicomic of his early adventures in north-east Arnhem Land. One night he was bogged with the old tractor in a swamp, the crocodiles' eyes plainly visible in the torchlight as Christopher and Tom calmly stuck planks under the wheels for traction. He waded down a deep creek with steep muddy sides with Yilarama and heard what he thought was a crocodile barking, but Yilarama said it was a jabiru, until rounding a bend they saw a four-metre croc slide into the water. Yilarama turned abruptly, saying, 'This is his place!' and they waded back down the creek. He camped one evening in jungle swarming with mosquitoes. Determined to have no advantage over his hosts, Neville left his mosquito net in his pack, and endured the ravening insects all night. At first light, through eyes that were mere slits in the puffy, reddened flesh of his face, he saw his companions were all sleeping soundly under mosquito nets. For breakfast they had a 'huge furry feral cat' the men had knocked out of a tree the night before. Out hunting, Yilarama told him not to move a muscle as he stalked a wallaby with his spears, so Neville stood stock still in a marsh while the species of stinging caterpillars that caused the Great Serpent to vomit the Wagilak sisters attacked his bare feet and legs.

About 11 pm, as we lay in our tents, we heard a car on the airstrip but, looking out, could not see it. Next morning, we found it had been Tom arriving from Nhulunbuy with young Marcus. The drive had been slow because the car had no lights, and they had only starlight to see by. Tom laughed and rolled his eyes about the trip. It was nothing to the time when Christopher, finding his vehicle jammed in reverse gear, drove backwards from Walker River to Donydji – a journey of 200 kilometres that takes six hours in a vehicle travelling forwards.

A meeting on the deck of the old school, called to explain the visit of the lawyers and the deputy vice chancellor, became an open airing of grievances. The whole community came, children and all. Tom was the last to arrive, driven the 100 metres from his house by Neville in his rented Toyota. He stepped out dressed as I had never seen him before, in jeans and shirt. He sat on a small chair from the classroom, his face with its ironic smile ringed by beard and hair.

Ricky, asserting himself as never before, began haltingly but grew fluent as his frustrations spilled over. The things they needed never came – not from Laynhapuy and not from Marthakal before it. Too many people at Donydji were not working. Everything was left to him and David. David of the gaunt and beautiful face, the sorrowful eyes, the broken teeth, the long, shapely fingernails, the quiet drollery, sat in silence while his eight-year-old daughter, as beautiful as he, alternated between stroking his head and Tom's in turn, and hanging off each of their necks. David was recently back from some nightmare in a hub-town, saying this was where he wanted to stay, this was what Donydji should be, one big family, Black and white, working together.

Ricky had barely finished when Tom's sister Wanakiya suddenly joined the fray, slapping a metre-long length of poly-pipe on the deck and in fierce rasping tones denouncing those in the community who stole fuel from the generator and left the women in the old houses without power. Neville translated: There should be solar panels on all the houses, so no one had to rely on the generator. Why did they always have to depend on Neville White and his friends to get things done?

Tom rose and Neville translated as he spoke. He wanted to see the children educated, in both their own culture and the balanda ways, in their own language and in English. He wanted the young men to learn skills. He wanted solar power for every house. In all the years of Donydji, governments had done nothing. Marthakal and Laynhapuy had been no good either. The vets had done everything, and the people from Melbourne who had given money, and now these lawyers from Melbourne. The people listened in solemn silence.

Then Hayden Stephens from Slater and Gordon stood up to say how impressed he and his colleagues were with Donydji, and, with a diplomatic nod to Tom, how grateful they were for the community's hospitality. They would give the community any help they could, he said. They would draft letters to Laynhapuy, Shepherdson College and Centrelink, asking why services they are obliged to provide had not been provided to their client, the Donydji Association. They would provide legal advice regarding Cowboy's efforts to gain control. As a parting gesture, Hayden handed Tom a wad of notes for having them on his land, and the meeting wound up with an unlikely round of applause. As we walked away, Ricky said with a grin, 'Does this mean I can go and be bad and they'll be my lawyers?'

The Telstra man arrived unannounced. He could have phoned the school or the public booth to make sure Tom and Christopher, the custodians, were at home, but since when was it necessary to make an appointment with a 'bush black'? He had come to 'consult' with the community about the cable Telstra were running from Nhulunbuy to Katherine. The Yolngu consultant he brought with him was amiable, but at Donydji he was regarded with suspicion. As the meeting got underway, Ricky had his head under the bonnet of a beat-up Toyota with a smashed windscreen that he'd been trying to get going for hours. The women were talking, weaving and tending their hearths. Ronnie was using the angle grinder in the workshop. Ringo the bull was chewing his cud under a mango tree.

Tom did not want the cable because it would cut through ancient pathways or 'Dreaming tracks' that connected sacred sites. He said he could show them where the paths went; where, for example, the ancestral dog pathway was, and where the dogs, travelling underground, with an anthropomorphic figure travelling above them, stopped to drink. He said to avoid the pathway the cable should be laid in a shallow trench, and he tapped just below his knee to indicate the maximum depth. The consultants nodded. The thing could be encased in a fireproof pipe, Tom said. The consultants kept nodding. The idea was a good one, they said.

But Tom came from the meeting downcast. He was sick of people 'pushing and pulling' him. He didn't want what happened to Yilarama to happen again. These men had nodded when he tapped his knee, but he didn't trust them. He was right. Like the mining companies and the road-makers before them, Telstra ignored the connections and treated the sites as discrete. When Tom was consulted, the cable was already being laid a metre deep.

No one approached Tom – or Neville – when the meeting was over, and the men had driven away. No one asked what had been decided. They went on with what they were doing. Yet, as usual at such times, I had the feeling that everyone in the camp knew what the meeting had been about, and already knew the result of it. The engine of the beat-up Toyota suddenly burst into life.

A few months later Ricky showed us the place where the dogs stopped to drink. Here they spoke in the Ritharrngu-Wagilak dialect. Wherever they stopped they spoke in the language of the owning clan. The pathways thus linked the clans, the water systems and the dialects. This place had been a pond with pandanus growing on an island in the centre of it, but buffalo had churned it into a bog. The road had separated the site from a patch of plants the clans ate and, they believed, could only taste when taken in combination with the water from the pond. Further along their ancient path, sections of which were now marked by yellow Telstra signs indicating the path of the cable, the dogs sat down and, as Ricky mimetically demonstrated, scratched their fur and brushed their whiskers. The stand of elegant Carpentaria palms that grow there sprouted from the dross they shed.

In June 2010, Neville met the Northern Territory member for Nhulunbuy, a Yolngu woman much liked and admired. Neville had been at Donydji for several weeks with a couple of the vets. I arrived in Nhulunbuy the night before and went to the meeting with him. Neville did most of the talking. We met her at her office. Out the window the mining town looked sleek, like the office.

Was it the policy of the Northern Territory Labor government to close the homelands? he asked. That was not the policy – emphatically not, she said. Then why was the government doing so little to help them? He offered some examples. The ALPA store in Gapuwiyak, which is supposed to provide for the homeland communities, refused to operate a food card system for Donydji, and rejected Neville's suggestion that they consider delivering food to the homelands. He told the local member that the ALPA store 'lost' more than $3000 of Joanne's food money and refused to acknowledge any responsibility. When, at Neville's request, Slater and Gordon wrote asking for an explanation, the reply was to the effect that if there were any more legal interventions of this kind, the store would not deal with Donydji at all. He offered several more examples of things not done or done badly.

They are hungry at Donydji, Neville said. The local member was sympathetic, concerned, even shocked. She told Neville that to solve the problems he must do this and that, phone this person, and that person. An hour or so later, Neville recalled the conversation. 'She said, "Ring that person and this person." She didn't say, "*I* will ring this person and that person."'

After the meeting, I saw Harvey Creswell, a veteran of the Territory working at the Miwatj medical centre. True, he said, Donydji was isolated and did not have the food resources the coastal clans had, or the access to Yirrkala for their artworks. But regardless of their advantages, some homelands just ran more smoothly. One reason for this, he thought, might be that they were not led by Yolngu as conservative and intractable as Tom. Not long before this, Leon White, another Arnhem Land veteran and the first teacher at the Yirrkala school, told me he thought Donydji would be better without Tom and Christopher: they were clinging to power and frustrating willing and talented young men.

Neville knew he had kept his promise to Tom and Tom's father and mother. The school and all the other buildings spoke for that. So did the absence of alcohol, gunydja and kava. But 'I haven't been able to secure the futures of the children . . . and the young men,' he wrote in his journal. Myopic and incompetent bureaucrats, and vandalism and pilfering by Yolngu, meant that the workshop had never become the enlivening force that he and the vets and Tom and Ricky hoped for.

I wondered sometimes if, somewhere in his mind, Neville believed he could only succeed if he did not look too hard at the dimensions of the problem. Was he the cargo in a cargo cult: not God, but His inexhaustible, ever-providing vicar? If, as the functionalists say, culture is the vehicle all societies use to carry out their everyday lives, was Neville the flywheel in the vehicle? Had he made himself an indispensable part of the culture itself?

I never found a satisfactory answer to any of these questions. All I knew was that when the lawyers and academics, teachers, students and charitable donors left – when the vets left – he was still up there filling out forms, putting money in accounts, listening to complaints and holding on in that infernal phonebooth while he tried to resolve their problems with an air-conditioned bureaucrat.

At Donydji, Neville found Ricky outside his house crying, and Joanne and Sonya repeatedly hurling themselves on the ground, keening and wailing. Their mother had been ill for some time and news of her death in Darwin hospital had just reached them. Sonya appeared to knock herself out. Neville was not the only one to worry that the sisters would do themselves serious injury – the men put their axe-heads out of reach. Many Yolngu women are shockingly scarred by mourning.

The woman, of the Ritharrngu-Gulungurr clan, had been treated by a traditional Yolngu doctor at Numbulwar, where, Neville said, it was whispered in the usual way that her children at Donydji were to blame for her illness. But when she returned weighing just 28 kilograms, the people at Donydji were inclined to blame Numbulwar. This made it even more likely that the funeral contingent from there would be a large one.

When a person died it had been the custom at Donydji to lay the body on a platform in the bush, cover it with branches and leave it there for six months to a year. When time and the elements had wasted it sufficiently the bones were collected, cleaned, covered in ochre and placed in a log that had been hollowed out by termites and painted in the appropriate clan design. When the bones were brittle enough, they were taken from the hollow log, broken up, painted sometimes, and placed in a bag, an intimate travelling ossuary, which the women of the clan carried for years.

The Donydji clans gave up hollow log funerals around the time the homeland was established. Ricky and Joanne's mother would be buried in the Westernised way that had been practised ever since.

The ceremony had been put off until the vets had finished renovating the green house in which a dozen women slept. When that was done and the moon was full again, the body would be flown back, and the funeral would begin in earnest.

I got to Donydji as the first preparations were underway. Everything was shipshape except the tractor, which looked like it had been attacked and beaten senseless. Every light on it was broken, every panel dented, and one front wheel was twice as the big as the other. But the day after we arrived a mechanic came to fix it and was good enough to involve Ricky in the work. Dave Glyde and a team of helpers had resuscitated the garden. It had been infested with highly flammable mission grass – a rampant weed introduced by government but blamed on the missions – and a fire had mysteriously swept through it a few months earlier.

Ricky said, 'This is a sad time for me.' I said I understood. Despite his sadness, in the absence of Tom, who was sick and sleeping on a floor in Gapuwiyak, and Christopher (who was rarely sighted at Donydji these days), Ricky's star had risen. He took us out to his country and a little quarry from which the clans traditionally got heavy quartzite spear heads, like the famous Ngilipitji variety.

We inspected the rock art near the entrance to the homeland. There were paintings of barramundi and catfish – swamp fish – birds' feet, and a couple of human figures with arms raised and fingers outstretched. Like others Neville had shown me, these seemed to have been painted over pictures made in a different style, suggesting the ancestors of the present clans displaced an earlier culture. Unlike Tom and the older generation of Donydji men and women, Ricky acknowledged the difference between the paintings, but he did not see the older ones as Neville saw them. He saw crocodiles we couldn't see. The figures with outstretched arms were warriors warning away intruders who had come to steal or harm the children.

Hoyas cascaded from the rocks, and pink hyacinth grew here and there between them. As we left, Ricky pulled up a root of a flowering succulent to plant in his garden.

As if aware that Tom was away and they were not threatened by his slingshot, a flock of mudlarks had been moving up and down the airstrip all week. In the evening a dozen Torresian crows gathered to clean up Neville's leftover curry. But the star performer was a plover – a rare species that Neville couldn't find in his bird book – that took up residence on the strip 15 metres from our camp. All day it repeated the same mesmerising ritual: stand motionless for several minutes, then a 360-degree spin, and stand still again. Shriek. Then dash 10 metres, return and make like a statue again. Repeat the procedure in the opposite direction. Fly 20 metres for no purpose other than to expose the colour on the underside of beautiful, jagged wings. Stand still again. Shriek.

We went into Gapuwiyak, to see Tom and to sort out why Dolly, who must be sixty years old, was on a New Start Youth Allowance, and why it had been taken away. Some anomalies were probably inevitable, but others defied reason. Years later, Betty would be told that government records showed she was sixty-three and too young to apply for a pension. The records were wrong, Neville would say: she was at least seventy, and she had been raising children and feeding a community for at least fifty of those years. What did they expect her to do? 'Retrain,' they said. 'Retrain as what?' Neville managed to ask. They looked on the computer, 'There is a vacancy in hairdressing,' they said.*

The local kids moped along the streets in their NBA singlets and long baggy shorts. The gambling schools were in full swing out the front of the houses.

Expecting a visit from the local member of parliament, the authorities had cleaned up the town. Empty wheelie bins lay everywhere. A Yolngu man said to Neville: 'They do anything for a politician, nothing for the Yolngu.'

Tom was in Dick's house; generous, roguish Dick. Ricky's handsome son, Lance, was sitting on the verandah outside in the heavy shade of the trees. There were people in the hallway. Tom was in a room off to the right. Neville went in first. 'My friend, I am all buggered up,' Tom said. Tom was kneeling on a bed of blankets, in his shorts and brown check shirt. A bit of crumbled bread lay in a bowl by the bed. His left elbow was bandaged, and his arm was held in a ragged sling. I knelt in front of him. He smiled broadly and took my hand and held it as he told me in words, very few of which I understood, that he had grown dizzy and fallen over and broken his arm at Donydji. He needed to have an X-ray at Nhulunbuy, then he hoped to go back to Donydji. We hoped so too. It was grotesque to think he might die in that miserable room. Dick said he and his family would take him back to the homeland and look after him until he died.

The nurses at the health centre 300 metres up the road said that they visited Tom once or twice a week. It might have been unfair, but we wondered why they – someone – could not have gone more often and taken him a bowl of soup.

                                *

---

* Around this time Betty and Dhulutarama's son Donald, who worked with the vets on the building program, was killed by a punch from a drunk white man in a Darwin street.

The first mourners were beginning to arrive, and the preliminary rituals were underway. At night we heard the women chanting over at the green house, and from another direction the sounds of yidaki and clapsticks, which are no less eerie and affecting for being so familiar. It was Ricky and David, Neville said.

Funerals bring the clans together, preserve and pass on knowledge and maintain cultural practices. Like other ceremonies they are 'rituals of diplomacy' (to borrow from anthropologist Les Hiatt). They are a binding force, reinforcing trust and mutual understanding. They are both commemorative and initiatory, the means by which the creed, the law and the historical bases of religion and cosmology are passed intact from generation to generation. At the same time, funerals are poetic expressions of being, homages to the 'everywhen'. Families drive great distances to attend, and frequently stay for days or even weeks to fulfil their ceremonial duty. At funerals, clans from the same moiety as the dead person, whose lands are crossed by the sacred pathways, are expected to come and sing. It is considered an obligation and there are penalties for failing to honour it.

But funerals disrupt life in the homelands. The hosts must feed the visitors, and weather any damage to their buildings and equipment, and any delinquency among the children. Funerals constantly take children out of school, or cause parents to leave them for long periods in other communities that may not have the ready resources to feed and care for them. In the homelands funerals are a conundrum with no apparent solution.

Then one night bathed in soft moonlight and caressed by a kind breeze we heard singing. Neville recognised the Ritharrngu words in the song, but not the singer. He thought the singer had come from another homeland to sing his part of the cycle. And, sure enough, a minute or two after the music stopped, the singer's work done, an old Toyota went bouncing onto the airstrip and chugged up the rise heading for home, one headlight pointing to the sky.

For now, the singing was confined to the nights. By day, Neville buzzed about, invigorated by the progress the vets were making on the houses. The grass was mown, the airstrip impeccable. The vets had put shelves into the single men's houses, built an all-weather cookhouse for the women and installed grills for all their fires.

As if to give substance to the impression of an agrarian village, John Atari flew in wearing a hat reminiscent of Katharine Hepburn's in *The African Queen* and made straight for the garden. The Methodist mission had brought him to Arnhem Land from Fiji in the 1960s. He brought a passion and a genius for gardening, and a dislike for the way white people treated the Yolngu. This day he had with him sweet potato cuttings, cassava stalks and taro seedlings, and he soon set about the soil with his immaculate spade.

Each day several young men laboured happily with the vets, refurbishing the women's house, while Neville, battered and thin, scurried here and there sorting out the funeral. The dogs looked fatter than he did. Since their desexing they had never looked so sleek. Except for one, mortally ill, laying at Djikambur's fire, a heap of bones, raw flesh gaping on its back leg, not discernibly breathing. David and I were collecting a trailer load of building rubbish to take to the tip. We paused at the dog. I thought it was going on the load, but it flinched, and David said softly, with a fleeting, broken-tooth smile, 'No, still alive.'

An almost full moon shone at one end of the airstrip and the evening star shone at the other. A sou'-easter ruffled the windsock. Tom's elegant brown and white dog trotted up the strip, its turquoise eyes glowing in the near dark. Another dog, black and tan, tail curled over its back, followed a minute later.

Out of the silence, from the direction of David's house, singing. It was Christopher, 'expressing the inexpressible', for us at least, but not perhaps for Christopher. His voice filled the night, the whole world. The moon went into half-eclipse. No one seemed to notice.

Later, when we were in our tents, the singing stopped and the dogs took over, one pack after another, until it seemed that every dog in Arnhem Land had joined the choir and the overlapping sounds were orchestrated and rehearsed. The DNA of all dingoes shows so little variation that the founding population must have been small, possibly just a single pregnant female arriving from Indonesia about 5000 years ago. They or she must have been domestic dogs. Their offspring became dingoes as they spread wild across the continent, and it is reasonable to think their haunting harmonic abilities grew from a desire to stay in touch with their relations.

And somewhere, faintly, in a moment's lull, a cow bellowed.

In the Edenic peace of Donydji in the morning, David asked Neville for the gun and two bullets. 'Bullocky,' he said. He had heard the cow too. The women went after fish, and wood for their fires. New shades were built. With the tractor Christopher graded a patch of ground for dancing. Three hours after leaving with the gun, David returned and, with a grin, gave Neville one bullet. Soon after he set off on the tractor, and a couple of hours later arrived with the bleeding carcass. The mourners would be fed.

TWELVE

Soon enough, there would be another funeral. At night beneath a waxing moon the Donydji clans sang songs for Tom. Always accompanied by the yidaki and clapsticks, they sang of the koel, the spotted nightjar, the tawny frogmouth, the whistling kite, the sulphur-crested cockatoo, the butcherbird, the heron and a crimson finch that sits in the top of pandanus trees; of the goanna, the antilopine kangaroo, the long-necked turtle, the green tree frog, a small light brown frog, the spider, mosquitoes, sandflies, the yabbie, the saratoga fish and the diving duck; of the east wind, the north wind and the north-east wind; of dews and mists, of waterways, trees, ancestral beings, spirits. They sang of the 'wandarra', a small, flat fish that swims near the riverbank and is hard to spear because it darts sideways, like a dancer. They sang of a mollusc that lives where the saltwater meets the freshwater in the rivers and, when the tide goes out, dribbles a little saltwater on the sand which assures the tide's return. They sang about raindrops, a mist and the junction of two creeks.

Men, women and children took part in dances through which the connection between clans was illustrated by the habits of the parrot fish and a grub that it eats. They danced, the men and the women, the old and the young. As the day of the burial grew closer, the people sang and danced in the morning as well as the evening.

Carloads of singers and dancers from other parts – all connected through the totemic relationships celebrated in the song cycles – came bouncing down the airstrip. A group of expert dancers from Gapuwiyak introduced new themes to their routines: flags, knife fights, smoking gunydja, drunkenness. The songs were interspersed with the clatter of diesel engines fading into the night as the performers returned to their homes.

In all the time Neville had known him, Tom would never sing just a fragment of a song. The whole song should be sung, or not sung at all. He spoke of the words 'hitting the ground', as if only the whole song would reach the ancestors.

Among other things, the ethnographers say, songs are ecological maps. They contain intimate knowledge of Country and keep that knowledge alive in the generations that walk the land. Songs are mnemonic devices explaining existence and describing all manner of phenomena, from animals and birds to certain moments, a certain time of the year, a certain light at a certain time of the day. The songs referred to scores of living things and places; to seasonal change and the clans' movement in accordance with it; to what grew where and when it was to be harvested; to the paths they followed, and the paths followed by the ancestral beings.

They are transmogrifying instruments: a song about where the koel ('guak') goes is also a song about where the clans go, and where the souls of men and women go. They are rich in symbolism and metaphor, linguistically complex, nuanced, poetic. As things in nature come in abundant shades of green, naming the things makes the word 'green' unnecessary. There is no word for blue, but there are duck eggs. There are many shades of grey in the world, and one of them is 'an ant bed in a seasonal swamp'.

These nights of singing and ceremony brought such a haunting peace to the camp, all were as if united in the poetry of a common understanding. In the dawns Neville sat and watched the women, gaunt and straight in bright dresses, moving about their hearths. Smoke drifted up from their freshly lit fires. A woman walked out of the bush carrying a bundle of wood on her head. No sign of the men at this hour. And, therefore, no sign of the simmering quarrels.

The days grew hotter. The camp lay in perfect silence, save the faint rattling of dead leaves on the boughs of the four funeral shades. The Torresian crows swaggered about with open beaks.

When Christopher was singing as if to 'elucidate the soul' of his people (to borrow Barry Hill's words), and Djikambur's yidaki was filling the moonlit air with melancholy, Neville recorded the songs and gleaned what information the singers were prepared to disclose. A lot of information is locked up in the words, including ecological information. He had always been keen to unlock them for what they might reveal about Yolngu cultural and material life and the links between them. The senior men would tell him the stories, and the words of the songs, but they would not sing them out of a ceremonial context. To do that, Tom said, would 'hurt the ears of the spirits'.

Some words they could not have translated even if they had wanted to: archaic words which time had leached of meaning, and as obscure to Tom as Brythonic is to English speakers – though not, presumably, to the spirits.

With the passing of the old ways, the old knowledge remains in the songs to be passed on to the young at ceremonies, including funerals. But many of the links between spiritual life and material existence have been broken. The songs make sense to the old people whose understanding is rooted in experience and the know-how needed to survive in the environment. They cannot make the same sense to young people who have not walked the country and will never walk it as the old people did. Without experience, the young can only learn so much. All the more reason why Neville wanted to record the songs and ceremonies, and why the older people were willing to help.

The Yolngu sang into the night. Neville lay on his mat remembering his travels with Tom. He'd walk with him, in silence mostly, and when he stopped to ask questions, Tom would grow impatient and stride off. He was very fast over the ground and often Neville lost sight of him. He'd stop, hear something and, walking in the direction of the sound, find Tom tapping on a tree, pretending he had found sugar bag, or some other invented pretext for making a noise.

Neville thought about all his years trying to understand his enigmatic hosts. He had always wondered if Tom was unforthcoming because he didn't want to divulge secrets, or because he didn't want to simplify matters that were too complex or too ambiguous to settle on definitively. He learned from him despite his caginess, his admonishments whenever his pupil forgot what he had been told, and his stubborn refusal to tell him a second time. And it had been exhilarating to bit by bit discover another culture, another cosmos.

Neville had lost not only a friend, but his chief source of cultural information. One side of the story – the intellectual side – would soon be over. Tom's death would be depressingly like the end of the adventure. All that remained was responsibility.

Authority had fallen by chance to stern, unbending Tom. With Dhulutarama gone and Yilarama choosing exile, authority had devolved to him gradually. Tom the knowledgeable. Tom the believer in the Rhum. Rhum was the equivalent of divine law, given in the form of unbreakable custom and order – Themis – the order which, in Neville's mind, Vietnam had ruptured. Tom and Neville had this in common: they believed in a moral order and the obligation to preserve and obey it. The order had been upset. It was crumbling.

They came together in satisfaction of their need to restore the collective conscience, the primary rules of human society.

Tom's brothers had not thought the Yolngu at Yirrkala or Blue Mud Bay were 'like kids' who didn't know the rules; or the non-Yolngu on the north coast were 'like dogs' who flouted the few they had. But that was what Tom thought. The differences in personality and outlook among the Bidingal fathers and brothers meant that good participant observers should not mistake the rules of a society for its reality. That was what Bernhard Schebeck meant about the limits of 'systemised' anthropology. All the brothers acknowledged the same unbreakable law that Christopher, the great rule *breaker*, demonstrated by squeezing a rock in his hand. All were members of a culture which, as anthropology would have it, shaped their minds and how they saw the world. But if it had been Yilarama – or Christopher – who inherited the leadership, instead of Tom, Donydji would have been a different place.

The women went after fish, and wood for the hearths. The men went after wallaby and bullocky. New shades were built. And then, as always, as if by magical prearrangement, the sticks began, the yidaki, the singing and keening. Everything in its proper place: the beat, the words, the order of proceeding, the participation of old and young, male and female, clan and clan.

At two o'clock in the morning, when the songs were over for the night, the mourners danced into the room at the old school where Tom lay in a rosewood coffin. They came in a 20-metre line joined by a piece of string tied to the hair of the man leading. Their song told of the Pacific black duck, which in myth flew from Elcho to Donydji and laid its eggs there, the Djawk stones that the homeland was established to protect.

The body had come the day before from Nhulunbuy, where Tom had died in hospital. From the women's houses came the strains of Christian hymns. The women, painted up with yellow and white and red ochre, clothed in white sheets, lay resting on their elbows 'like a pride of lions,' Neville wrote in his diary, 'looking so quiet and docile'. Neville painted up with the men.

Burrukala led the men to the plane. Three times they went and three times they returned. Carrying his bathi, Neville went with them as part of Christopher's group. Burrukala rapped on the plane's door three times, the third time 'theatrically'. When the door opened Christopher and his companions started on clapsticks ('makbar'). The coffin emerged and Djikambur led Neville forward to place his bathi on the coffin beside two plastic wreaths.

Young men in red ochre came forward and in a shuffling gait bore the coffin towards the room in the old house where his father once lived. They did not take it directly, but at Burrukala's direction they pulled it from side to side, as if suggesting some kind of conflict. The women, on their knees by the walkway that leads to the coffin room, keened and cried and yelled and threw themselves heavily on the hot ground and the even hotter concrete as the procession passed. The men pressed into the coffin room, wailing and weeping, 'tears drenching their cheeks, in real grief, not ritualized emotion'. They wiped their tears and sweat on the coffin. Women pushed into the room and threw themselves on the coffin. They stayed there as the men left. Neville went to Roy Ashley, who was sitting cross-legged under a mango tree, tears streaming down his face. In a 'quavering voice' he thanked Neville for 'coming and always helping'.

Hundreds had come to Donydji. The songs and dancing had gone on for a fortnight before the body arrived, and the disputes for almost as long. Mangay demanded a 'deep shade' or 'closed shade' funeral, a 'madayin'. Christopher and Djikambur were adamantly opposed. Christopher recalled his father's funeral, which ended with a woman speared to death. The most recent one at Donydji had caused big arguments, and left Cowboy fearing for his life. Christopher said madayin was like poison from a snake. They were finished at Donydji, he said.

Mangay refused to come. He was angry with Neville and with everyone at Donydji. Neville heard that people were questioning his status, and that they wanted the bathi. He knew it was Cowboy and probably his sons. Out of sight, he practised his old boxing manoeuvres.

But Cowboy changed his mind. He sent a message to Neville, saying he wanted to be friends and put their differences behind them. He brought Sandy to Donydji, and they set up camp near Neville. He connected a long electrical lead to the school, and day after day sat in his director's chair and watched the ceremonies with a fan in front of him playing on his face.

One night, the men were advancing in a procession, 'hunched, tapping, and hooting and groaning'. The women were kneeling on either side of the column and keening. A man came out of the dark, bare-chested, shouting.

Some of the women shouted back. The singers stopped. The man, Neville realised, was Ricky. Another man wrestled with him. Tom's sisters appeared out of the dark, waving machetes. Wanakiya rushed at Ricky with a gleaming blade raised. Ricky bent and lowered his head, offering it to her. She raised the machete higher, lunged at him and brought it down fiercely, but somehow managed to miss his neck and the blade curved over his back. And as the shouting continued, Christopher got the sticks and the yidaki going.

Ricky left the ceremony and rampaged past the women's houses. He threw burning logs at the workshop. He threw them at houses and cars. Neville went after him, calling on him to stop. But Ricky didn't stop until he reached his own house, where he hauled his possessions onto the verandah and set fire to them. He told Neville he would leave that night and never return. Neville walked him to Wanakiya's house and left him there, sitting on the ground, his head on Wanakiya's shoulder, crying.

He had been excluded from the funeral arrangements. No one had asked his opinion. Just as no one respected his work for the homeland. It went deeper than that. He had never been allowed to rise to a position equal to his talent and ambition. It unmanned him. It ground his soul.

On and off for years, when tensions rose, Wanakiya had complained that the Guyulas, Ricky's family, were trying to be the bosses. But Donydji was Bidingal land. Tom's clan, her clan, owned it. Now the same Wanakiya lent on Ricky, her head on his and her arm around his shoulders. 'She was crying and keening and tearfully calling her regrets.'

The Guyulas *were* taking over. Wanakiya's brothers had not produced children. Now there were more Guyulas than Bidingals, and their Djambarrpuyngu language was the dominant one. It must have happened countless times: one clan usurps control, not by conquest but by marriage and reproduction.

Fearing the wrath of Tom's sisters, and seeing no end to the discord, Joanne and Sonya told Neville they had decided to leave the homeland. Neville said, 'We'll leave together.' He was in despair.

Neville looked around the camp at seven o'clock one morning, saw the curls of smoke from the hearth fires lit by the women at daybreak and wondered if it was all over. The years had left him 'worn out'. 'I've had enough, I think. What have I really accomplished for these people? What have I helped to create?' The funeral had exposed Donydji's original divide that, symbolically in the bathi, and materially in his work and presence, Neville was expected to bridge. Again and again, he had proved himself a dutiful son, a faithful brother, a good citizen. Whenever he was knocked down, he had got up off the canvas. But when Ricky went berserk and

Tom's sisters took up machetes, it was more than failure. It seemed
to him that he had brought about the chaos. It was his obsession, his
sense of moral duty and his refusal to walk away. He had persisted
in the face of every doubter. As if persisting had become the point
of it all. Persisting to the point of absurdity. 'To what end?' he
wrote. 'This?'

Simone Weil believed that 'attention' unimpeded by ego or
presupposition was both the only way to understand humanity, and
the 'rarest and purest form of generosity'. But humanity at Donydji
was trapped between the need to preserve tradition and the need
to create a viable future, and Neville's 'attention' was not enough to
extricate them from that contradiction. When the people tipped into
mayhem, it was all he could do to stop himself from tipping with them.
Generosity and attention unimpeded by ego perhaps, but in swinging
between sublime order and grim disorder, Donydji sometimes seemed
to parallel the swings in Neville's psyche.

What was there to do but start again?

A young man went out and shot a wallaby. He came back with one
and gave a piece to Neville, who promptly took it to Joanne and Sonya,
but they already had a piece. It briefly cheered him up to see that the
meat had been shared.

Roy Ashley, Tom's brother-in-law, walked through the homeland
with his spear thrower, calling out, 'Put your problems behind you
and show respect for the barpurru [funeral]. There should be dancing
all day.'

Then, with the dancing underway, Roy implored Neville to help
him start a new homeland for his family at Dhupawamirri. He would
give him a 'really strong bathi'. It would tie all the families together,
like his bathi had at Donydji. And could he help him get his boat back
to Gapuwiyak? It was a good time of the year for stingrays, he said.
Beautiful fat, he said.

He sat down on Roy and Sarah Ashley's blanket. When he first arrived in the homeland, Roy had been in the Wagilak camp where Neville lived for some time and where he 'became' Wagilak himself. The women had helped him with his ethno-botany.

After a year or so, the Wagilak had decamped down the creek to Dhupuwamirri and there they stayed. Roy got the English surname, because, like Cowboy, he was raised on a Roper cattle station; and like Cowboy, he once envisaged running cattle on the Donydji lands. Now he was telling Neville that pigs and buffalo were destroying his country. They were dangerous. Would Neville arrange to have them shot? Would he do for Roy and Sarah what he had done for Donydji? Would he build houses, an airstrip, a school, a workshop? The bathi 'brought you back and look what you built for these people,' Roy said, casting around. 'Everything here is from you and Melbourne. Now please take time and help me . . . at Dhupuwamirri.'

The night before the burial Djikambur sang in a haunting voice, one that was 'not his own', a 'faraway' voice. The lights went out and in total darkness a dozen or more men danced into the coffin room. They chanted 'like Buddhists', stomped in unison, uttered 'guttural grunts', made 'unsettling' noises. There was 'throat singing' – 'a harsh expiration from the back of the throat'. A man's voice called sacred names. The point of this ceremony, Terrance Rithmurrwuy told Neville, was to say to the dead person, 'You're not alone. We're with you. Don't be sad.'

An extensive sequence of Ritharrngu songs had to be got through: the magpie goose, the rainbow bird, the koel. The dew. It went on until 2 am.

In an interval, the Ganhalpuyngu performed a tobacco bunggul.

In the crowd near the coffin room, Wanakiya keened. With yidaki, sticks and singing, they came forward, men and women on their knees. Each raised a hand holding a plastic flower, to be placed by the carers on the coffin. Plastic flowers would once have been traditional feathered sticks and strings. Men in the coffin room began to crawl out to the passageway, where they sat up on their knees, raised their arms and fell forward. Then, on their haunches, sweating heavily, they moved slowly away from the building. A weeping woman threw herself sideways onto the ground. A young woman went to her and held and comforted her. Three dhapi danced bravely. Cowboy watched it all with the fan sweeping back and forth. A shooting star fell blazing in the west.

The mourners left the coffin room and walked around the camp, chanting names and stopping at the places where Tom had liked to sit. All the while they called, 'Guak! Guak!' the sound of the totemic koel. Then the women danced with flaming paperbark torches, waving them in time to the music and 'perilously close to their bodies'.

In the morning, as the women silently went about their hearths, painted *narambiya* (carers of the body) sat facing the coffin, and the strains of Christmas carols sailed across the homeland, then Cliff Richards' rendition of the Lord's Prayer. Christopher had arranged for a Yolngu Christian minister to come from Elcho.

Amid the singing, a blue tarpaulin was stretched from the house to the vehicle, and the women knelt on either side of it. As the coffin was carried to the vehicle they wailed, and in the hysteria Wanakiya threw dirt at Neville. Some women threw themselves on the coffin and stopped the men from loading it onto the canopy-shaded tray of the Toyota. Neville wrote: 'Raw grief and desperate attempts at self-harm, with clubs, sharp tins and rocks, with some throwing themselves sideways onto the hot, hard ground . . . screams; people, mainly the women, trying to hold others intent on hurting themselves: dust: yidaki, clapsticks and singers. Chaos!'

The coffin was loaded, with plastic flowers and Neville's bathi placed on top. Tom's possessions in bags, and a pole from Yilarama's funeral, were loaded into the back of Neville's vehicle. Ricky's brother

Bunbuma and Christopher wept. Neville held them both and 'they cried openly' on his shoulders. The mourners followed the vehicles up the airstrip to the grave, and there being 'fundamental needs of the human soul that Christ alone can satisfy', the Christian minister delivered a reading and a prayer in English, then a speech in Yolngu and the coffin was lowered into the grave. The pit was rapidly filled in and, as dusk descended, a Geelong Football Club flag was tied between two sticks in the ground at one end of the grave, and the Warramirri of Elcho Island put up their flag at the other.

That night the camp resounded to yidaki and sticks and vehicles departing. In the morning, the coffin room and the mourners of the day before were washed and smoked. The house of the deceased, the car that carried the body, and all the mourners were smeared with red ochre.

Tom had lived for another year after we saw him on that floor in Gapuwiyak. His emphysema could be monitored there, so he became one among the many Yolngu in that grim town disjoined from their clan lands and the foundations of their dignity. Neville took him out to Donydji for a few days. For the 'air' that he had asked for, and 'for meat'. There were people in his house, so he slept in the big tent that Neville had given him.

On a balmy evening, when nganda, his darling breeze, was blowing, Tom left his slingshot behind and sat cross-legged in the middle of the airstrip with his transistor radio. The evening star was bright in the sky. A little further up the bush on the far verge a fire was burning gently. Fire is like a pet, tamed long ago, a faithful servant and companion ever since. Tom's tape deck played Yolngu music. A cat wandered over and sat in front of him. He gave it a skerrick of something. Another cat joined them. And another – and a dog. A teenage boy in blue rode out on a bicycle and stopped to talk to him. Djikambur walked over slowly and sat down next to him. The radio played yidaki. Then the yidaki gave way to an exuberant hymn sung by a women's choir. Two little boys ran out and sat down next to Tom and Djikambur, the cats and the dog.

A young couple with a baby strolled up the airstrip, perfectly groomed, laughing. In the soft south-easterly, they promenaded. It's the same gentle evening ritual that Italians perform in their towns. More people joined the parade.

Tom now had six children gathered around him, and three cats.

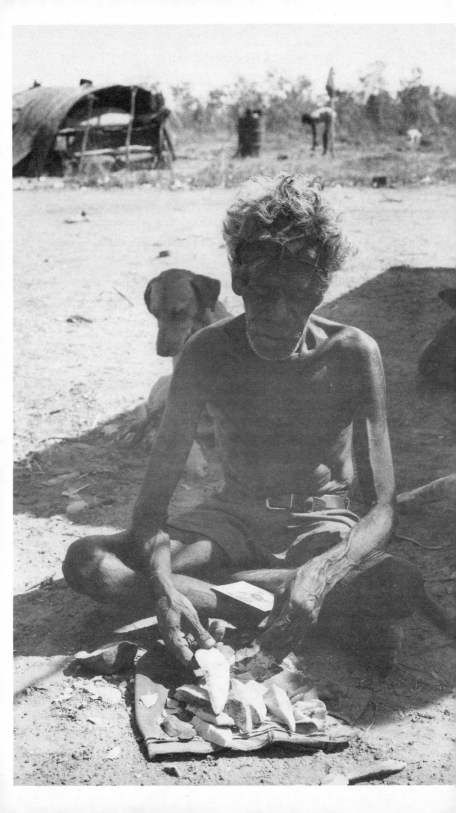

CODA

When Tom's funeral was over Neville wrote in his diary that he thought Donydji was over too. It would 'wilt and die'. He took his bathi and went into the bush with Christopher, David and Ricky. He showed them the contents as 'proof' that Dhulutarama had given it to him because he wanted the clans to live together.

The men vowed to live in harmony. But Neville knew how fragile the agreement was, and how contrary to the traditional relationships and the old ways of managing tensions. He also knew that there were Yolngu – Cowboy for instance – who wondered how any balanda could have the influence Neville had; how a man who had not come 'from the belly of the clan' could be treated as if he had. He begged Christopher to lead, but the man was no leader and they both knew it. Christopher said he was going away for a while, and in the six years before he died of kidney failure, he came and went from Donydji and took little apparent interest in the place.

Tom's death also persuaded Neville that he was finished with the homeland. 'I can't keep going. I know that for sure,' he wrote in his journal.

But he did. Every year before he went back. And when he was not there, every day it seemed he spoke to someone at the homeland, or to several people – Joanne, Ricky, Djaypi, the formerly exiled Kevin Gunyanbirrirr. To fix something. He would be telling me the latest news in a café and his phone would ring and for the next ten minutes he'd yell down the phone in Ritharrngu-Wagilak. Though every time he went he said it would the last, year after year Dave Glyde kept going back too.

Late in July 2019, Neville reported from Donydji that a dried-out and peaceable Ricky had the place looking good. The workshop was immaculate, the grounds clean and mowed, the garden hoed and sprouting.

Joanne had bought a second-hand vehicle in Darwin for $17,000, money she had saved from her teaching assistant's salary, and set out for Donydji. In the middle of the night, on the lonely road three hours from home, the car broke down. She rang the schoolteacher and the schoolteacher raised Ricky, who from his sister's description deduced which part was defective. By torchlight he removed the same part from a defunct vehicle, drove (without a licence in an unregistered vehicle) the three hours, and by torchlight jacked up Joanne's car, replaced the faulty part, and escorted her back to Donydji. All, one imagines, with barely a word or a glance, because that is the rule with brother and sister.

But Ricky was in strife. He had brought his new wife and her baby girl to Donydji. His wife Joy was Wagilak, Dhuwa like Ricky, which meant the marriage was 'wrong'. She spoke and wrote English fluently and was a good teaching assistant, but Joanne, outraged at Ricky's apostasy, would not have her at the school.

Ricky was in breach of more than Yolngu law. With supplies running low at Donydji, he had pieced a car together and headed for Gapuwiyak to get food for his stepchild and Joy's elderly mother. On the way back the car caught fire, and while it was burning, the police happened by. They discovered that the car was not registered, and the driver was disqualified – and not for the first time. Ricky was facing a couple of months in gaol.

Neville arranged for legal aid, but Ricky told the lawyer that he preferred to take the gaol sentence and 'come out a free man'.

Neville and I both wrote references for him. So did Peter Duncan (AO) of Melbourne Rotary and David Walter Glyde (JP) of Brisbane. In November 2019, Neville and I went up for the court case at Gapuwiyak.

Nothing seemed to have changed, except at the turn-off on the Yirrkala-Nhulunbuy road a NASA space station was being built. At Gapuwiyak, the women were still playing cards, the flags were flying, the youths still wandering about. The usual crowd was gathered at the store in the mind-numbing heat.

The town did seem neater and more orderly, but a man at the art gallery told us chroming, petrol sniffing and gunydja, which had seemed under control for a while, were a big problem again, and humbugging was worse than ever.

At a little gallery, Lucy, a Wagilak woman from Donydji, was thrilled to see Neville and hugged him fiercely. Lucy Malirrimurruwuy Wanapuyngu is a brilliant weaver of baskets and mats – 'woven art', the gallery calls it. She had recently been to the United States where her work had been exhibited. She and Neville talked for some time about the old days, the people who had died, the sick ones, the sad state of the young people. They spoke mainly in dialect, but some of the names I recognised. Lucy is Joy's sister. When Ricky's name came up, she tapped the side of her head, to indicate he was unstable.

Ricky had been hearing voices for years. He had often told Neville about them. But the health services at Gapuwiyak do not include *mental* health.

He came to the courthouse in new green work trousers and a bright blue T-shirt with a picture of a four-wheel drive and the

words 'Rugged Off Road' emblazoned on the front. He brought the
strikingly beautiful Joy, and her baby girl, and left them in the shade
of a tree while he joined Neville and the lawyer. I hadn't seen him
for seven years. He looked tired and knocked about, smaller than
I remembered him, yet for all the damage done he was as he'd always
been, still with the faintest trace of a smile on his face, still speaking
gently, thoughtfully, often as if he was ahead of your thoughts and
waiting for you to catch up. His 'Yo' extends the vowel, giving it a kind
of musical weight.

But standing before the law, he looked spiritless and numb,
as if indifferent to both the proceedings and the judgement that
was coming. Asked if he understood the charges, he nodded to His
Honour. The judge said he noted the difficulties the defendant had
faced and the shining testaments to his good character, and though
Ricky's record of offending justified a custodial sentence, he would
instead place him on a good behaviour bond and fine him $1570. He
wanted Ricky to know that further offences or failure to pay the fine
would mean gaol. Did he understand? Ricky did.

At 7:30 in the morning, the kids were washing their faces and
cleaning their teeth in the stainless-steel trough at the front of the
Donydji school. Joanne was supervising. A couple of the mothers
in bright skirts stood by. There were cooking fires burning at half a
dozen hearths. A stand of bamboo shaded one house from the sun,
and a healthy crop of cassava grew behind a buffalo-proof fence.
A new fence ringed the garden, new irrigation pipes and sprinklers
had been installed and the plot had been cleared of mission grass. By
9.30 am, that soft breeze was casting its benign spell on the place.
There were women in the shade of the old single men's quarters
weaving dyed pandanus leaves into baskets, and another washed
clothes in the washing machine outside the ablution block. A man
was watering his cassava. Two others in ranger's overalls were pruning

a bush apple tree to let light onto solar panels. David, second son of Dhulutarama and Betty, called to them: 'Leave that tree alone! My father planted it!'

The breeze rustled the leaves of the lemon grass Ricky had planted outside Tom's old house, which had become his since Ronnie had departed. A colossal domestic duck, weirdly white and monstrous, apparently from Roper River, sat on its haunches in the dust. Not a sound from the kids in the classroom. Only a nearby crow calling glumly from a tree, and a few moments later, a faint, even glummer reply.

Donydji had the appearance of a peaceful and well-ordered village. The impression could not have been lost on Neville as, like a spry old parish priest, and with his army slouch hat, his totem, he visited each house in turn. The gait was as busy as it had always been, but slower. He leaned forward at the waist, possibly because of an untreated hernia, and his trembling hand – he has developed a condition called essential tremor – he held bent and higher than the other. Sitting with him the previous evening, I noticed his right foot bouncing up and down, but I realised it had always done that. It was an old nervous twitch, not a new neurological condition.

Idyllic as the scene appeared – if idylls ever come with cawing crows and flea-bitten, furiously scratching dogs – troubles simmered. Poor Joanne, who had spent unavailing years trying to get the qualification she needed to teach, remained only an assistant. To those duties, caring for old Betty and three children not her own had been added. Most responsibilities, including the provision of food from the Gapuwiyak store, fell to her. For this reason, Christopher's vehicle became hers when he died, but the men pressured her and soon took it over. That was why she had bought the car in Darwin. Then they pressured her for that, until in despair she smashed every window and light on it. Joanne was trapped and ground down and regularly told Neville that she must leave. That prospect was almost as sad for Neville as it was for her.

Ricky was warring with his brother Bunbuma. Neville called a meeting, but after three minutes, Ricky said he was leaving Donydji for good and got up to go. Neville settled things down. He reminded them that the old men of Donydji were also brothers, and they often argued, but after a few days they got back together. They learned how to live with each other. They had come to an agreement: this would be their place, they would live here not as single strands, which are weak, but as strands woven together for strength. Those old men made Neville promise to look after it, and to make sure it didn't fall apart with fighting. Now Neville was asking Ricky and Bunbuma to honour the old men, and by resolving their differences live up to the example they set.

It all ended happily. The brothers stood up and shook hands, and borrowing Neville's gun, went off to hunt flying foxes. They came back a few hours later with forty and soon every hearth was cooking them. The day before, the women had brought turtles, and Mangay's son-in-law had arrived with fish. With school out, the children headed for the creek. We could see their loose-limbed, straight-backed bodies moving among the lime-green cycads and the slender tree trunks.

Ricky was happy when we left. But Joanne rang Neville a day after we returned and said he'd gone berserk again. He has been in the long grass for most of the last two years.

In July 2022, Neville went to meet a Wagilak man in Gapuwiyak who said he could help Neville fill in a few missing sites on his maps of traditional lands in the southern reaches of Wagilak Country. It turned out the man knew of no sites that Neville hadn't already identified, and he didn't know several that Neville had been shown by the old Wagilak men years before. Djikambur told Neville he must not give his maps to anyone because there were people who will use them to claim country that isn't theirs.

Neville went on up to Ramingining to talk to the rangers, ten of whom came from Donydji. The rangers wanted to see his maps to better know the country they were tending. They didn't know it half as well as he did. David Burrumarra had been right when he told him, back in 1974, that the clans at Donydji were the last of the Yolngu to live in the traditional way and to truly know their country. And Neville had learned from them. Most of the rangers' work was burning, which they mainly did from helicopters. Neville told them that while cool burning was essential, the old men also let patches grow for hot fires – hunting fires.

Back at Donydji, the people were pleased to see him. And they had been pleased to see Dave Glyde a few months earlier. Dave had gone to Arnhem Land on a fishing trip with his partner, Jill, and he drove the three hours out to Donydji so she could see where he'd been going and what he'd been doing all those years. They were treated, as Donald Thomson had been eighty years earlier, with warmth and courtesy.

Neville found Donydji in good shape. Now a shady hamlet nestling in the vast savanna, the place gave the impression of tranquility, order and permanence. Abidingness, perhaps. It had outlived Bayman, Dhulutarama and Rayguyun, and nearly all their children. It is mainly a Guyula place now. Of the Donydji Bidingal, David is the only man remaining.

Neville took heart. There were more than twenty children in the school, with Joanne and a full-time teacher. The Yolngu looked well. Everything was working. (If only he could persuade the right people to set up a simple food delivery system from Gapuwiyak, the idea he'd been pushing for a couple of decades at least.) He gave Betty cigarettes and two dresses.

No one can say what Donydji will be in five years time, or ten, or a hundred. The sites will remain sacred, of course, the south-east breeze will rustle the leaves and the koel will continue to call. But it's just as certain that the mining companies will want to frack and drill, and some Yolngu with ceremonial links to the place will wonder if they might move in for the royalties. Neville's oral and visual record of the old people's fight against mining, and his documented knowledge of the country, will be vital defences against all other claims.

But the best insurance will be the place itself, the physical proof of the clans' determination to stay and strike a balance between the old ways and the new. The people have not left. Whether it endures or fades, Donydji will never be less than a refuge and always a miracle: an epic of perseverance, the houses, the school and the workshop, the cooking shelters, the laundries and the old caravan, will go on speaking for the dogged hope that put them there.

ACKNOWLEDGEMENTS

A book as long in the making as this one has been, naturally accumulates many debts. In the beginning, when the idea was still sketchy, Rod Morrison saw the possibilities and had faith in it and me. For that trust I am deeply grateful. My thanks also to Sophie Hamley for her enthusiastic agenting in those days, and for their continuing support, Jane Cameron, Jeanne Ryckmans, and Catherine Chittick. For all she did on my behalf, I thank Jo Butler.

For their friendship and assistance of various kinds, Toby and Juliana Hooper, Jovelyn Barrion and Eddel Gauten, Jaye Kranz and Angeliki Androutsopoulos, Bernard Galbally and Emma Goodsir, Jan and Helen Senbergs, Tosca Looby and Hayden Stephens, Murray Bail and Louise Home, Rob Watson and Annette Phillips, Ellie Watson, Meredith Curnow, Morry Schwartz, Con Tam and Charlotte and Deb and their colleagues.

My thanks to Dave Glyde, Dave Bryan, Charlie Howe, Tom and Robyn Donovan, Alan Osborne and Dave Coates for so frankly sharing their experience with me. And Ruth Dunne who shared her knowledge of PTSD.

Several hours memorably spent in the droll, incisive company of the late Neville Scarlett (he died in August this year) at once sharpened my perspective and broadened it. For similar reasons the redoubtable Leon White has my thanks. And for further enlightenment,

Harvey Creswell. The late Stephen Kerr was also a friend of this project. On Neville's behalf, I must acknowledge Melbourne Rotary's sustained support for his work at the Donydji homeland, and thank especially Peter Duncan and John Mitchell.

For his trust, patience, wise counsel and conversation I thank Ben Ball. Elizabeth King edited and organised with flawless efficiency, calm and good humour. I am grateful beyond measure for the editorial care and counselling Isabel Moutinho brought to the manuscript in its final stages. Thanks also to Julian Welch and Mark Evans; and at Simon & Schuster, Michelle Swainson and Anna O'Grady. For invaluable help with the photographs, David Rapsey and Glenda Hambly.

Chloe Hooper lent me her great gift for storytelling and for this and a world of other things I thank her here.

There remain two other great debts. The first is to the people of Donydji for their unfailing hospitality over the years and for allowing me to see something of their lands and their lives. Above all, I wish to acknowledge the generosity of the late Tom Gunaminy Bidingal, and for warmly consenting to the publication of this book, Joanne Yindiri Guyula, David Bidingal and Peter Wanamal Guyula.

Though its flaws are entirely mine, this book owes more to Neville White than I can express here. I can only thank him for his boundless generosity, his friendship, and his revelations.

NOTES

The principal sources for this book were Neville White's PhD thesis, 'Tribes, Genes and Habitats' (La Trobe University, 1979), his published work on the ethnography of the Donydji clans and the development of their homeland, some of his hundreds of notebooks, numberless conversations with him, and my own observation of his projects.

ONE

5.   **Neville had about him a bit of the 'Anthropologist as Hero'** ... Susan Sontag, 'A Hero of Our Time', *New York Review of Books*, 28 November, 1963.

9.   **The explorer David Lindsay told** ... David Lindsay, 'Explorations in the Northern Territory of South Australia' [1887], *Proceedings of the Royal Geographical Society of Australasia (South Australian Branch)*, Third Session, 1888, p. 14.

10. **It was the gist of Claude Lévi-Strauss's** ... Claude Lévi-Strauss, *Tristes Tropiques* [1955], translated by John Russell (New York: Criterion Books, 1961), p. 45.

13. **'sometimes in little hordes ...'** Donald Thomson, *Donald Thomson in Arnhem Land*, introduced by Nicolas Peterson (Victoria: Currey O'Neill Ross, 1983), p. 67.

14. **'swarming with wildfowl ...'** Lindsay, *op. cit.*, p. 13.

15. **'measured, weighed and modelled ...'** Patrick Wilcken, *Claude Lévi-Strauss: The Poet in the Laboratory* (New York: Penguin, 2010), p. 263.

16. **The venerable Australian anthropologist** ... W. E. H. Stanner, 'The Dreaming', in *The Dreaming & Other Essays,* edited by Robert Manne (Melbourne: Black Inc., 2009), p. 72.

16. **The Wagilak Sisters were ever present in their minds** . . . See: W. Lloyd Warner, *A Black Civilization: A Social Study of an Australian Tribe* (New York: Harper and Brothers, 1937), p. 238. See also: Les Hiatt, 'High Gods', in *Aboriginal Religions in Australia: An Anthology of Recent Writings*, edited by M. Charlesworth, F. Dussart and H. Morphy (London: Routledge, 2017), p. 52.

20. **'Dreaming is an active continuous time . . .'** Kim Mahood, 'The Seething Landscape', *Songlines: Tracking the Seven Sisters*, edited by Margo Neale (Canberra: National Museum of Australia, 2017).

20. **'nexus of adjacencies, chains of . . .'** Ian Keen, *A Place for Strangers: Towards a History of Australian Aboriginal Being* (Cambridge, UK: Cambridge University Press, 1993), p. 272.

20. **'Man never creates anything truly . . .'** Claude Lévi-Strauss, *Tristes Tropiques* [1955], translated by John and Doreen Weightman (Harmondsworth: Penguin Classics, 1976), p. 536.

24. **'We must advance as nature prescribes . . .'** Jane Ellen Harrison, *Alpha and Omega* (London: Sidgwik, 1915), p. 33.

TWO

26. **The legendary boxing impresario Jimmy Sharman** . . . Richard Broome, 'Theatres of power: Tent Boxing Circa 1910–1970', *Aboriginal History* 20 (1996), pp. 1–23.

29. **Australians born in the decade after World War II** . . . For Australia's post-war foreign policy concerns, see: Allan Gyngell, *Fear of Abandonment: Australia in the World Since 1942* (Carlton: La Trobe University Press, 2017).

31. **'Asian nations are imbued with . . .'** quoted in *Warwick Daily News*, 17 March, 1952, p. 1. For more manipulation of Australia's Asia phobia before World War I, see: Greg Lockhart, 'Race Fear, Dangerous Denial', *Griffith Review* 32 (May 2011).

32. **'direct military threat'** . . . Menzies, Ministerial Statement, Commonwealth Parliament Debates, 25 April, 1965.

33. **'Your motives will be misrepresented . . .'** Calwell, quoted in *A Certain Grandeur: Gough Whitlam's Life in Politics* by Graham Freudenberg (Melbourne: Sun Books, 1983), pp. 52–53.

33. **'bearing in mind all the various commitments . . .'** Menzies, quoted in Sue Langford, 'The National Service Scheme 1964–72', Encyclopedia Appendix, Australian War Memorial (n.d.).

34. **Report for National service . . .** Mark Dapin, *The Nashos' War: Australia's National Servicemen and Vietnam* (Melbourne: Penguin, 2017), and Langford, *op. cit.*

36. **'Discipline,' Field-Marshal Montgomery reckoned . . .** quoted in Ben Shephard, *A War of Nerves: Soldiers and Psychiatrists, 1914–1994* (London: Jonathon Cape, 2000), p. 238.

36. **'They need to be trained not to care' . . .** Pat Barker, *The Regeneration Trilogy* (London: Penguin, 1998), p. 593.

37. **'The one thing that doesn't abide by majority rule . . .'** Harper Lee, *To Kill a Mockingbird* [1960] (New York: Harper, 2002), p. 107.

37. **The argument was at least as old as Saint Augustine . . .** Saint Augustine of Hippo, 'Homily VII', *Homilies on the Gospel of John* (Grand Rapids, Michigan: W. M. B. Eerdmans, 1956).

39. **'Once for all, then . . .'** Saint Augustine, *op. cit.*, p. 504.

47. **'come into view' . . .** Westmoreland, quoted in Nick Turse, *Kill Anything that Moves: The Real American War in Vietnam* (New York: Metropolitan Books, 2013), p. 64.

THREE

54. **'first affluent societies' . . .** Marshall Sahlins, *Stone Age Economics* (Chicago: Routledge, 1972), p. 11.

65. **Australian and US soldiers alike . . .** Johnathan Shay, *Achilles in Vietnam: Combat Trauma and the Undoing of Character* (New York: Simon & Schuster, 1995), p.17. For American weaponry, see: Nick Turse, *op. cit.*

67. **'This will bring about a moment . . .'** Henry Westmoreland, quoted in Nick Turse, *op. cit.*, p. 64.

68. **'the incommunicable experience of war . . .'** Oliver Wendell Holmes Jr, 'The Soldier's Faith', Memorial Day Address at Harvard University, 30 May 1985.

70. **He believed he had killed 'hundreds of men'. . .** A. B. Facey, *A Fortunate Life* (Ringwood, Victoria: Penguin, 1986), p. 258.

70. **Bert wrote that he was wounded . . .** *ibid.*, p. 274.

71. **'no such thing as shell shock . . .'** General George Patton, quoted in David Oshinski, 'The Human Mind Was Not Made for War', *New York Review of Books*, 13 February, 2020.

71. **Yet, despite unprecedented measures to ease . . .** See: Shephard, *op. cit.* The French campaign against the Algerian independence war makes a

useful comparison with Vietnam – an estimated 350,000 returning French servicemen suffered PTSD. See: Adam Shatz, 'Dynamo Current, Feet, Fists, Salt', *London Review of Books*, 18 February, 2021.

71. **'that gall of anger that swarms . . .'** Homer, *The Illiad*, XVIII, 108–110.

72. **The inward symptoms of the syndrome . . .** See: Shephard, *op. cit.*

74. **A psychologist who worked for many years with Vietnam vets . . .** Conversation with Ruth Dunne, 10 December, 2019.

75. **'Danger of death and mutilation . . .'** Jonathan Shay, *Achilles in Vietnam, op. cit.*, p. 10.

75. **Myth it largely was . . .** Ffion Murphy and Richard Nile, 'The Many Transformations of Albert Facey', *M/C Journal* 9:4 (2016).

76. **'I have often thought . . .'** *ibid.*

FOUR

78. **But the story of the Makassans . . .** See: Campbell MacKnight, *The Voyage to Marege* (Melbourne: Melbourne University Press, 1976); 'Studying Trepangers', in *Makassan History and Heritage: Journeys, Encounters and Influences*, edited by Marshall Clark and Sally K. May (Canberra: ANU E-Press, 2013); Ian S. McIntosh, 'Missing the Revolution! Negotiating Disclosure on the pre-Makassans (Bayini) in North-East Arnhem Land', in *Exploring the Legacy of the 1948 Arnhem Land Expedition,* edited by Martin Thomas and Margo Neale (Canberra: ANU E Press, 2011); and Alan Walker and R. David Zorc, 'Austronesian Loanwords in Yolngu-Matha of Northeast Arnhem Land', *Aboriginal History* 5:2 (1981).

78. **'The medical function of trepang . . .'** Marshall Clark and Sally K. May (eds.) 'Understanding the Macassans: A Regional Approach,' in *Makassan History and Heritage: Journeys, Encounters and Influences* (Canberra: ANU E Press, 2013), p. 20.

79. **'When the first lightning came, the Makassar . . .'** Warner, *op. cit.*, p. 448.

81. **'exploit [them] without any control or supervision' . . .** Thomson, *op. cit.*, p. 81.

82. **Warner concluded that . . .** Warner, *op. cit.*, p. 421.

82. **In the Wuramu ceremony . . .** Ian S. McIntosh, 'Islam and Australia's Aborigines', in *Aboriginal Religions in Australia: An anthology of recent writings*, edited by M. Charlesworth, F. Dussart and H. Morphy (London: Routledge, 2017).

82. **the Yolngu were on 'a path of natural . . .** Regina Ganter, 'Histories with Traction: Makassan Contact in the Framework of Muslim Australian history', in Clark and May, *op. cit.*, p. 60.

83. **'some of the tribes suffered . . .'** Lindsay, 'Explorations', *op. cit.*, p. 15.

85. **The Roper River Anglicans called it . . .** 'Roper River', Bringing Them Home website, <https://bth.humanrights.gov.au/node/119>. Accessed: 6 September, 2022.

86. **'They adhere tenaciously to their superstitions . . .'** quoted in Mickey Dewar, *The Black War in Arnhem Land: Missionaries of the Yolngu 1908–1940* (Darwin: ANU North Australian Research Unit, 1995), p. 10.

86. **'some of the blacks sat with their . . .'** Elsie Masson, *An Untamed Territory: The Northern Territory of Australia* (London: Macmillan and co. 1915), p. 139.

87. **'practice of "promising" . . .'** Elicia Taylor, 'Beloved Benedictines? Vulnerable Missions and Aboriginal Policy in the time of A. O. Neville', *Aboriginal History* 42 (2018), p. 117.

88. **The missionary Theodor Webb . . .** Theodor Webb, *The Aborigines of East Arnhem Land* (Melbourne, 1934).

91. **'a cross between . . .'** 'David Lindsay', Obituary, *Sydney Morning Herald*, 19 December, 1927.

92. **'An Anglican missionary said . . .'** quoted in Andrew Markus, *Governing Savages* (Oxon: Routledge, 2020), p. 75.

92. **In October 1935, having received . . .** Thomson, *op. cit.*

93. **'There is something indefinable . . .'** Thomson, *op. cit.*, p. 67.

93. **'the whole gamut of our culture . . .'** Reverend Edwin Smith, 'Anthropology and the Practical Man', *The Journal of the Royal Anthropological Institute of Great Britain and Ireland* 64 (Jan–Jun, 1934), p. xxvii.

94. **Donald Thomson told the government . . .** Thomson, *op. cit.*, pp. 79–80.

95. **Cook worried about 'the problem . . .'** 'The Problem of the Half Caste', *Memorandum: Aboriginal Protection Acts*, Queensland, 1934. See also: Tim Rowse, 'Cecil Evelyn Aufrere (Mick) Cook 1897–1985', in *Australian Dictionary of Biography*, Vol. 17, 2007. For Cook and Baldwin Spencer, see: Barry Hill, *Broken Song: T. G. H. Strehlow and Aboriginal Possession*, (Sydney: Knopf, 2002) pp. 266–67.

96. **Baldwin Spencer, who was . . .'** Baldwin Spencer, quoted in Noah Jed Riseman, 'Defending Whose Country? Yolngu and the Northern Territory Special Reconnaissance Unit in the Second World War', *Limina* 13 (2007), pp. 83–84.

96. **'disorganisation of their social order . . .'** Thomson, *op. cit.*, pp. 77-83.

96. 'treated with contempt and ridicule . . .' Paul Strzelecki, *Physical Description of New South Wales and Van Diemen's Land* (London: 1845), pp. 350–356.

97. 'It would be a pity,' the Northern Territory Crown . . .' quoted in *NT News*, 4 September, 1952.

97. The federal Labor member Kim Beazley Sr . . . 'Dispossession and Disease: or Dignity?' *Provocative Pamphlet* 115, (September–October, 1964), p. 7.

98. It was John Wesley's view . . . John Wesley, *Doctrine of Original Sin* (Bristol: 1757), p. 463.

100. Ninety-six per cent of the 1000 . . . Australian Bureau of Statistics, 2016 census material.

101. kava as a remedy . . .' See: Peter Botsman, 'The Sublime Tragedy of Kava in Arnhem Land', Peter Botsman's Working Papers, 11 May, 2015. Botsman suggests that kava may have been introduced as early as 1946.

101. The World Health Organization . . . 'Kava: A Review of the Safety of Traditional and Recreational Beverage Consumption', Food and Agriculture Organization of the United Nations and World Health Organization, Rome, Italy. 2016.

102. The Aboriginal Affairs minister said police had . . . Nigel Scullion, Indigenous Affairs Minister, quoted in '"It Paralyses Everything": PM's Kava Plan Flies in the Face of Elders' Concerns and Police Evidence', by Stephanie Zillman, ABC News, 4 February, 2019. <https://www.abc.net.au/news/2019-02-04/morrisons-kava-import-plan-flies-in-face-police-evidence-elders/10775068>

103. 'Everyone else,' the few . . . Les Hiatt, *Kinship and Conflict: A Study of Aboriginal Community in Northern Arnhem Land* (Canberra: ANU Press, 1965), p. 11.

105. '[W]hy do they come again and again . . .' David Burrumarra, quoted in Ronald Berndt, *An Adjustment Movement in Arnhem Land* (Paris: Moulton, 1962), p. 40.

105. Burrumara, an elder of the Warramirri . . . See: Ian S. McIntosh, 'David Burramurra', *Australian Dictionary of Biography*; and Claire Hunter, 'David Burramurra: An Unforgettable Man', Australian War Memorial blog, 9 July, 2021. <https://www.awm.gov.au/articles/blog/david-burrumarra>.

FIVE

115. Pama Nyungan . . . Richard Evans and Patrick McConvell, 'The Enigma of Pama Nyungan Expansion in Australia', in *Archaeology and Language II: Archaelogical Data and Linguistic Hypotheses*, edited by Roger Blench and Matthew Spriggs (London: Routledge, 1998).

117. **survey investigating the extent of genetic variation** . . . Neville White, Honours thesis, La Trobe University, 1971.

123. **Franz Boas told Lévi-Strauss** . . . See: Patrick Wilcken, *Claude Lvi-Strauss: The Poet in the Laboratory* (New York: Penguin, 2010).

123. **'We now have definite schemes . . .'** Speech by Dr Rivers, F.R.S., at the Annual Meeting in England, *Southern Cross Log: Australia and New Zealand Edition*, 5 February, 1910, pp. 140–144.

124. **'the civilised races of man . . .'** Charles Darwin, *The Descent of Man* (London: 1871), p. 201.

124. **Harvard biological anthropologist Joseph Birdsell** . . . For Birdsell's 'trihybrid' theory, see: John Mulvaney and Johan Kamminga, *The Prehistory of Australia* (Sydney: Allen & Unwin, 1999), pp. 153-55.

126. **Franz Boas, a German Jewish anthropologist** . . . See: Francis Gooding, 'G&T's on the Verandah', *London Review of Books*, 4 March, 2021.

126. **'The crucial differences which distinguish . . .'** Ruth Benedict, quoted in *An Anthropologist at Work: The Writing of Ruth Benedict*, edited by Margaret Mead (Boston: Houghton Mifflin, 1959), p. 440.

127. **For David Hume it was 'certain instincts . . .'** David Hume, *Treatise of Human Nature*, Book II (Oxford: Oxford University Press, 1888), p. 417.

128. **linguist Bernhard Schebeck** . . . See: Bernhard Schebeck, *Dialect and Social Groupings in Northeast Arnhem Land* [1968] (Munich: Lincom Europa, 2002).

130. **Albert Camus' 'universe of jealousy . . .'** Albert Camus, *Myth of Sisyphus and Other Essays* (New York: Knopf, 1955), p. 8.

132. **'totality of all social, cultural and psychological . . .'** Bronisław Malinowski, *Argonauts of the Western Pacific* (London: George Routledge & Sons, 1932), p. xvii.

133. **'accomplished that inner revolution . . .'** Sontag, *op. cit.*

135. **It was rather like the challenge Simone Weil** . . . See: Robert Zaretsky, 'Simone Weil's Radical Conception of Attention', *LitHub*, 9 March, 2021.

136. **'Mobility and property are in contradiction . . .'** Sahlins, *op. cit.*, p. 11.

137. **According to Warner and the Berndts** . . . See: Warner, *op. cit.* and Ronald M. Berndt and Catherine H. Berndt, *The World of the First Australians* (Canberra: Aboriginal Studies Press, 1999).

143. **The white cockatoo** . . . Yilarama Bidingal, translated by Neville White.

150. **She lived 'a long, long, long time ago . . .'** Alan Thorne, quoted in Mulvaney and Kamminga, *op. cit.*, pp. 161–62.

SIX

153. 'the architect raises his structure in imagination . . .' Karl Marx, *Capital: A Critique of Political Economy,* Vol. 1 (Chicago: C. H. Kerr & Co, 1906), p. 198.

154. 'magicians, both evil and good . . .' Warner, *op. cit.,* pp. 183–233.

155. 'Every religious dogma . . .' Jane Ellen Harrison, 'The Influence of Darwinism on the Study of Religions', in *Darwin and Modern Science,* edited by A. C. Seward (Cambridge: Cambridge University Press, 1909), p. 510.

157. 'a number of these soul stealers . . .' Warner, *op. cit.,* pp. 183-233.

159. 'at one and the same time, the reward . . .' Lévi-Strauss, quoted in Wilcken, *op. cit.,* p. 138.

159. **When the Methodist missionary Keith Cole** . . . Keith Cole, *From Mission to Church: The CMS Mission to the Aborigines of Arnhem Land, 1908–1985* (Bendigo: Keith Cole Publications, 1985).

SEVEN

169. 'sandstones and bimodal volcanics . . .' R. K. Jones, *Independent Consulting Geologist's Report: Uranium Interests of Top End Uranium,* September 2007.

173. 'called a woman and held in contempt' . . . Warner, *op. cit.,* p. 151.

174. **In the novelist Pat Barker's hands** . . .' Pat Barker, *The Regeneration Trilogy* (London: Penguin, 1998), p. 211.

177. **Australian Heritage Council: 'exceptional natural** . . .' Website, <https://www.dcceew.gov.au/parks-heritage/heritage/about/national>.

EIGHT

182. **In the Ritharrangu-Wagilak diet** . . . Neville White, 'In Search of the Traditional Australian Aboriginal Diet: Then and Now', in *Histories of Old Ages: Essays in Honour of Rhys Jones,* edited by A. Anderson, I. Lilley and S. O'Connor (Canberra: Pandanus Books, 2001) and 'Food Intake Patterns in a Traditionally-Orientated Aboriginal Community: Dietary Fat as an Example', in *Proceedings of the Nutrition Society of Australia* 15 (1990).

184. **The missionary Wilbur Chaseling noted** . . . quoted in White, 'In Search of', *op. cit.,* p. 345.

184. **Decades later, Rhys Jones and Jim Bowler** . . . Rhys Jones and Jim Bowler, quoted in White, 'In Search of', p. 349.

184. **Bernhard Schebeck found a clue** . . . quoted in White, 'In Search of', *op. cit.*, p. 349.

185. **Nicolas Peterson found at least 60 per cent** . . . quoted in White, 'In Search of', p. 346.

186. **'always [had] good teeth . . .'** Lindsay, *op. cit.*, p. 15.

189. **'strong feelings of remorse'** . . . Lévi-Strauss, *Tristes Tropiques*, *op. cit.*, p. 509.

189. **He could be a 'critic at home'** . . . Sontag, *op. cit.*

193. **'affluent hunters with high gastronomic . . .'** Betty Meehan, *Shell Bed to Shell Midden* (Canberra: AIAS, 1982).

197. **An alarmingly perfunctory one-page report** . . . Australian Transport Safety Bureau, Investigation No. 200202656, Bell Helicopter Co 206B(II), VH-PHA, 6 January, 2003.

199. **'A mental health condition triggered by . . .'** Mayo Clinic, 'Post-traumatic stress disorder', 6 July 2018, <https://www.mayoclinic.org/diseases-conditions/post-traumatic-stress-disorder/symptoms-causes/syc-20355967>.

200. **'ruinous, ever-present past . . .'** Bessel A. van der Kolk, *The Body Keeps the Score: Brain, Mind, and Body in the Healing of Trauma* (London: Penguin, 2015). See also: Iain McGilchrist, *The Master and his Emissary: The Divided Brain and the Making of the Western World* (London: Yale University Press, 2009), pp. 146–47.

201. **'All is disgust when one leaves his own nature . . .'** Sophocles, *Philocetes*, line 902.

202. **William Rivers wondered** . . . See: Tim Bayliss Smith, *The Ethnographic Experiment: A. M. Hocart and W. H. R. Rivers in Melanesia*, edited by Edvard Hviding and Cato Berg (New York: Berghahn Books, 2014), and 'Doctor who treated Siegfried Sassoon "pioneered" anthropology', by Alison Flood, *Guardian*, 7 November, 2014.

202. **'Terror is the normal state of any oral society . . .'** Marshall McLuhan, *The Gutenberg Galaxy* (Toronto: Toronto University Press, 1962), p. 32.

204. **'To love and be loved . . .'** John Winthrop, 'A Model of Christian Charity' [1630], *The Journal of John Winthrop 1630–1649* edited by Richard S. Dunn and Laetitia Leandle (Cambridge, Massachusetts: Belknap, 1996), p. 7.

204. **From empathetic connections** . . . See: Bessel A. van der Kolk, *op. cit.*

204. **That might help explain why for some people altruism** . . . See: Larrisa MacFarquhar, *Strangers Drowning: Voyages to the Brink of Moral Extremity*, (London: Penguin, 2018).

NINE

220. Joanne Guyula, the young, dedicated ... For one example among others of Joanne's scandalous mistreatment by the education authorities: Letter from General Manager, Human Resource Services, Northern Territory Department of Education to Joanne Guyula 13 January 2015, informing her that her 'fellowship with the More Indigenous Teachers Initiative (MITI) and your contract of employment with the Department ... has been terminated.' And Neville's letter to the Chief Executive of the Department, pointing out the injustice of the decision and begging him to reconsider, 15 March, 2015. (Neville White, private collection).

223. 'not particularly interested in ...' Warner, *op. cit.*, p. 452.

231. 'the failure of Northern Territory governments ...' Marcia Langton, 'Trapped in the Aboriginal Reality Show', *Crikey*, 3 September, 2008. <https://www.crikey.com.au/2008/09/03/essay-trapped-in-the-aboriginal-reality-show/>.

TEN

237. 'The Aboriginal aesthetic ...' Peter Sutton, 'The Morphology of Feeling', in *Dreamings: The Art of Aboriginal Australia* edited by Peter Sutton (Ringwood: Viking, 1988), p. 62.

251. 'prioritise the actions and outcomes according to ...' Northern Territory Department of Education website.

ELEVEN

260. 'a strong and relevant education system ...' Syd Stirling, Minister for Employment, *Education and Training, Indigenous Education Strategic Plan 2006–2009.*

263. 'A philosophy of life ...' W. E. H. Stanner, *The Dreaming & Other Essays*, (Collingwood: Black Inc., 2010), p. 69.

264. 'Long-grassers' are outcasts ... See: Tom Danks, 'Katherine Unites to Find Vulnerable Residents a Home', *Katherine Times*, 30 July, 2020, and 'Contested Spaces: The "Long-Grassers" Living Private Lives in Public Places', *The Conversation*, 20 March, 2017.

279. 'rituals of diplomacy' ... See: John Mulvaney, 'Conflict and the Rituals of Diplomacy: Les Hiatt and the AIAS' in *Scholar and Sceptic: Australian Aboriginal Studies in Honour of L. R. Hiatt*, edited by Francesca Merlan, John Morton and Alan Rumsey, (Canberra: Aboriginal Studies Press, 1997).

280. 'expressing the inexpressible' . . . Aldous Huxley, *Music at Night and Other Essays* (New York: Doubleday, 1931), p. 17.

TWELVE

285. 'elucidate the soul' . . . Barry Hill, *op. cit.*, p. 6. See also: pp. 434–438.

Descriptions of the funeral are taken from the notebooks of Neville White.

SELECT WORKS OF NEVILLE WHITE

'A history of Donydji Outstation, North-east Arnhem Land', in *Experiments in Self-determination: Histories of the outstation movement in Australia*, edited by N. Peterson and F. Myers. Acton: ANU Press, 2016.

'In search of the traditional Australian Aboriginal diet: Then and now', in *Histories of Old Ages: Essays in Honour of Rhys Jones*, edited by A. Anderson, I. Lilley and S. O'Connor. Canberra: Pandanus Books, 2001.

'Meaning and metaphor in Yolngu landscapes, Arnhem Land, Northern Australia', in *Disputed Territories: Land, Culture, Identity in Settler Societies*, edited by D. S. Trigger and G. Griffiths. Hong Kong University Press, 2003.

'Genes, languages and landscapes in Australia', in *Archaeology and Linguistics: Aboriginal Australia in Global Perspective*, edited by P. McConvell and N. Evans. Melbourne: Oxford University Press, 1997.

Donydji rock art project, 1995 season: A Report to the Australian Institute of Aboriginal and Torres Strait Islander Studies. 1995-1996.

'Inside the Gurrnganngara: Social processes and demographic genetics in north-east Arnhem Land, Australia,' in *Human Populations: Diversity and Adaptation*, edited by A. J. Boyce and V. Reynolds. New York: Oxford University Press, 1995.

'Genetic diversity' and 'Genetics and disease', in *Encyclopaedia of Aboriginal Australia: Aboriginal and Torres Strait Islander history, society and culture*, edited by David Horton. Canberra: Aboriginal Studies Press, 1994.

'Food intake patterns in a traditionally-orientated Aboriginal community: Dietary fat as an example', in *Proceedings of the Nutrition Society of Australia* 15. Nutrition Society of Australia, 1990.

'Cultural influences on the biology of Aboriginal people: Examples from Arnhem Land', in *The Growing Scope of Human Biology: Proceedings of the Australasian Society for Human Biology* 2, edited by L. H. Schmitt, L. Freedman and N. W. Bruce. Nedlands: University of Western Australia, 1989.

'Sex differences in Australian Aboriginal Subsistence: Possible implications for the biology of hunter-gatherers', in *Human Sexual Dimorphism,* edited by J. Ghesquierre, R. D. Martin and F. Newcombe. London: Taylor and Francis, 1985.

'Some observations on an Evangelical movement at Donydji outstation, April-June 1980'. Paper presented at the Symposium on Contemporary Aboriginal Religious Movements, Australian Institute of Aboriginal Studies. Canberra, 1981.

'The use of digital dermatoglyphics in assessing population relationships in Aboriginal Australia', in *Dermatoglyphics: Fifty Years Later,* edited by W. Wertelecki and C. C. Plato, *Birth Defects: Original Article Series* 15:6 (1979).

'Changing life-styles and dietary patterns in a north-eastern Arnhem Land community: Some observations and comments.' Submission to the House of Representatives Standing Committee on Aboriginal Affairs. *Hansard,* 1978.

'A preliminary account of the correspondence among genetic, linguistic, social and topographic divisions in Arnhem Land, Australia', *Mankind* 10 (December 1976).

[With Meehan, B] 'Arafura Wetlands and surrounds: "...this is no ordinary place – this is my country"'. Statement of significance for full listing on the register of the National Estate, prepared for the Australian Heritage Commission, Canberra, 1999.

[With A. C. Huntsman] 'Modernization in Bali, Indonesia and the influence of socio-economic factors on the nutritional status of preschool children in 1989/90: An anthropometric study', *Annals of Human Biology* 34:4 (July 2007), pp. 411-424.

[With G. Wearne] *Supporting Natural and Cultural Resource Management in the Arafura Wetlands and Catchment: A Community Based Approach.* Report to the Centre for Indigenous Natural and Cultural Resource Management. Darwin: Northern Territory University, 1998.

[With C. O. H. Jones] 'Adiposity in Aboriginal people from Arnhem Land, Australia: Variation in degree and distribution associated with age, sex and lifestyle', *Annals of Human Biology* 21:3 (May-June 1994).

[With G. Flannery] 'Immunological parameters in northeast Arnhem Land Aborigines: Consequences of changing settlement patterns and lifestyles', in *Urban Ecology and Health in the Third World*, edited by L. M. Schell, M. T. Smith and A. Bilsborough. Cambridge, UK: Cambridge University Press, 1993.

[With B. Meehan] 'Traditional ecological knowledge: A lens on time', in *Traditional Ecological Knowledge and Sustainable Development*, edited by N. M. Williams and G. Baines. Canberra: Centre for Resource and Environmental Studies, ANU, 1993.

[With B. Meehan, L. Hiatt and R. Jones] 'Demography of contemporary hunter-gatherers: Lessons from Arnhem Land', in *Hunter-Gatherer Demography: Past and Present*, edited by B. Meehan and N. White. Sydney: University of Sydney Press, 1990.

[With A. Polakiewicz and K. Semmens] 'Beliefs, behaviour and community health in Arnhem Land', in *Is Our Future Limited by Our Past?: Proceedings of the Australasian Society for Human Biology* 3, edited by L. Freedman. Nedlands: University of Western Australia, 1990.

[With K. O'Dea, and A. J. Sinclair] 'An investigation of nutrition-related risk factors in an isolated Aboriginal community in Northern Australia: advantages of a traditionally-orientated lifestyle', *The Medical Journal of Australia* 148:4 (January 1988).

[With R. Jones] 'Point blank: stone tool manufacture at the Ngilipitji Quarry, Arnhem Land, 1981', in *Archaeology with Ethnography: An Australian Perspective*, edited by B. Meehan and R. Jones. Canberra: Australian National University, 1988.

[With W. Beck, R. Fullagar] 'Archaeology from Ethnography: The Aboriginal use of cycad as an example', in *Archaeology with Ethnography: An Australian Perspective*, edited by B. Meehan and R. Jones. Canberra: Australian National University, 1988.

[With N. Peterson] *Skeletal Material in the Donald Thomson Ethnographic Collection: Report on its scientific significance*. Report commissioned by the Council of the National Museum of Victoria, 1985.

[With A. Thorne, B. Meehan and J. Golson] 'Australian Aboriginal Skeletal Remains: Their heritage and scientific importance', *Australian Archaeology* 19 (December 1984).

[With M. Howard] 'Report on the physical anthropology of the Robinvale human skeletal material', in *Archaeological Investigation of a threatened*

Aboriginal Burial Site near Robinvale, on the Murray River, Victoria, edited by S. Bowdler. Melbourne: Victorian Archaeological Survey, 1983.

[With N. Scarlett, and J. Reid] '"Bush Medicines": The Pharmacopoeia of the Yolngu of Arnhem Land', in *Body, Land and Spirit: Health and Healing in Aboriginal Australia,* edited by J. Reid. St Lucia: University of Queensland Press, 1982.

[With S. M. Stanley and P. A. Parsons] 'Populations, habitats and colonizing strategies in Australia', *Search* 12 (1981).

[With P. A. Parsons] 'Population genetic, social, linguistic and topographical relationships in northeastern Arnhem Land, Australia', *Nature* 261 (May 1976).

[With P. A. Parsons] 'Variability of anthropometric traits in Australian Aborigines and adjacent populations: Its bearing on the biological origin of the Australians', in *The Origin of the Australians,* edited by R. L. Kirk and A. G. Thorne. Canberra: Australian Institute of Aboriginal Studies, 1976.

[With P. A. Parsons] 'Genetic and socio-cultural differentiation in the Aborigines of Arnhem Land, Australia.' *American Journal of Physical Anthropology* 38:1 (January 1973).

[With P. A. Parsons] 'Genetic differentiation among Australian Aborigines with special reference to dermatoglyphics and other anthropometric traits', in *The Human Biology of Aborigines in Cape York,* edited by R. L. Kirk. Canberra: Australian Institute of Aboriginal Studies, 1973.

SELECT BIBLIOGRAPHY

In addition to those cited in the endnotes, the following works were among those consulted.

Anderson, Warwick. *The Cultivation of Whiteness: Science, Health and Racial Destiny in Australia*. Melbourne University Publishing, 2002.

Elkin, A. P. *The Australian Aborigines: How to Understand Them* [1938]. Sydney: Angus & Robertson, 1961.

Flood, Josephine. *The Original Australians: Story of the Aboriginal People*. Crows Nest, NSW: Allen & Unwin, 2006.

Fussell, Paul. *The Great War and Modern Memory*. Oxford University Press, 1975.

Griffiths, Billy. *Deep Time Dreaming: Uncovering Ancient Australia*. Carlton, Victoria: Black Inc., 2018.

Harrison, Jane Ellen, *Themis: A Study of the Social Origins of the Great Religions*. Cambridge University Press, 1927.

Hastings, Max. *Vietnam: An Epic Tragedy, 1945–1975*. London: Collins, 2018.

Herman, Judith. *Trauma and Recovery: The Aftermath of Violence from Domestic Abuse to Political Terror*. New York: Basic Books, 2015.

Junger, Sebastian. *Tribe: On Homecoming and Belonging*. London: 4th Estate, 2017.

Komer, Robert W. *The Malayan Emergency in Retrospect: The Organization of a Successful Counter Insurgency Effort*. Report to RAND Corporation, 1972.

Lévi-Strauss, Claude. *The Savage Mind* University of Chicago Press, 1966.

Maddock, Kenneth. *The Australian Aborigines: A Portrait of their Society*. London: Allen Lane/Penguin, 1972.

Maraniss, David. *They Marched Into Sunlight: War and Peace Vietnam and America, October 1967*. New York: Simon & Schuster, 2003.

Meagher, Robert Emmet. *Killing from Inside Out: Moral Injury and Just War.* Eugene, Oregon: Cascade Books, 2014.

Meehan, Betty, Rhys Jones and Annie Vincent. 'Gula-kula: Dogs in Anbarra society Arnhem Land', *Aboriginal History* 23 (1999).

Morphy, Howard. *Aboriginal Art.* London: Phaidon, 1998.

O'Brien, Tim. *The Things They Carried.* Boston: Houghton Mifflin, 1990.

Østby, Hilde and Ylva Østby. *Diving for Seahorses: The Science and Secrets of Memory.* Sydney: New South Books, 2018.

Phillips, Adam (ed.). 'On Not Making It Up', in *Side Effects.* London: Hamish Hamilton, 2006.

Scarlett, Neville H. and Neville White. 'Human Ecology Project: North-east Arnhem Land', Alphabetic Index, names of plants, Yolngu botany, etc. Canberra, AIATSIS, MS 2376, 1971–1978.

Scott, Wayne J. 'Posttraumatic stress disorder (PTSD), a Vietnam veteran's experience', Vietnam Veterans Association of Australia, April 2001.

Shay, Jonathan. *Odysseus in America: Combat Trauma and the Trials of Homecoming* New York: Scribner, 2002.

Sutton, Peter. *The Politics of Suffering.* Melbourne University Publishing, 2011.

Thomson, Donald. *Children of the Dreamtime: Traditional Family Life in Aboriginal Australia.* Melbourne: Penguin, 1989.

Trugden, Richard. *Why Warriors Lie Down and Die: Towards an Understanding of Why the Aboriginal People of Arnhem Land Face the Greatest Crisis in Health and Education Since European Contact.* Darwin: Aboriginal Resources and Development Services, 2000.

Walker, David. *Stranded Nation: White Australia in an Asian Region.* Nedlands: University of Western Australia Publishing, 2019.

Warner, Marina. 'Spellbound', *London Review of Books*, 2 July, 2020.

Williams, Nancy. *The Yolngu and Their Land: A System of Land Tenure and the Fight for its Recognition.* Canberra: AIAS, 1986.

Wright, Ronald. *A Short History of Progress.* Melbourne: Text, 2004.